Business Plans Made Easy

It's Not As Hard As You Think!

Entrepreneur MAGAZINE'S

Business Plans Made Easy

It's Not As Hard As You Think!

By Mark Henricks

ENTREPRENEUR MEDIA INC.
2392 Morse Ave., Irvine, CA 92614

Managing Editor: Marla Markman
Copy Editor: Bonnie Datt
Proofreader: Mimi Kusch
Production Design: Coghill Composition Company
Illustrations: John McKinley
Cover Design: Olson Kotowski & Co.
Indexer: Alta Indexing

This publication is designed to provide accurate and authoritative information in regard to the subject matter covered. It is sold with the understanding that the publisher is not engaged in rendering legal, accounting or other professional services. If legal advice or other expert assistance is required, the services of a competent professional person should be sought.

Library of Congress Cataloging-in-Publication Data
Henricks, Mark.
Business plans made easy: it's not as hard as you think! / by Mark Henricks.
    p. cm.
   ISBN 1-891984-05-5
   1. Business planning.   2. Industrial management.   3. Strategic planning.
4. Small business—Planning.   5. Success in business.
   I. Entrepreneur (Irvine, Calif.)   II. Title.   III. Title: Entrepreneur magazine's business plans made easy.
   HD30.28.H474   1999
   658.4'012—dc21   98-52831
                                         CIP

Printed in Canada

09 08 07 06 05 04 03 02 01 00   10 9 8 7 6 5 4 3 2

Acknowledgments

This book could not have been written without the enduring support of the editorial staff of *Entrepreneur* magazine, including Rieva Lesonsky, Maria Anton Conley, Maria Valdez Haubrich, Peggy Reeves Bennett and Karen Axelton, now with *Business Start-Ups*, who have helped sustain me for almost a decade while I learned to write about business. Marla Markman, a largely unseen ally on the copy desk at *Entrepreneur* for much of that time, has now stepped to the fore editing books at Entrepreneur Media. She has proven herself more valuable than I could have asked. Bonnie Datt's uncannily skillful copy editing of the manuscript saved me from many errors. Those that remain, of course, are mine alone. To the countless entrepreneurs and business planners who have contributed their expertise and experiences to this book in bits and pieces, some small and some large, I offer my enduring thanks. And to Barbara, Kate and Corey, who have labored with me through so many books now, I give gratitude and hope that future projects will be as enjoyable in the writing as this one.

Table of Contents

Chapter 13

INTRODUCTION

Some people get lucky and fall into a business that they love and that works and succeeds. But many other people don't, and some of them miss out not because they're unlucky, but because they were unprepared when luck descended. Fortune, says an axiom that has lasted for centuries, favors the prepared mind. What this book will help you do is be prepared when luck—good or bad—looks your way.

You'll learn how to create your own business plan, to use it to better understand your business, to manage and control your business, to analyze and evaluate other plans and, of course, to use it to obtain the financing that so many businesses need to get going and keep going until they are self-sustaining.

Each chapter in this book is devoted to analyzing, explaining and, wherever and whenever possible, making entertaining an important concept relating to business plans. The chapter topics range from why you even need a plan to what do with it when you're finished. You'll learn techniques for figuring your break-even ratio and tips for approaching potential investors. You'll hear stories about the business plans of famous entrepreneurs and even a few entrepreneurs admitting that they don't write plans—willingly, at least.

Along the way, you'll find sprinkled definitions of important terms, contact information for useful resources, warnings of especially common or serious mistakes, and pointers to steer you in the right direction. When you've finished reading the book, you'll be prepared to write a sound, comprehensive, convincing plan for almost any business, whether it's a brand-new start-up or an existing company. More important, however, you'll be the owner of a thoroughly prepared mind and need just the slightest nod from good fortune to proceed.

Following is a chapter-by-chapter summary of the book. The chapters are intended to be read in sequence, with exercises, work sheets and samples to be studied, completed and examined along the way. If, after finishing, you need more help with a particular section, the chapters can be reviewed as self-contained tutorials on their particular topics.

Chapter 1: Business Plan Basics

This chapter shows that there are many compelling answers to the question, Why write a business plan? It explores the basic definition of a business plan and when and why to write one. It provides detailed information on sources of capital and techniques for using your plan to raise money. It also describes using a plan as a tool for marketing your company to prospective partners, suppliers, customers and even employees.

Chapter 2: Money Hunt

Writing a business plan is an activity closely tied to the idea of raising money for a start-up business. This chapter examines sources of funding and explains how business plans can be used to help entrepreneurs obtain financing from the most commonly used sources.

Chapter 3: The Big Picture

One of the most important purposes of a business plan is to evaluate a business proposition's chances for success. This chapter shows how to use a plan to see if a new venture is likely to achieve the desired results.

Chapter 4: Set Your Course

No two plans are the same, but they all follow similar routes to creation. This chapter tells how to navigate the major steps, including determining your personal goals and objectives and how they figure in planning. It also provides a first, brief look at the major plan elements: Executive Summary, Management, Product or Service, Marketing, Operations and Financial Data, along with brief explanations of each.

Chapter 5: Match Game

You're unique and, in all likelihood, so is your plan. Plans differ among industries, for one thing, and they also have different purposes. You want to pick the general type of plan that fits your needs and your company. This chapter explains how to do that, as well as presents descriptions of the major types of plans, such as working plans, miniplans and presentations.

Chapter 6: Sum It Up

The Executive Summary is the most important part of your plan. This chapter tells you why, and details exactly what should go into a well-conceived summary.

Chapter 7: Team Work

The section of your business plan where you describe your management team is likely to be one of the first readers turn to. You'll need to explain what each member of your team does, how you plan to grow it if necessary, and even tell who your advisors are. This chapter explains the techniques and underlying import of all these tasks of the management section.

Chapter 8: Announcing . . .

Most entrepreneurs really enjoy describing the product or services that is their business's reason for being. This chapter tells how to channel that enthusiasm into answering the questions investors and other plan readers most often ask.

Chapter 9: Field Notes

Every business plan has to make the industry in which it will operate crystal clear. In this section you'll also describe the state of your industry, using market research, trend analysis and competitive factors to explain why you picked this industry, whether it's growing or shrinking, and what makes you better.

Chapter 10: Marketing Smarts

No matter how great your product or services are, if you don't know how to persuade someone to buy them, and show that you know it in your business plan, your plan will get short shrift. This primer in marketing strategy will tell how to employ the four P's of traditional marketing, as well as prepare a follow-up marketing plan for the next generation of products.

Chapter 11: The Works

Operations is another area few entrepreneurs have trouble mustering enthusiasm for. As usual, however, the entrepreneurial enthusiasm has to be directed at the right targets if the plan is to generate maximum impact among its readers. This chapter tells how to write operations sections for manufacturers, service firms and retailers, with special considerations for each.

Chapter 12: State Your Case

The most intimidating part of a business plan for many entrepreneurs is the required financial statements, including historical and projected balance sheets, income statements and cash flow statements. This chapter dispels fear by clearly presenting explanations of the major financial statements and analytical ratios, along with instructions on how to prepare them and common pitfalls.

Chapter 13: Extra, Extra

Many plans have important information that doesn't fit into the major sections. This chapter tells you what to consider for a plan's appendix, including employee resumes, product samples, press clippings and the like.

Chapter 14: Looking Good

Good presentation can make a good plan even better. You need to pick the proper stationery, printing and design for your plan. You need to make sure that you use charts, graphs and tables when appropriate, without overdoing it. This chapter provides straightforward tips for doing that, along with hints on multimedia presentations and other elements of a plan package such as cover sheets and cover letters.

Chapter 15: Help Line

There is as much information and assistance available on business plan writing as any entrepreneur could hope for. This chapter describes some of it, including software for writing business plans, books and how-to manuals, Web sites, trade groups and associations, business plan consultants and even business plan competitions.

Appendices A–D: Sample Business Plans With Comments

The appendices include four sample plans for several fictional firms, including a start-up retailer seeking seed money, a high-tech firm after second-round financing, a manufacturer courting a strategic partner and an established company seeking working capital. Each sample is a fully worked-up example following, where appropriate, the recommendations of this book.

Finally, at the end of the book, there are two resource listings chock-full of business resources that list contact addresses and phone numbers:

1. Our "**Government Listings**" appendix provides contact information for Small Business Development Centers, Small Business Administration district offices and state economic development departments across the country.

2. And, if you need financing, you'll definitely want to check out our listing of "**Small-Business-Friendly Banks**."

Scattered throughout the book you'll find various tip boxes. Each will provide useful information of a different type.

Plan Of Action

Here, we direct you to sources for more information and guidance.

Plan Pointer

This box offers advice on ways to improve your plan.

Fact Or Fiction?

Get straight answers about common business plan questions.

Plan Pitfall

This box warns you of common errors made by plan writers.

Buzzword

This box offers brief definitions of terms you'll run into in the process of writing your plan.

CHAPTER 1

BUSINESS PLAN BASICS

Why you absolutely need a business plan

A business plan is a written description of your business's future. That's all there is to it—it's a document that tells what you plan to do and how you plan to do it. If you jot down a paragraph on the back of an envelope describing your business strategy, you've written a plan, or at least the germ of a plan.

Business plans can help perform a number of tasks for those who write and read them. As noted, they are used by investment-seeking entrepreneurs to convey their vision to potential investors. They may also be used by firms that are trying to attract key employees, prospect for new business, deal with suppliers, or simply to understand how to manage their companies better.

Having said that, there are some generally accepted conventions about what a full-grown business plan should include and how it should be presented. And if you follow these conventions, you're going to need an awfully big envelope to hold your plan. Maybe that's not all bad. Jay Valentine, CEO of software start-up Info Glide Inc., says that when it comes to plans, the bigger, the better. "Venture capitalists only look at one thing," he scoffs. "And that is, how thick is it?"

Basically, however, a plan should cover all the important matters that will contribute to making your business a success. These generally include the following:

1. your basic business concept;
2. your strategy and the specific actions you plan for implementing it;
3. your products and services and their competitive advantages;
4. the markets you'll pursue;

1

5. the background of your management and key employees and, last but far from least;

6. your financing needs.

Buzzword

Competitive advantage is what makes you different from and better than the companies you are competing with. Lower price, higher quality and better name recognition are examples of competitive advantages.

You'll express most of this information in words—in plain English, and the plainer the better. There also almost certainly will be a lot of numbers in budgets and other financial reports. Tables, graphs, drawings and photographs are also not uncommon. A few plans include actual product samples.

What else is in a good business plan? Hopes, certainly, are there. Dreams, probably. Quite possibly there is passion. But it's worth noting now that none of these essential motivators will have a high profile in your business plan. They have to be there for you to succeed in business, to be sure, but few if any of the people who are likely to read it are interested in your private emotions about your business.

A business plan is a place to stick to facts instead of feelings, projections instead of hopes, and realistic expectations of profit instead of passion. Keep this in mind while writing your plan and you have a better chance of injecting it with perhaps the most important component of all—namely, credibility.

How Long Should It Be?

A useful business plan can be any length, from a scrawl on the back of an envelope to, in the case of an especially detailed plan describing a complex enterprise, more than 100 pages. A typical business plan runs 15 to 20 pages, but there is room for wide variation from that norm.

Much will depend on the nature of your business. If you have a simple concept, you may be able to express it

Fact Or Fiction?

All business planning experts say you must have a plan. Do you? Not necessarily. A study by Coopers & Lybrand found 32 percent of fast-growing firms had no written business plan.

COCKTAIL NAPKIN BUSINESS PLAN

Business plans don't have to be complicated, lengthy documents. They just have to capture the essence of what the business will do and why it will be a success.

The business plan for one of the most successful start-ups ever began with a triangle scrawled on a cocktail napkin. The year was 1971, and Herb Kelleher and Rollin King were formulating their idea for an airline serving Houston, Dallas and San Antonio. The triangle connecting the cities was their route map—and the basis of the business plan for Southwest Airlines.

The two entrepreneurs soon expressed their vision for Southwest Airlines more fully in a full-fledged business plan and raised millions in start-up capital to get off the ground. Eventually, they went public. Along the way, the airline expanded beyond the three cities to include other Texas destinations and today flies coast-to-coast.

Southwest now serves 50 cities in 24 states with 2,100 flights daily and revenues of $3.8 billion. It's the nation's fifth-largest airline and the only major airline that specializes in low-cost, no-frills, high-frequency service. Which, if you just add some lines to that original triangle, is the same strategy mapped out on that cocktail napkin.

in very few words. On the other hand, if you are proposing a new kind of business or even a new industry, it may require quite a bit of explanation to get the message across.

The purpose of your plan also determines its length. If you want to use your plan to seek millions of dollars in seed capital to start a risky venture, you may have to do a lot of explaining and convincing. If you're just going to use your plan for internal purposes to manage an ongoing business, a much more abbreviated version should do fine.

WHEN SHOULD I WRITE IT?

The fact that you're reading this book means you suspect it's about time to write a business plan. Odds are you are at or near one of the many occasions when a business plan will prove useful.

One good time is when you are picking a new venture to pursue. A business plan is a very good way to explore the feasibility of a new business

PUMPING UP A PUNY PLAN

Jay Valentine doesn't like business plans, doesn't believe in them and doesn't write them for start-ups he's involved in. "It's ridiculous for a start-up to make these plans and projections," he says. Valentine prefers to wait until he's conferred with a number of customers and booked a few sales. Then he knows how he'll sell his product and what revenues are likely to be.

But as CEO of InfoGlide Inc., a database technology start-up, Valentine was responsible for coming up with a plan that would please the venture capitalists InfoGlide was asking for several million dollars from to bring the technology to market. So he wrote one. "It was maybe 15 pages," says Valentine. "Just me writing about the company and what we were trying to do."

That wouldn't please number-crunching venture capitalists, Valentine knew. So he hired a consultant to prepare a five-year financial forecast. Then he sent it in, sight unseen. "I never even looked at the financials," he says. "But it was thick—and that's what the venture capitalists like to see." Crazy? Maybe. But the pumped-up plan landed $3 million from a big venture capital firm.

without actually having to start it and run it. A good plan can help you see serious flaws in your business concept. You may uncover tough competition while researching the market section, or you may find that your financial projections simply aren't realistic. On the other hand, a careful business plan that doesn't predict failure can be a rare comfort and motivator to proceed.

You are also likely to need a business plan when you are seeking financing. Bankers, venture capitalists and other financiers rarely provide money without seeing a plan. Less sophisticated or less unbiased investors, such as friends and family, may not require a business plan, but they probably deserve one. Even if you're funding the business with your own savings, you owe it to yourself to plan how you'll expend the resources you're committing.

It's also a good idea to realize that a

Buzzword

"Business concept" is a term referring to the basic idea around which you build your business. For instance, Federal Express is built on the idea of overnight delivery, while Amazon.com is based on the idea of selling books over the Internet.

business plan is not a one-time exercise. Just because you wrote a plan when you were starting out or raising money to get under way doesn't mean you are finished. A business plan should be rewritten or revised regularly to get maximum benefit from it. Commonly, business plans are revised yearly.

WHO NEEDS A BUSINESS PLAN

About the only person who doesn't need a business plan is one who's not going into business. You don't need a plan to start a hobby, or to moonlight from your regular job. But anybody beginning or extending a venture that will consume significant resources of money, energy or time, and that is expected to return a profit, should take the time to draft some kind of plan.

Start-ups

The classic business plan writer is an entrepreneur seeking funds to help start a new venture. Many, many great companies had their starts on paper, in the form of a plan that was used to convince investors to put up the capital necessary to get them under way.

Most books on business planning seem to be aimed at these start-up

---

NO PLAN, NO PROBLEM

When six Stanford University students started calling on venture capitalists looking for money to fund an Internet start-up called Architext, they had only a rough outline for a company that would help people find information on the World Wide Web.

Yet the six were able to convince seasoned Silicon Valley venture capitalists that the idea was sound. So sound, in fact, that co-founder Joe Kraus reports, "we raised our first $3 million without a written business plan."

Kraus' company went on to be renamed Excite Inc. and to become one of the most successful of all Internet start-ups. Excite garnered more financing and went public in 1996, raising $34 million and making instant millionaires out of the six co-founders.

This experience shows that there is an exception to every rule, and also that if your idea is strong enough, you don't need a lot of complicated spreadsheets and market analyses to get help to start your company. However, we can't stress enough, you do need some sort of business plan.

Fact Or Fiction?

The typical image of a business planner is an entrepreneur seeking to lure investors to a hot start-up. But most plans are not written by entrepreneurs or even business owners. Nor are they usually ever seen by anyone outside the company. They're written by corporate managers for corporate managers and are used for internal planning and control.

business owners. There's one good reason for that: As the least experienced of the potential plan writers, they probably are most appreciative of the guidance. However, it's a mistake to think that only cash-starved start-ups need business plans. Companies and managers find plans useful at all stages of their existence, whether they're seeking financing or trying to figure out how to invest a surplus.

Corporate Managers

If you've ever held a managerial position of any stature in a large corporation, you know well the rounds of five-year, three-year, annual, quarterly and even monthly budgets, forecasts, reports, analyses and plans you are expected to draft. Many large companies employ sizable staffs that do nothing but plan and assist others in planning, and sometimes one round of planning seems to lead directly into the next, with precious little time for actually implementing all the schemes.

Some people enjoy all this corporate paperwork; others consider it a good argument for entrepreneurship. Either way, it's hard to imagine running an organization that may employ tens of thousands without careful documentation and controls. Plans serve this purpose in big companies, which is why most business plans are written by employees, not entrepreneurs.

Established Firms Seeking Help

Not all business plans are written by multinational managers or starry-eyed entrepreneurs. Many are written by and for companies that are long past the start-up stage, but also well short of large-corporation status. WalkerGroup/Designs, for instance, was already well established as a designer of stores for major retailers

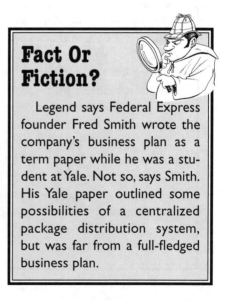

Fact Or Fiction?

Legend says Federal Express founder Fred Smith wrote the company's business plan as a term paper while he was a student at Yale. Not so, says Smith. His Yale paper outlined some possibilities of a centralized package distribution system, but was far from a full-fledged business plan.

when founder Ken Walker got the idea of trademarking and licensing to apparel makers and others the symbols 01-01-00 as a sort of numeric shorthand for the approaching millennium. Before beginning the arduous and costly task of trademarking it worldwide, Walker used a business plan complete with sales forecasts to convince big retailers that promising to carry the 01-01-00 goods would be a good idea. It helped make the new venture a winner long before the big day arrived. "As a result of the retail support up front," Walker says, "we had over 45 licensees running the gamut of product lines almost from the beginning."

These middle-stage enterprises may draft plans to help them find funding for growth just as the start-ups do, although the amounts they seek may be larger and the investors more willing. They may feel the need for a written plan to help manage an already rapidly growing business. Or a plan may be seen as a valuable tool to be used to convey the mission and prospects of the business to customers, suppliers or others.

CHAPTER 2

MONEY HUNT

Using your plan to raise capital

A business plan is almost essential for entrepreneurs seeking to raise money to help fund their companies. In fact, business plans are so closely tied to fund-raising that many entrepreneurs look at them as only suited for presenting to investors and overlook the management benefits of planning. "We don't have a formalized business plan, mainly because we aren't seeking capital," says Jeff Musa, president and founder of Cutting Edge Software Inc. "You're not going to refer to your business plan when you're going to make some microdecision about the way your company's running," he adds. "In a three-person company, we sit down at a roundtable with a couple of beers and make decisions."

But for those entrepreneurs who are seeking funding, a business plan accomplishes several things. First, it helps convince potential sources of funding that the entrepreneur has thought the idea through. It also gives any actual investors a set of financial benchmarks for which the entrepreneur can be held accountable, should performance fail to measure up.

In a real sense, a business plan is a ticket to enter the financial dance. It would be oversimplistic to say that you invariably must have a plan to get funding. There are exceptions to that rule, as to many others. But it's not too simplistic to say that a good plan will help you to raise your funds more quickly, more easily and more completely than you could without it.

VENTURE CAPITALISTS

Venture capitalists represent the most glamorous and appealing form of financing to many entrepreneurs. They are known for backing high-risk companies in the early stages, and a lot of the best-known entrepreneurial success stories owe their early financing to venture capitalists.

When many entrepreneurs write a business plan, obtaining venture capital backing is what they have in mind. That's understandable. Venture capitalists, or VCs, as they're also known, are associated with business success. They can provide large sums of money, as much or more advice, and considerable prestige by their mere presence. Just the fact that you've obtained venture capital backing means your business has, in their eyes at least, considerable potential for rapid and profitable growth.

Venture capitalists both lend to and make equity investments in young companies. The loans are often expensive, carrying rates of up to 20 percent. They sometimes also provide what may seem like very cheap capital.

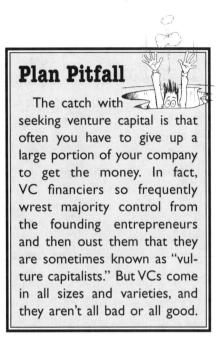

Plan Pitfall

The catch with seeking venture capital is that often you have to give up a large portion of your company to get the money. In fact, VC financiers so frequently wrest majority control from the founding entrepreneurs and then oust them that they are sometimes known as "vulture capitalists." But VCs come in all sizes and varieties, and they aren't all bad or all good.

tal. That means you don't have to pay out hard-to-get cash in the form of interest and principal installments. Instead, you give a portion of your or other owners' interest in the company in exchange for the VC's backing.

What Venture Capitalists Want

While venture capitalists come in many forms, they usually have very similar goals. The main similarities are that they want their money back, and they want it back with a lot of interest.

VCs typically only invest in companies that they foresee being sold either to the public or to larger firms within the next several years. As part owners of the firm, they'll get their cash back when that sale goes through. Of course, if there's no sale or if the company goes bankrupt, they don't get their money back.

That's exactly what happens with many venture capital investments. The firms, despite their promise, turn out to be unsuccessful and produce a dead loss for their investors. VCs aren't quite the plungers they may seem, however. They're willing to assume risk, but they want to minimize it as much as possible. Therefore, they typically look for certain features in companies they are going to invest in. Those include:

1. rapid, steady sales growth

2. a proprietary new technology or dominant position in an emerging market

3. a sound management team

Plan Pointer

Some VCs specialize in a field, such as retail, biotechnology or high-tech. Others have a regional focus. But whatever his or her special interests, almost any venture capitalist will admit to desiring the four basic characteristics in an investment.

4. the potential to be acquired by a larger company or taken public in a stock offering

Rates Of Return

Like most financiers, venture capitalists want the return of any funds they lend or use to purchase equity interest in companies. But VCs have some very special requirements when it comes to the terms they want and, especially, the rates of return they demand.

Venture capitalists require that their investments have the likelihood of generating very high rates of return. A 30 percent to 50 percent annual rate of return is a benchmark many venture capitalists seek. That means if a venture capitalist invested $1 million in your firm and expected to sell out in three years with a 35 percent annual gain, he or she would have to be able to sell the stake for approximately $2.5 million.

These are quite high rates of return compared with the 6 percent or so usually offered by U.S. Treasury instruments and the 10 percent historically returned by the U.S. stock market. Venture capitalists justify their desires for such high rates of return by the fact that their investments are highly risky.

Most venture capital-based companies, in fact, are not successful and generate losses for their investors. But venture capitalists gamble that their successes will outweigh their failures.

Cashing Out Options

Clearly, one of the key concerns of venture capitalists has to be the existence of a way to cash out their investment. This is typically done

Buzzword

Rate of return is the income or profit earned by an investor on capital invested into a company. It's usually expressed as an annual percentage.

through a sale of all or part of the company, either to a larger firm through an acquisition or to the public through an initial offering of stock.

In effect, this need for cashing out options means that if your company isn't seen as a likely candidate for a buyout or an initial public offering (IPO) in the next five years or so, VCs aren't going to be interested.

Going Public

Some fantastic fortunes have been created in recent years by venture-funded start-ups that went public. Initial public offerings of their stock have made multimillionaires, seemingly overnight, of entrepreneurs such as Marc Andreessen of Netscape Communications and Yahoo! co-founders Jerry Yang and David Filo. Less obvious but equally, if not more, important is the fact that the same IPOs have made many millions for the venture investors who provided early-stage financing.

The stringent requirements for IPOs leave out most companies, including those that don't have audited financials for the last several years, as well as those who operate in slow-growing or obscure industries such as car washes or paper-clip manufacturing. And IPOs take lots of time. You'll need to add outside directors to your board and clean up the terms of any sweetheart deals with managers, family or board members as well as have a major accounting firm audit your operations for several years before going public. If you need money today, in other words, an IPO isn't going to provide it.

An IPO is also probably the most expensive way to raise money, in terms of the amounts you have to lay out up front. The bills for accountants, lawyers, printing and miscellaneous fees for even a modest IPO will easily reach six figures. For this reason, IPOs are best used to raise amounts at least equal to millions of dollars in equity capital. Venture capitalists keep all these requirements in mind when assessing an investment's potential for going public.

Fact Or Fiction?

Many entrepreneurs dream of going public. But IPOS are not for every firm. The ideal IPO candidate has a record of growing sales and earnings and operates in a high-profile industry. Some have a lot of one and not much of the other. Low earnings but lots of interest, for instance, characterizes many biotech and Internet-related IPOs.

Being Acquired

A much faster and more common way for venture capitalists to cash out is for the company to be acquired, usually by a larger firm. An acquisition can occur through a merger or by means of a payment of cash, stock, debt or some combination.

Mergers and acquisitions don't have to meet the strict regulatory requirements of public stock offerings, so they can be completed much more quickly, easily and cheaply. And buyers will probably want to see audited financials, but you—or the financiers who may wind up controlling your

Buzzword

Due diligence refers to all the things an investor should do to check out an investment. It has a legal definition when applied to the responsibilities of financial professionals, such as stockbrokers. In general, it includes such things as requiring audited financial statements and checking warehouses for claimed inventory stocks.

company—can literally strike a deal to sell the company over lunch or a game of golf. About the only roadblocks that could be thrown up would be if you couldn't finalize the terms of the deal, if it turned out that your company wasn't what it seemed or, rarely, if the buyout resulted in a monopoly that generated resistance from regulators.

Venture capitalists assessing your firm's acquisition chances are going to look for characteristics such as proprietary technology, distribution systems or product lines that other companies might want to possess. They also like to see larger, preferably acquisition-minded, firms in your industry. For instance, Microsoft, the world's largest software firm, frequently acquires small personal-computer-software firms that possess talented personnel or unique technology that it desires. Venture capitalists looking at funding a software company are almost certain to include an assessment of whether Microsoft might be interested in buying the company out someday.

Plan Of Action

The National Association of Certified Valuation Analysts is the trade group for people whose business is deciding what businesses are worth. It can help you find a valuation analyst as well as learn the basics of figuring a business's worth. Contact NACVA at 1245 Brickyard Rd., Salt Lake City, UT, 84106-2559, (801) 486-0600, fax: (801) 486-7500, www.nacva.com.

Management Control

A very important consideration when dealing with venture capitalists is their penchant for taking control. Many VCs insist on placing one or more directors on the boards of companies they finance. And these directors are rarely there merely to observe. They frequently take an active role in running the company.

VCs are also reluctant to provide financing without obtaining majority or controlling interest in the companies they back. This can make them just as influential as if they had a majority of the directors on the board, or more so.

The frequent end result of venture capitalist management activism is that

EZ VC

When you have a hot business concept that promises big things, sometimes you can dictate terms to venture capitalists instead of them dictating to you. Before Yahoo! went public in 1996, the co-founders of the Internet directory service provider sold 30 percent of the company to giant Japanese publishing conglomerate Softbank.

Yet even though Yahoo! founders Jerry Yang and David Filo—who at the time were Stanford University graduate students—were running a brand-new business concept in an unproven industry, they were able to strike a favorable deal with their Japanese financiers. That was especially true, Yahoo! COO Jeff Mallett says, when it came to the matter of control.

Softbank came on board the Yahoo! train just a month before an IPO raised $35 million for the start-up. Yet despite Softbank's sizable ownership share and the inexperience of the co-founders, Softbank pretty much lets them run the company the way they want to, Mallett says.

"They have no hands on [our] operation, save one board seat," says Mallett. "We have lots of discussions with Softbank, but at the end of the day they give us the reins to run our own company."

the entrepreneurs lose control of the company. This appears unfortunate to outside observers, and may be plain heartbreaking to an entrepreneur who's worked hard for years to get an idea off the ground, only to see the controls snatched away just as it's about to take off.

When Venture Capital Is An Option

Venture capital is something many entrepreneurs dream about. And it may be an option for many companies at various stages of their lives. Venture capital is most often used to finance companies that are young without being babies, and that are established without being mature. But it can also help struggling firms as well as those that are on the edge of breaking into the big time.

Following are the major types and sources of capital, along with distinguishing characteristics of each:

◆ **Seed money:** Seed money is the initial capital required to transform a business from an idea into an enterprise. Venture capitalists are not as likely to provide seed money as some other, less tough-minded financing sources, such as family inventors. However, venture capitalists will back seedlings if the idea is strong enough and the prospects promising enough.

VCs are less likely to provide equity capital to a seed-money stage entrepreneur than they are to provide debt financing. This may come in the form of a straight loan, usually some kind of subordinated debt. It may also involve a purchase of bonds issues by the company. Frequently these will be convertible bonds that can be exchanged for shares of stock. Venture capitalists may also purchase shares of preferred stock in a start-up. Holders of preferred shares receive dividends before common stockholders, and also get paid before other shareholders if the company is dissolved.

Seed money is usually a relatively small amount of cash, up to $250,000 or so, that is used to prove a business concept has merit. It may be earmarked for producing working prototypes, doing market research or otherwise testing the waters before committing to a full-scale endeavor.

◆ **Start-up capital:** Start-up capital is financing used to get a business with a proven idea up and running. For example, a manufacturer might use start-up capital to get production under way, set up marketing and create some actual sales. This amount may reach $1 million.

Venture capitalists frequently are enthusiastic financiers of start-ups because they carry less risk than companies at the seed-money stage but still offer the prospect of the high return on investment that VCs require.

◆ **Later-round financing:** Venture capitalists may also come in on some later rounds of financing. First-stage financing is usually used to set up full-scale production and market development. Second-stage financing is used to expand the operations of an already up-and-running enterprise, often through financing receivables, adding production capacity or boosting marketing. Mezzanine financing, an even later stage, may be required for a major expansion of profitable and robust enterprises. Bridge financing is often the last stage before a company goes public. It may be used to sustain a growing company during the often lengthy process of preparing and completing a public offering of stock.

Venture capitalists even invest in companies that are in trouble. These turnaround investments are riskier than start-ups and therefore even more expensive to the entrepreneurs involved.

When you get down to it, venture capitalists are likely to do almost anything and to back almost any venture. That's partly because they don't have the legal requirements of public offerings or the bureaucratic overhead of bankers. It's also because they come in so many varieties themselves, from well-established Wall Street firms, whose money comes from pension funds, to groups of what are essentially individual investors pooling their money to back what they hope will be big winners.

VCs aren't for everybody, but they provide a very important financing option for many young firms. When you're writing a business plan to raise money, you may want to consider venture capitalists and their unique needs.

BANKERS

While venture capitalists may seem sexier, far more successful businesses are financed by banks than by VCs. Banks can provide small to moderate amounts of capital at market costs. They don't want control—at least beyond the control exerted in the covenants of a loan document. And they don't want ownership. Bankers make loans, not investments, and, despite what you may fear, as a general rule they don't want to wind up owning your company.

Bankers provide only debt financing. That is, you take out a loan and pay it back, perhaps in installments consisting of principal and interest, perhaps in payments of interest only, followed by a balloon payment of the

Buzzword

"Turnaround" is the term used to describe a reversal in a company's fortunes that takes it from near death to robust health. For example, in the 1970s Chrysler had to be bailed out by the federal government. Then in the 1990s, Daimler-Benz bought the turned-around Chrysler in what was at the time history's biggest industrial buyout. Some turnarounds are faster, taking months or weeks. Some never happen at all.

Buzzword

A balloon payment is a single, usually final, payment on a loan that is much greater than the payments preceding it. Some business loans, for example, require interest-only payments the first year or two, followed by a single large payment that repays all the principal.

principal. One of the nice things about debt financing is that the entrepreneur doesn't have to give up ownership of his or her company to get it. The cost is clearly stated.

One nice thing about loans is that the bank can usually be counted on to want minimal, if any, input into how the business is run. Most of the time, as long as you're current on payments, you can do as you like. Get behind, however, and you're likely to find a host of covenants buried in your loan documentation.

Loan covenants may require you to do all sorts of things, from setting a minimum amount of working capital you must maintain to prohibiting you from making certain purchases or signing leases without approval from the bank. In fact, most bank loans contain so many covenants that it's difficult for a lender to avoid being technically in default on one or more of them at a given time.

Your loan officer is likely to ignore many covenant violations unless you stop, or seem likely to stop, making timely payments. Even then you'll probably get a chance to work out the problem. But if you remain in violation, you may find yourself declared in default in short order and the bank may demand all its money immediately, perhaps seizing your collateral and even forcing you to protect yourself by declaring bankruptcy.

What Bankers Want

As with other financiers, bankers' first concern is getting their money back, plus a reasonable return. To increase the odds of this, they look for certain things in the businesses they lend to. Those include everything from a solid explanation of why you need the money and what you're going to use it for, to details about any other borrowing or leasing deals you've entered into.

Bank-loan applications can be pretty voluminous, almost as long and complete as a full-fledged business plan. Plans and loan applications aren't exactly interchangeable, however. For instance, a banker may not be too interested in your rosy projections of future growth. In fact, when confronted with the kind of growth projection required to interest a venture capitalist, a banker may be turned off. On the other hand, a banker is likely to be quite interested in seeing a contingency plan that will let you pay back the loan, even in the event of a worst-case scenario.

◆ **Cash flow:** One of the most convincing things you can show a banker is the existence of a strong, well-documented flow of cash that will be more than adequate to repay a loan's scheduled principal and interest. Basically, you're going to have to show where you're going to get the money to pay back what you're borrowing.

You'll need more than a projection of future cash flow, by the way. Most bankers will want to see cash flow statements as well as balance sheets and income statements for the past three or so years. And don't forget your tax returns for the same period.

◆ **Collateral:** If you're just starting out in business, or if you're dealing with a banker you don't know well, you're unlikely to be able to borrow from a bank without collateral. (That's doubly true if, as is the case with many entrepreneurs, both descriptions apply to you.) Collateral is just something the banker can seize and sell to get back some or all of the money you've borrowed, in the event that everything goes wrong and you can't pay it back with profits from operations. It may consist of machinery, equipment, inventory or, all too often, the equity you own in your home.

Bankers are trained to sniff out collateral, naturally, because they want to make loans. But it's a good idea to take the initiative here and propose something that will be used if you suspect a banker will require it. Often the collateral will consist of whatever you're borrowing money to buy—production equipment, computers, a building, etc.

◆ **Management ability:** Bankers these days like to stress the personal aspect of their services. Many state that they are interested in making loans based on a borrower's character as well as his or her financial strength. And in fact, the borrower's track record and management ability are concerns for bankers evaluating a loan application. If you can show you've run one or more other companies successfully, it will increase your chances of landing a loan to get a start-up going.

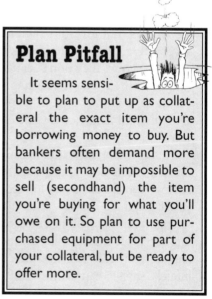

Plan Pitfall

It seems sensible to plan to put up as collateral the exact item you're borrowing money to buy. But bankers often demand more because it may be impossible to sell (secondhand) the item you're buying for what you'll owe on it. So plan to use purchased equipment for part of your collateral, but be ready to offer more.

Fact Or Fiction?

Can you borrow money for 100 years? Most business loans are for less than a year and, except for mortgages, few loans are for more than a few years. But some 19th-century railroad companies and, more recently, Walt Disney Co., have issued bonds not slated to pay off for a century. Disney, in fact, sold $350 million in 100-year bonds in 1993.

When Bank Financing Is Appropriate

Bank financing is most appropriate for up-and-running enterprises that can show adequate cash flow and collateral to service and secure the loan. Bankers are less likely to provide start-up money to turn a concept, even a well-proven one, into a business, and they are even less likely to put up seed money to prove a concept.

Bankers are also sensitive to the term or length of a loan. Most bank loans are of short to intermediate term, meaning they are due in anywhere from less than a year to five years. A short-term loan may be for 90 days, to finance receivables so you can get a big order out the door. A longer-term loan, up to 20 years, may be used to purchase a piece of long-lasting capital equipment.

Borrowing When You Really Need It

The old saw about bankers only lending to people who don't need to borrow is almost true. In fact, bankers prefer to lend to companies that are almost, but not quite, financially robust enough to pursue their objective without the loan. Remember: Bankers are lenders, not investors. Unlike, say, a venture capitalist who is taking an equity position, they don't get a higher return on their loan if you happen to be more successful than expected. Their natural tendency is to be conservative.

This is important to understand because it affects how and when you will borrow. You should try to foresee times you'll need to borrow money, and arrange a line of credit or other loan before you need it. That will make it easier and, in many cases, cheaper in terms of interest rates, than if you wait until

Plan Pointer

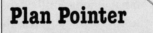

Lenders look for borrowers exhibiting the four C's of Credit: 1) *Character:* What's your reputation and record? 2) *Capacity or cash flow:* Do you have sufficient cash flow to repay principal and interest? 3) *Capital:* Does your business have enough capital to keep going if you can't pay the debt from earnings? and 4) *Collateral:* Do you own something valuable the banker can take if you can't pay the loan back?

you're a needier and, in bankers' eyes, less attractive borrower.

SMALL BUSINESS ADMINISTRATION

Sometimes the government really does want to help. The Small Business Administration (SBA) is a branch of the Department of Commerce that truly is devoted to helping small-business people. One of its most valuable offerings is a set of financial assistance programs that aim to help you raise the money you need to get started and keep going.

> ## Buzzword
>
> Factoring is the flip side of trade credit. It's what happens when a supplier sells its accounts receivables to a financial specialist, called a factor. The factor immediately pays the amount of the receivables, less a discount, and receives the payments when they arrive from customers. Factoring is an important form of finance in many industries.

There are more than a dozen SBA loan programs, each with unique characteristics. For instance, the Specialized Pollution Control Program is set up just to provide small businesses with loan guarantees to fund the planning, design or installation of pollution control equipment. There's also a Microloan Program that helps businesses get loans for as little as $100. The primary SBA financing program, however, is the 7(a) Loan Guaranty Program. In fact, the pollution control loan guarantee program, as well as several other special efforts for minority and women-owned businesses, exporters and veterans, is part of 7(a).

The SBA sometimes lends money directly to small businesses, but most of its financing help is in the form of loan guarantees. That is, the SBA, using the full faith and credit of the U.S. government, guarantees a lender will get back most—but not all—of the money lent out, even if the borrower can't pay. A typical loan guarantee covers 80 percent of the loan. You will find it easier to borrow money, and usually get a lower finance rate, if you can get an SBA guarantee. To do that, you need to meet the SBA's definition of a small business and put up pretty much all the business's assets as collateral. Most banks handle SBA-backed loans and can tell you more about the programs. Or, call your local SBA office for information (see Appendix E for a state-by-state listing of district offices).

OTHER WAYS TO BORROW MONEY

Banks and venture capitalists aren't the only lenders around. Lending, rather than that other activity, may in fact be the oldest profession, and

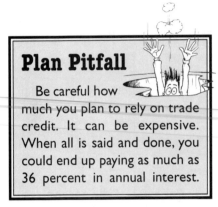

Plan Pitfall

Be careful how much you plan to rely on trade credit. It can be expensive. When all is said and done, you could end up paying as much as 36 percent in annual interest.

through the ages a bewildering variety of ways to borrow have come into being. People have financed new or growing ventures through everything from cash advances on personal credit cards to borrowing from friends.

Corporate Bonds

There are two kinds of debt financing: straight loans like those you get from a bank and bonds. Bonds give you a way to borrow from a number of people without having to do separate deals with each of them. If you need to borrow $500,000, for instance, you can issue 500 bonds in $1,000 denominations. Then you can sell those bonds to anyone who'll buy them, including family, friends, venture capitalists and other investors.

Corporations use a bewildering variety of bonds for financing, but the most common type simply calls for you to pay a stated amount of interest on the face amount for a certain period. After that time, usually five years, you pay back the face amount to the buyer.

Bonds give you the great advantage of being able to set the interest rate and terms and amount you're trying to raise, instead of having to take whatever a lender offers. The problem with bonds is that they are regulated similarly to public stock offerings. So although they're widely used by big companies, very few small companies issue them.

Trade Credit

You don't need a loan application, permission from the Securities and Exchange Commission or even a note from your mother to take advantage of one of the most useful and popular forms of financing around—that is, trade credit, the credit extended to you by suppliers who let you buy now and pay later.

You can measure the amount of trade credit you have outstanding by simply adding up all your accounts payable, or the amount of unpaid bills on your desk. Any time you take delivery of materials, equipment or other

Plan Pitfall

Family members offer tempting capital sources. But emotions can interfere with judgment when dealing with relatives and can lead to hurt feelings as well as possible lawsuits and other entanglements. Minimize the risk of misunderstanding by fully documenting interest rates, terms and other details for loans and equity investments from family.

valuables without paying cash on the spot, you're using trade credit.

For many businesses, trade credit is an essential form of financing. For instance, a clothing store owner who receives a shipment of bathing suits in April may not have to pay for them until June. By that time she can hope to have sold enough of the suits to pay for the shipment. Without the trade credit, she'd have to look to a bank or another source for financing.

Fact Or Fiction?

Think Daddy's money is no way to start a business? Consider that Eddie Bauer had to have his father co-sign a $500 loan to open his first tennis shop in Seattle. Spiegel purchased Bauer's catalog operation in 1988 for $260 million.

OTHER INVESTORS

When you're looking for money, it may seem that investors are as scarce as hen's teeth. But the real problem may be that you're not looking in enough places for potential financiers. You may find investors as close as your immediate family, and as far away as the other side of the country.

Investors come in many shapes and sizes, as well as with various needs and intentions. Odds are you can find someone to help you with your business's financing needs if you cast your net wide enough.

Family And Friends

The most likely source of financing are the people closest to you. Spouses, parents, grandparents, aunts, uncles and in-laws, as well as friends and colleagues, have reasons to help you that arm's-length financiers lack. For that reason, they may back you when no one else will.

Willingness to take risk doesn't mean family and friends are foolish investors, however. Money from family and friends has backed many a successful business venture. Here are a few:

◆ **Albertson's Inc.:** Co-founder Joe Albertson borrowed $7,500 from his aunt to get his $12,500 contribution to the partnership that began the grocery store that grew to sales of more than $2 billion a year.

◆ **Pizza Hut Inc.:** Co-founders Frank and Dan Carney borrowed $600 from an insurance fund left by their late father to start the pizza chain.

◆ **Eckerd Corp.:** Jack Eckerd raised $150,000 from family members to purchase three failing Florida drugstores, the cornerstone of a

Plan Pointer

If you're after angels, it's in your interest to guard their interests. Unsophisticated angels may, for instance, give you money without specifying exactly what, such as percentage of ownership, they're buying. Such angels can be taken advantage of. But you may want more help someday. So make it legal, make terms clear, and take care of their interests as well as your own.

company whose sales would one day top $9 billion a year.

Family and friends may not be able to raise millions of dollars, but they can provide long-term financing to highly speculative endeavors that more mainstream financiers wouldn't touch.

Why Even Families Need A Plan

If you're financing your venture with family money, you may think all you need is a smile and a polite request to raise what you need. In the short term, that may work, and produce the funds you need. But over the long term, even family-financed enterprises will benefit from having a business plan.

A business plan sets out in writing the expectations for the company. It shows family members who are putting up the money what they can expect for their contribution. And it helps keep the entrepreneur—you—mindful of responsibilities to family members who backed you, and on track to fulfill your obligations.

Angel Investors

If you are having trouble getting funding for your venture under the right terms, or under any terms at all, you'll be glad to know about the existence of angels in the investment world. Angels are individuals who invest their own money as opposed to institutions or professional money managers who invest other people's money. Many angels are well-off professionals, such as doctors and lawyers. Others are successful small-business owners who have made a bundle with their own entrepreneurial efforts and are now interested in letting their money work for them in someone else's venture.

Fact Or Fiction?

The term "angel investor" sounds like it was bestowed by a happy entrepreneur whose venture was saved by the arrival of one of these well-heeled, risk-welcoming investors. Actually, however, the term comes from the theater, where the label was applied to backers who rescued shows that no one else was willing to finance.

A PIE-EYED PLAN

Gordon Weinberger of Londonderry, New Hampshire, likes to call himself the 6-foot, 9-inch Pie Guy. A better name for the founder and CEO of Top of the Tree Baking Co. might be the dollar-at-a-time guy.

Weinberger started his company as a bakery, making and marketing all-natural apple and other pies. After a few years, he decided he needed to concentrate on the marketing alone, and he contracted out the manufacturing of the pies to larger commercial bakeries. The only problem was, it would take money to reposition his company from being a manufacturer to being a marketer of already-cooked pies. So he took to the road in a gaudily painted school bus. He traveled to spots as disparate as Aspen, Colorado, and wealthy Connecticut suburbs, in search of the haunts of the rich and investment-minded. When he rolled up, he presented his business plan and asked for backers.

By the time he pulled out his thumb, Weinberger had raised several hundred thousand dollars, primarily in small amounts. And he was well on the way to a successful restructuring of his 10-person company.

Since angels invest their own money, you might think they were the most discriminating, difficult-to-please investors of all. But nothing could be further from the truth. They are, as a rule, much more willing to take a flier on a risky, unproven idea than are more sober professional investors and lenders. In fact, angel investors are so well-known for backing shaky ventures that some experts feel the very sight of well-heeled doctors or dentists in the vicinity suggests that an investment is likely to fail.

In addition to being willing to go with unproven ideas, angels are also more open to seat-of-the-pants business plans. They don't usually require even a fraction of the documentation that a more demanding investor, such as an institutional venture capitalist, does. This sometimes means, of course, that they get into businesses that aren't well thought out or that have faulty underlying structures.

Another common characteristic of angels is that they usually are friends, acquaintances, colleagues, relatives or in some other way are tied to you in an informal, personal way. One reason for that is that angels don't generally advertise their existence, certainly in the way a bank might with a newspaper ad or billboard on the freeway offering loans. Another reason is that angels are usually swayed more by personal concerns than by financial ones. They may hope to make a killing, but they're really investing in your enterprise because they like and believe in you. With professionals, that attitude is uncommon, and suspect when it crops up.

The angel investment community is getting more sophisticated in recent years. ACE-Net, for example, is an electronic network of angel investors sponsored by the SBA. It helps angel investors and small businesses seeking capital meet online, turning the informal angel investment community into a 21st century Internet-based securities listing service. Learn more about ACE-Net by contacting the SBA at (800) 8-ASK-SBA or visit the ACE-Net Web site at www.sba.gov/ADVO.

You may be an appropriate vehicle for angel investors if you have been unsuccessful at finding financing elsewhere, yet you still have a valid business concept. Angels are, above all else, unconventional. If 20 banks turn you down, chances are the 21st will too. That's because all bankers have pretty much the same training and use the same formulas and requirements to evaluate loans—within broad guidelines, of course. Most angels, on the other hand, have no training whatsoever in evaluating business ideas. If 20 angels turn you down, it doesn't mean a thing. Until you've gone through the last name in your Rolodex, you still have a chance of landing an angel backer.

You may also fit angel guidelines if you don't need a whole lot of money. Institutional venture capitalists can, by pooling the funds of several different groups, raise vast sums. It's not unheard of for venture capitalists to invest nine-figure sums—more than $100 million—in relatively new, unproven ventures. Even Bill Gates or Warren Buffett is unlikely to feel comfortable sinking that kind of money into anything uncertain. Your angel's capacity will vary, of course, but few angels can come up with more than a few tens of thousands of dollars at least at the outset. If you need more, you may need more than one angel.

CHAPTER 3

THE BIG PICTURE

Now that you have a plan, what do you do with it?

There are few things to equal the sensation of filling in all the numbers on a cash flow projection, hitting the recalculate button, and scrolling to the bottom of your spreadsheet to see what the future holds. If the news is good, and you see a steady string of positive cash balances across the bottom row, then you know that, assuming your data is good and your assumptions reasonable, your business has a good chance of making it.

Lisa Angowski Rogak is an entrepreneur who has started several newsletters in much the same way: She devised a plan, focusing on marketing strategy and cash flow projections to see if she could come up with a way to sell the newsletters while keeping her bills paid, then prepared a sample issue to be used in a direct mail and publicity campaign. "Planning is the key to the success of your newsletter," says Rogak, whose latest venture is Williams Hill Publishing. "It's the single most important thing you can do to ensure the success of your newsletter."

That's the kind of encouragement that helps entrepreneurs persevere, whether they have an existing concern that's hitting a rough spot or a start-up concept that nobody else seems to believe in. Numbers can lie, of course, and nobody can create a spreadsheet that really tells the future. But evaluating financial data is to entrepreneurship what evaluating lab results is to a medical doctor. If your vital signs are good, odds are your future will be as well.

But what if the odds don't look so favorable? What if the first pass through your cash flow projection or income pro formas contains more red than a fire station paint locker? Sure, you can go back and look for an error or an overly pessimistic or conservative assumption. You can even try altering a few of the inevitable numbers that you really have no way of estimating accurately, to see where the pressure points are if nothing else.

But what if you do that, even pushing your alterations past the point of credibility, and your plan still doesn't make sense? Well, in that case, you've probably done yourself the really big favor of finding out something isn't going to work before you sink your money into it. Nobody knows exactly how often this happens, but it's safe to say that a lot of businesses are never attempted because the plan convincingly says that they shouldn't be.

Is that bad? Well, it may feel bad. But think how much worse you would feel if you went ahead with the venture and things turned out as the plan forecast. Business planning is a powerful tool for evaluating the feasibility of business ventures. Use it.

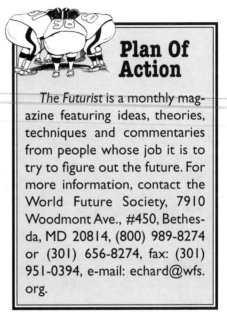

Plan Of Action

The Futurist is a monthly magazine featuring ideas, theories, techniques and commentaries from people whose job it is to try to figure out the future. For more information, contact the World Future Society, 7910 Woodmont Ave., #450, Bethesda, MD 20814, (800) 989-8274 or (301) 656-8274, fax: (301) 951-0394, e-mail: echard@wfs.org.

Do The Numbers Add Up?

Many businesses fail because of events that are impossible to foresee. If you'd begun a car dealership specializing in yacht-sized gas guzzlers right before the Arab oil embargo in the 1970s, you would be in the same position as a driver heading at 100 miles per hour into a brick wall—through no fault of your own. The same might go for a software start-up that comes out with a new program just before Microsoft unveils a top-secret, long-term development effort to create something that does the same job for a lot less money.

It's probably not a bad idea, as part of your business planning process, to try to get some information about the activities or intentions of the potential embargos and Microsofts in your business plan. If nothing else, crafting a scenario in which the unthinkably awful occurs may help you to deal with if it does. But some things are just wild cards and can't be predicted. For these you just have to trust the luck of the draw.

So what numbers have to add up? Certainly you have to be selling your products and services at a profit that will let you sustain the business long-term. You'll also have to have a financial structure, including payables and receivables systems and financing, that will keep you from running out of cash even once. Depending on whether you have investors who want to sell the company someday, you may need a plan with a big number in the field for shareholders' equity on the projected balance sheet.

When you're asking yourself whether the numbers add up, keep the needs of your business and your business partners, if you have any, in mind. Even if it looks like it'll take an air strike to keep your business from getting started, you don't want to do it if the numbers say that long-term it's headed nowhere.

Where Are You Going?

Your partners aren't the only ones whose concerns should be addressed in your plan. You also need to think of what you want and whether your plan's findings suggest you'll get it. For instance, say you desire above all else the feeling of freedom from control by other people. If your plan shows that you'll have to take on several equity partners, each of whom will desire a chunk of ownership, you may need to come up with a business whose capital needs are not so intensive.

Or let's say you really want a company that will let you do your work and get home at a reasonable hour. The only problem is, your business plan requires you to squeeze your labor costs down so much, you're going to be doing the work of two people (and possibly getting paid for less than one, but that's another story). Again, whether or not this business survives and prospers, it may not be a winner for you if the plan shows it won't take you where you want to go.

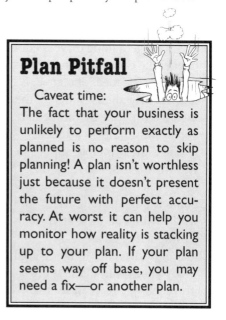

Plan Pitfall

Caveat time: The fact that your business is unlikely to perform exactly as planned is no reason to skip planning! A plan isn't worthless just because it doesn't present the future with perfect accuracy. At worst it can help you monitor how reality is stacking up to your plan. If your plan seems way off base, you may need a fix—or another plan.

MONITOR YOUR PERFORMANCE

Nothing ever succeeds as planned, the saying goes, and it's true enough to use as a working principle for business planning. A typical plan consists of thousands of words, numbers, formulas and assumptions. Many of these are of considerable importance to the eventual outcome of your business.

A seriously out-of-tune prognostication, or even a typographical error in entering a formula or number, may be enough to seriously damage your business somewhere down the line. The same can be true of a number of slightly off-track assumptions or data findings. When you add it all up, you can't speak in terms of more than probability about the place you think your business will be in a year or so. Some cynics would insist that the only thing you can be sure of is that you won't be exactly where you plan to be. Actually, it's not that easy. You may run according to plan, but there's an excellent chance you won't.

Using a business plan to monitor your performance has several benefits. If your cash flow is running much shorter than projected at the moment, even though you're not currently in trouble, it may help you to spot eventual disaster before it occurs. You may also, by comparing plan projections with actual results, gain a deeper understanding of your business's pressure points or the components of your operation that have the most effect on results.

Spotting Trouble Early

A teenager taking driver's education is told to look through the rear window of the car in front to try to see the brake lights on the vehicle ahead of that one. The idea, of course, is that if the novice driver waits until the car immediately ahead slams on the binders, it may be too late to stop. Looking forward, past the immediate future, helps traffic move more smoothly and averts countless accidents.

The same principle applies in business planning. You don't have to be a wizard to get some solid hints about the future beyond tomorrow, especially when it comes to the operations of your own business. (As we've pointed out, it's tougher to know what's going to happen in the outside world.) You can look at virtually any page of your business plan and find an important concept or number describing some expected future event that, if it turns out to be diverging from reality, may hint at future trouble.

Say your profit margins are shrinking, slowly but steadily and seemingly irreversibly. If you can see that within a few months your declining margins will push your break-even point too high to live with, you can take action now to fix the problem. You may need to add a new, higher-margin product, get rid of an old one, or begin stressing marketing to a more profitable clientele. All these moves, and many more you could take, have a good chance of working if your careful comparison of plan projections to actual results warns you of impending danger. Wait until the last minute, and you could be peeling yourself off the windshield.

Understanding Pressure Points

Not all tips that come from comparing plans with results have to do with avoiding danger. Some help you to identify profit opportunities. Others may show how seemingly minor tweaks can produce outsized improvements in sales or profitability. For example:

The plan for a one-person professional service business indicated that rising sales were not, in general, accompanied by rising costs. Fixed items such as office rent and insurance stayed the same, and even semivariable costs such as phone bills went up only slightly. The bulk of any extra business went straight to the bottom line, showing up as profit improvement. But one cost that didn't seem especially variable went up sharply as business volume climbed. That was the number of transactions.

Ordinarily this would be a given and not necessarily a matter of grave concern. A large enterprise would simply hire a few more modestly paid customer service reps, credit department staff or bookkeepers to handle the added orders forms, invoices and the like. For this single professional, however, added paperwork came at a very high cost—her own time.

Somehow, in her projections of steadily rising sales volume, she'd neglected to note that more business meant more invoices to be sent out, more account statements to be mailed, more slow-payers to be reminded, and, even when the money came in quickly, more deposit slips to be filled out, checks to be endorsed, and trips to be taken to the bank. All this work, while not necessarily unpleasant (especially the check-cashing part), was taking up more and more of her time.

As a part of checking her plan against results, she noticed this unexpected increase in transactions and figured out what it meant. Calculating that, taking all paperwork into account, she spent around an hour on each transaction no matter how large or small it was, she realized that one of the most important pressure points in her business was related to the size of a transaction. By refusing small engagements and seeking clients who could offer big jobs, she would reduce the amount of time spent on otherwise unproductive paperwork, and increase the time she could spend completing client requirements.

Ultimately, she was able to trim what had been 100 annual transactions down to 75, even while increasing the amount of her dollar revenue. The result was a free 25 hours to spend working on more business or just vacationing. That's the kind of pressure point that, if you can see it and relieve it, can really take off the pressure.

ATTRACTING GOOD PEOPLE

It takes money to make money, sure, but it also takes people to make a company. That is, unless you're a one-person company, and sometimes even then a plan can be an important part of your effort to attract the best partners, employees, suppliers and customers to you.

Prospective Partners

Partners are like any other investors, and it would be a rare one that would come on board without some kind of plan. Partners want to know your basic business concept, the market, and your strategy for attacking it; who else is on your team; what your financial performance, strengths, and needs are; and, basically, what's in it for them. Luckily, these are exactly the same questions a business plan is designed to address, so you're likely to please even a demanding prospective partner by simply showing him or her a well-prepared plan.

One difference: A plan probably won't contain the details of a partnership agreement. And you'll need one of these to spell out the conditions of your partnership, no matter how well you and your prospective partner know, understand and trust one another.

Prospective Employees

Although employees may not be making cash contributions to your business, they're making an investment of something equally important—their own irreplaceable time. The kinds of employees you probably want are careful, thorough, good at assessing problems and risks, and unwilling to leap into hazardous waters. As it happens, these are just the kind of people who are going to want to see a written plan of your business before they come on board.

Now, it's not going to be necessary, if you're running a restaurant, to show your full business plan to every waitperson or assistant dishwasher who fills out a job application. It's the most desirable employees—the talented technologists, the well-connected salespeople, the inspired creative types, and the grizzled, seen-it-all managers—who are most likely to feel they can and should demand to see details of your plan before they cast their lot with you. So even if you don't show your plan to more than a few prospective employees, when you need it you may really need it bad. Make sure you're ready when a promising but inquisitive job candidate shows up at your doorstep.

Another thing: As we've pointed out, not all businesses have plans. So by having one, you'll be making yourself a more desirable employer.

Suppliers And Customers

Increasingly, companies large and small have been trying to trim the number of suppliers and customers they deal with, and develop deeper and stronger relationships with the

Plan Of Action

The Employee Benefit Research Institute (EBRI) conducts regular studies and surveys to find out what employees want and what employers are giving them. To learn more about what benefits you should offer to attract the best, contact EBRI at 2121 K St. NW, #600, Washington, DC 20037, (202) 659-0670.

ones they keep. An essential part of this is getting to know more about existing and prospective vendors and clients. So don't be surprised if one day, when you're trying to set up a new supplier relationship or pitch a deal to a big company, the person you're negotiating with asks to see your business plan along with your order or price sheet.

Why do suppliers care about business plans? Suppliers only want to sell to people who can pay, which is one important reason a new supplier is likely to want to see your business plan before taking a big order. Remember, if a supplier is selling to you on credit—letting you take delivery of goods and pay for them later—that supplier is in effect your creditor. Suppliers who sell for other than cash on delivery have the same legitimate interest in your business's strategy and soundness as a banker.

Suppliers are also interested in doing business with the same companies over and over. If you want to be successful, you probably will take much the same attitude because far and away the best customers are long-time customers. It's easier to sell to someone you've sold to before, and easier to satisfy someone you've satisfied before. That's one of the reasons for identifying and targeting market niches, and building and sticking to core competencies.

There are some exceptions to the rule about the extreme desirability of repeat customers, such as in the case of a gas station on an interstate freeway, where most of its customers are only passing by and may never visit again. But doing what you're best at and selling to people you know you can sell to is a good recipe for success.

One way suppliers can find the best customers is to simply sell to everybody and see what happens. The customers that last over time will turn out to have been good bets, while those who place an order and are never heard from again will be less valuable. But a better approach is for a company to try to figure the typical characteristics of its longest-lived customers, then find more customers like them.

Say a supplier's analysis of customer records shows it has a knack for developing long-term profitable relationships with moderate-sized companies that emphasize excellent service, price at a premium level and sell only the best merchandise. Business plans provide all the information such a company will need to find and clone its best customers. So if a supplier asks to see your plan, be willing to share it. It could be the start of a long and mutually beneficial relationship.

Customers And Business Plans

Why should a customer care about your business plan? Shouldn't it be enough that your price, product and service are good enough to win his or her business? Not necessarily. These days customers, too, are interested in

FITTING WITH FORD

The automobile industry provides one of the clearest examples of the extent to which big companies are trying to cut the number of suppliers they deal with. Ford Motor Co. has gone especially far in reducing the number of suppliers it does business with. "In one of our vehicles, we now have one overall supplier, plus four other suppliers, for a total of five," says C. W. Graning, procurement strategy manager for purchasing and supply development and strategy at Ford. "In the past we had a total of 27."

When you look at the bigger picture, it's even more startling. In 1983, Ford had more than 1,800 suppliers. By 1993 it had 825. By 1998, the number had shrunk to 600. What that means for the losing suppliers, of course, is that they had to replace the sales to the Dearborn, Michigan, giant or perish.

But for those who made the cut, they got even more business from Ford than before. How did they pass Ford's muster? The answer is, by fitting into Ford's management system. That means lots of reports, lots of analysis and lots of planning. In fact, a comprehensive business plan, describing how the supplier will work with Ford in every aspect of the supplier-customer relationship, is one of the key criteria of the automaker in selecting companies to become its long-term bosom buddies.

It's not exactly going with the low bid, but for those whose have the ability to prepare convincing plans, seeking business from big companies who are cutting the number of their suppliers can be rewarding indeed.

developing strategic relationships. They want fewer suppliers, and better ties to those they have. That can be good—if you're one of the suppliers who gets picked, you can expect a lot more business than before. But to play in this game, you have to be willing to share more information than may be contained in a sales brochure.

Customers are likely to be concerned about how well your respective strategies fit together. For instance, say your mission statement states that you intend to produce the best-in-the-world example of your product no matter what the cost. Your customer, meanwhile, is a high-volume, low-price reseller of the type of products you make. Even if, for some reason, your offering fits the customer's need this time, odds are good that the relationship won't work out over the long haul. If, on the other hand, a look at your business plan reveals that your companies share the same kind of strategies and have similar objectives in type if not scope, then it's an encouraging sign.

What A Business Plan Can't Do For You

The author of a book on business plans is likely to dream up a lot of benefits to writing one. And a business plan can, in fact, do a lot for you. But it would be a disservice to claim that a good business plan is all you need to succeed. Even a perfectly planned business can fail if fortune fails to smile on it.

Predict The Future

It may seem dishonest to say that a business plan can't predict the future. After all, isn't that what a plan is supposed to do? What are all those projections and forecasts, if not attempts to predict the future? There is a difference, however, even if it is subtle. And that difference is mainly determined by the degree to which you believe in those projections.

The fact is, no projection or forecast is really a hard-and-fast prediction of the future. It's simply an attempt to show what will happen if a particular scenario occurs. That scenario has been determined, by your research and analysis, to be the most likely one of the many that may occur. But it's still just a probability, not a guarantee.

While you're running your business during the future period that is covered by your plan, you'll need to keep in mind that your sales forecasts, market trends and other projections are merely likely, not certain, to occur. Stay alert to events that may change the odds, and adjust your expectations accordingly. If the scenario starts looking as if it will probably play out a lot differently than you expected, you may need to go back and rework your plan to figure out a way to deal with it.

Guarantee Funding

There are all kinds of reasons why a venture capitalist, banker or other investor may refuse to fund your company. It may be that there's no money to give out at the moment. It may be that the investor just backed a company very similar to your own and now wants something different. Perhaps the investor has just promised to back her brother-in-law's firm, or is merely having a bad day and saying no to everything that crosses her desk. The point is, the quality of your plan may have little or nothing to do with your prospects for getting funded by a particular investor.

But what about the investment community as a whole? Surely if you show a well-prepared plan to a lot of people, someone will be willing to back you. Again, not necessarily. Communities, as well as people, are subject to fads, and your idea may be yesterday's fad. Conversely, it may be too far ahead of its time. The same is true of the availability of funds. At times, banks everywhere seem to clamp down on lending, refusing to back even clearly superior borrowers. In many countries, there is no network of venture capitalists to back fledgling companies. Even in the United States, where the VC community is large and active, that was true not too many years ago.

By all means, do the best job you can on your plan. And send it to prospective investors with confidence. But don't consider it a guarantee of funding. There is many a slip twixt cup and lip when it comes to getting backing for a venture. As a rule, you can only count on funding when the money has been deposited to your account.

Raise All The Money You'll Need

Even if you are successful in finding an investor, odds are good that you won't get quite what you asked for. There may be a big difference in what you have to give up, such as majority ownership or control, to get the funds. Or you may simply find you can't snare as large a chunk of cash as you want.

In a sense, a business plan used for seeking funding is part of a negotiation taking place between you and your prospective financial backers. The part of the plan where you describe your financial needs can be considered your opening bid in this negotiation. The other information it contains, from market research to management bios, can be considered supporting arguments. If you look at it in that way, a business plan is an excellent opening bid. It's definite, comprehensive and clear.

But it's still just a bid, and you know what happens to bids in negotiations. They get whittled down, the terms get changed and, sometimes, the whole negotiation breaks down under the force of an ultimatum from one of the parties involved. Does this mean you should ask for a good deal more than you need in your plan? Should you, for example, expect to follow some sort of halve-the-difference strategy with financiers who don't want to pony up all you're asking for?

Actually, that may not be the best strategy either. Investors who see a lot of plans are going to notice if you're asking for way too much. That may make you appear greedy, ill-informed or simply naive. Such a move stands a good chance of alienating those who might otherwise be enthusiastic backers of your plan. It's probably a better idea to ask for a little more than you think you can live with, plus slightly better terms than you would really prefer. That will recognize the fact that you aren't likely to get everything you want, while maintaining your credibility and giving you some negotiating room.

Fool People

A professional financier such as a venture capitalist or bank loan officer will see literally hundreds of business plans in the course of a year. After this has gone on for several years, and the financier has backed some percentage of those plans and seen how events have turned out, he or she becomes very good at rooting out inconsistencies, deflating overblown projections, and zeroing in on weaknesses, including some you'd probably rather not seen highlighted.

In short, most financiers are expert plan analyzers. You have little chance of fooling one of them with an overly optimistic or even downright dishonest plan. That doesn't mean you shouldn't make the best case you honestly can for your business. But the key word is "honestly."

You certainly shouldn't play down your strengths in a plan, but don't try to hide your weaknesses either. Intelligent, experienced financiers will see them anyway. Let's say you propose to open a small bookseller at an address directly across the street from a book superstore. An investor who knows this fact but doesn't see any mention of it in your plan may suspect you've lost your senses—and who could blame her?

Now think about the effect if your plan notes the existence of that big bookstore. That gives you a chance to differentiate yourself explicitly, pointing out that you'll be dealing only in rare antiquarian titles—which the superstore doesn't carry but many of its customers may want. Suddenly that high-volume operator becomes a helpful traffic-builder, not a dangerous competitor.

So recognize and deal appropriately with the weaknesses in your plan. If you do it right, this troubleshooting can become one of the strongest parts of the whole plan.

BUSINESS PLANNING RISKS

If a business plan is to be credible, it has to recognize the inevitable risks associated with any business venture. In the same way, this book has to point out that there are some risks associated with writing a business plan. That's right—while one of the main purposes of a business plan is to help you avoid risk, the act of creating one does create a few risks as well.

The risks you run by writing a plan include the possible disclosure of confidential material. You may lead yourself astray if, through the act of creating a plan, you come to believe too strongly in the many forecasts and projects it contains. If, on the other hand, you fill the plan with purposely over-optimistic prognostication, exaggeration or even falsehood, you may ruin your reputation, or worse. Some plans prepared for the purpose of seeking funds may run afoul of securities laws if they appear to be serving as prospectuses unblessed by the regulators. If you spend too much effort planning, you may not have enough energy or time to actually run your business. And, finally, if you include too much detail in a plan, you may not hurt yourself, but you may seriously dilute the effectiveness of your plan.

After considering all these risks, is writing a business plan worth it? The situation resembles the programs to administer vaccines to children to protect against chickenpox. A certain number of children are going to become ill from the vaccine. However, the idea is that far more would suffer much worse from complications of chickenpox if they weren't vaccinated.

Some parents are more concerned about the risk posed by the vaccine, and opt not to have their children inoculated. But most children do take the shots, and the overall result is positive. Will you inoculate your business against risk with a plan? The choice is yours.

Too Much Detail

Let's start with the least scary risk first. If you put too much detail into your plan, you run the real risk of overburdening anybody who reads it with irrelevant, obscuring detail. A plan isn't supposed to be a potboiler, but it should tell a story—the story of your business. Therefore, it should be as easy as possible to read. That means keeping technical jargon under control.

Explain any terms that may be unfamiliar to a reader who's not an expert on your industry. And never, never make the mistake of trying to overawe a reader with your expertise. There's a good chance someone reading your plan will know more than you. And if you come across as an overblown pretender, you can bet your plan will get short shrift.

It's easy to believe that a longer, more detailed plan is always better than a short, concise one. But financiers and others to whom you may send your plan are likely to be busy people. They may not have time to plow through an inches-thick plan and may in fact be put off by its imposing appearance. Better to keep it to a couple dozen pages, and stick to the truly important material.

Too Much Time

They call it analysis paralysis. It's a syndrome that occurs when you spend so much time planning that you never do anything. For a lot of businesspeople, this is a nonissue—they detest planning so much that there's no chance at all they'd forgo actually doing business and merely plan it.

But business planning can take on a life of its own. It's possible to spend so much time planning a start-up that you miss your window of opportunity or to schedule such frequent updates of a plan for an established business that it becomes difficult to administer the other details of the concern. Big corporations have large staffs who can devote themselves to year-round planning. As a small-business person, you have to be more selective.

Your planning may be approaching the paralysis stage if you find yourself soothing your nerves about starting a business by delaying the start-up date so you can plan more. If you notice yourself putting off crucial meetings so you can dig up more information for a plan update, suspect that planning has become overly important.

It can be difficult to tell enthusiastic planning from destructive planning. And such a judgment is always somewhat arbitrary. But at least know that it's possible. That way, if you fall victim to the overplanning trap, you'll at least have a chance of recognizing the problem before it becomes severe.

Fact Or Fiction?

Can you succeed as planned? A study of 150 start-ups found:

◆ 48 percent didn't achieve expected first-year revenues.

◆ 53 percent needed more capital than expected.

◆ 53 percent underestimated time spent on payroll, taxes, paperwork, recruiting and training.

◆ 55 percent weren't as successful overall as expected.

◆ 63 percent progressed more slowly than projected.

◆ 74 percent of owners earned a lower-than-expected standard of living.

It's A Plan, Not A Prophecy

You put a lot of work into your plan, so it's only understandable that you take it pretty seriously. But it's a mistake to believe too implicitly in the projections, forecasts and budgets that it contains. No matter how carefully you gather data and analyze trends, a plan is not a crystal ball. It's a plan, and it's almost certain that things won't work out quite as it describes.

What's the risk in believing too much in your plan? Plenty. If you bank that the assumptions you make are correct in every detail, you're more likely to miss it when things inevitably change, perhaps profoundly and disastrously. Also, if you take a too-rigid view of how things might turn out, you won't build in the contingency funds and other elements of flexibility that are hallmarks of successful planning.

So do your planning seriously, and take it seriously. But don't take it too seriously. Always ask yourself what will happen if you are wrong. Watch

Fact Or Fiction?

Every business is different, so every plan should be different, right? Not necessarily. Ken Olsen raised money to start Digital Equipment Corp. with the help of a plan copied out of a textbook; he just changed the name and a few numbers and other facts.

carefully as you put your plan into action and build in flexibility to account for change.

You Are Your Plan (So Be Careful How You Present Yourself)

There's no point in planning for failure, but there is a point in writing a business plan that is willing to admit the possibility of failure. It's only natural to hope to create a plan that will describe a roaring success, but you have to be careful not to present an overly optimistic view, especially of such elements as sales, costs and profit margins.

It's tempting to noodle around with the numbers until you come up with the desired result. And if you only make small changes here and there, it may seem all right. What difference does it make? Say you increase your projected market share by 1 percent here, reduce expected costs by 2 percent there, and lower your estimate of required start-up capital by a few percentage points as well.

A number of similarly small changes, in sum, can make a big difference in the bottom line of your plan and turn what otherwise looks like a loser into a projected winner. But don't be seduced. You may be asking for investments from friends and family you care about, as well as putting your own life savings into the enterprise. Arm's-length investors' feelings may not be so important, but if you mislead them in your plan, you may open yourself up to accusation of misrepresentation.

Looking at things through rose-colored glasses in your plan may even doom your business to failure if it causes you to seek insufficient start-up capital, underprice your product or service, or expect unrealistically rapid growth. Temper your enthusiasm. If your plan indicates that the business idea isn't sound, by all means look for mistakes. But don't make the mistake of skewing your plan to fit an idea that isn't sound.

USING YOUR BUSINESS PLAN

In a lot of ways, writing a business plan is an end in itself. The process will teach you a lot about your business that you are unlikely to learn by any other process. You'll spot future trouble spots, identify opportunities, and help your organization run smoothly, simply through the act of writing a plan.

It would be a shame to keep the benefits of a well-done plan to yourself, however. And you shouldn't. You can use your plan to find funding, of course. But a good plan can also help sell your products, services and your whole company to prospects and suppliers, too. And a plan is a valuable tool for communicating your visions, goals and objectives to other managers and key employees in your firm.

Finding Funding With Your Plan

We've discussed the fact that a plan can help you find funding, but how do you use your plan to do that? The first step, of course, is simply to have a plan. You could wait until a banker or investor asks you for one, then spend the weekend throwing something together. But it's far, far better to be able to reach into your briefcase and say, "Will this do?" So Rule 1 is: Be prepared.

Carrying a plan around in your briefcase in hopes that someone will ask you if you have a start-up you want to fund is, of course, not likely to be a successful strategy. So you'll want to present your plan proactively to a group of the kind of people you want to see it, whether they're potential investors, customers, suppliers, partners or other interested parties.

A plan is, in a sense, like an advertisement or a brochure. You can plan to handle it somewhat like a direct marketing piece. In other words, you'll want to come up with a mailing list, a calling list or, if you plan to present the plan in person, an address list of the people you want to pitch it to.

Check trade associations, industry directories, the Yellow Pages and, best of all, your personal business address book for contacts to send your plan to. Then, call, mail or drop in on them.

You don't want to broadcast your plan too widely, however. Odds are good that it will contain at least some sensitive information, ranging from your own salary to the secret ingredients of that margarita that's been packing them in down at your new bar and restaurant. Most venture capitalists and bankers are honest and discreet. But you never know who is working with a competitor— or thinking about becoming one. If you have any doubt about whom

Plan Of Action

The *Directory of Venture Capital* (John Wiley & Sons), by Catherine E. Lister and Thomas D. Harnish, is a thick volume listing the firm names, addresses, phones, partners' names, amounts available to invest and specialties of more than 600 venture capitalists across the country.

Plan Pointer

A confidentiality statement helps control the spread of proprietary information. It should say something like: "This document contains privileged information. Please don't show it to anybody else, and return to International Widgets when you're through." Get your attorney to help with the wording.

you're sending it to, check them out with a phone call: Ask one of the partners if there is any conflict of interest.

Selling With Your Plan

When you're selling with a business plan, using it to inform customers about your company's suitability to become a vendor, you must take a less proactive approach. It's hardly appropriate to be mailing out thick business plan binders to all your prospective customers, although you might do so with venture capitalists.

As a rule, your business plan is only likely to be required in the later stages of being selected as a supplier. At the very least, you should let the customer's process decide when or if you'll present your plan. As an added benefit, working your way through the early stages of vendor selection will give you a chance to rework your plan, if necessary, to stress the areas that you have learned are more important to your potential customer.

Managing With Your Plan

The spread of the open-book management theory means a lot more employees are seeing their companies' business plans than ever before. And that's a good thing, generally. When employees get the key information managers are using to make decisions, they understand management better and make better decisions themselves, and efficiency and profitability often increase.

Many companies hold annual meetings at which they present and discuss an edited version of their business plan to all employees. Others provide new hires with business plan-type information as part of their indoctrination in company culture. Both are effective approaches. You can also use bulletin boards or company newsletters to publish smaller sections of your plan, such as your mission statement or even some details of your financial objectives and how you're progressing.

One drawback to using a plan to help inform and manage your employees is that many won't understand it. Some firms provide employees with rudimentary training in such matters as how to read a financial report before they hand out the company's plans. Often this training is done by the CEO and can take considerable time. But don't be afraid to share details of your business plan with employees. They may turn out to understand it better than you.

Updating Your Plan

Writing a business plan is one of those skills that improves with practice. The first one or two times you create one, you may feel a little unsure of yourself and even less certain that what you're doing has value.

If you go on to start several ventures during your career, you'll naturally write several business plans, and each one will be better than the last. It's likely as well that with better planning skills will come improved business skills, boosting the odds that each successive company you start will do better than the one before.

But there's no reason that only serial entrepreneurs can get the benefit of regular business planning sessions. If you start just one company, or even if you never start a company at all, you can and should be constantly honing your business planning skills by updating and rewriting your business plan.

Updating a plan is normally easier than starting from scratch. Instead of trying to figure out what your basic business concept is, you only have to decide whether it's changing. Instead of wondering where you'll find the current market research you need, you just have to go back to the original source for updated figures. You'll usually be able to reuse the financial formulas, spreadsheets, management biographies and other more or less evergreen contents of your plan.

It's important, however, that a plan update not be a mechanical task, limited to plugging in the most recent sales figures. Take the time to challenge some of the core assumptions of your prior plan, to see if they still hold up. Have profit margins been higher than you expected? Then start planning how to make the most of any extra cash you generate. Is your new retail store unit not performing as well as others have or as you expected? Then now's the time to figure out why. Has competition for your new product arisen sooner than you guessed? Take a look at other products with an eye to seeing if they are also more vulnerable than you think.

In large corporations with strict planning routines requiring annual, semiannual, and quarterly plans and plan updates, managers are spending at least part of their time working on or thinking about a new plan or plan update. All that information flowing up to senior managers in the form of plans helps keep the brass informed. It helps those in the trenches too. It's a fact that everybody is judged by past performance. And the best way to ensure that a year from now you'll be looking back on your performance with satisfaction and pride is to plan now and often.

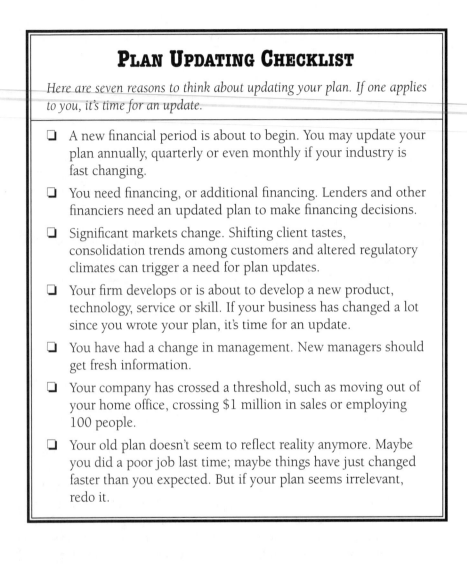

PLAN UPDATING CHECKLIST

Here are seven reasons to think about updating your plan. If one applies to you, it's time for an update.

❏ A new financial period is about to begin. You may update your plan annually, quarterly or even monthly if your industry is fast changing.

❏ You need financing, or additional financing. Lenders and other financiers need an updated plan to make financing decisions.

❏ Significant markets change. Shifting client tastes, consolidation trends among customers and altered regulatory climates can trigger a need for plan updates.

❏ Your firm develops or is about to develop a new product, technology, service or skill. If your business has changed a lot since you wrote your plan, it's time for an update.

❏ You have had a change in management. New managers should get fresh information.

❏ Your company has crossed a threshold, such as moving out of your home office, crossing $1 million in sales or employing 100 people.

❏ Your old plan doesn't seem to reflect reality anymore. Maybe you did a poor job last time; maybe things have just changed faster than you expected. But if your plan seems irrelevant, redo it.

CHAPTER 4

SET YOUR COURSE

Before you start, answer these basic questions

You've decided to write a business plan, and you're ready to get started. Congratulations. You've just greatly increased the chances that your business venture will succeed. But before you start drafting your plan, you need to—you guessed it—plan your draft.

Is planning a plan going too far? Not really, for a couple of reasons. Planning your plan will make it easier to write—and easier to live by. When Stratus Computer founder William Foster was writing the plan for the computer manufacturer, he projected sales in the fifth year would hit $75 million. When, five years later, Stratus hit that total almost to the dollar, Foster was left to wonder what would have happened it he'd planned for $125 million. "I don't think we would have made $125 million," he says, "but I bet we would have done more than $75 million."

One of the most important reasons to plan your plan is that you may be held accountable for the projections and proposals it contains. That's especially true if you use your plan to raise money to finance your company. Let's say you forecast opening four new locations in the second year of your retail operation. An investor may have a beef if, due to circumstances you could have foreseen, you only open two. A business plan can take on a life of its own. Thinking a little about what you want to include in your plan is no more than common prudence.

Second, as you'll soon learn if you haven't already, business plans can be complicated documents. You'll be making lots of decisions as you draft your plan, on serious matters, such as what strategy you'll pursue, as well as less important ones, like what color paper to print it on. Thinking about these decisions in advance is an important way to minimize the time you spend planning and to maximize the time you spend generating income.

To sum up, planning your plan will help control your degree of accountability and reduce time-wasting indecision. To plan your plan, you'll first need to decide what your goals and objectives in business are. As part of that, you'll assess the business you've chosen to start, or are already running, to see what the chances are that it will actually achieve those ends. Finally, you'll take a look at common elements of most plans to get an idea of which ones you want to include and how each will be treated.

DETERMINE YOUR GOALS AND OBJECTIVES

Close your eyes. Imagine that it's five years from now. Where do you want to be? Will you be running a business that hasn't increased significantly in size? Will you command a rapidly growing empire? Will you have already cashed out and be relaxing on a beach somewhere, enjoying your hard-won gains?

Answering these questions is an important part of building a successful business plan. In fact, without knowing where you are going, it's not really possible to plan at all.

Your plan may look beautiful, but without a solid understanding of your own intentions in business, it is likely to lack coherence and, ultimately,

---

BUSINESS PLANNING WITHOUT A NET

When former Lotus Development CEO Jim Manzi joined a young company called Industry Net Corp., he had big plans. He helped raise $25 million for the Pittsburgh-based online seller of industrial products, promising to turn it into the leader in Internet marketing.

But the company, renamed Nets Inc., wasn't able to fulfill its projections. Employment doubled to 300 as Manzi simultaneously tried to develop a market and the technology to handle complex online transactions. Soon the company was running through its investors' stake at the rate of $3 million a month. Meanwhile, revenues were less than $10 million a month.

After less than two years, Nets Inc. still hadn't developed either its technology or its market in the way its plans had forecast. And investors had tired of waiting. They refused to provide more funding, and Nets Inc. had to file for bankruptcy protection in 1997. The experience illustrates the importance of coming up with a plan that not only offers promise but can fulfill that promise as well.

Dream A Little Dream

Don't count out any source of guidance when it comes to pinning down what you want. Even the dreams you dream at night can help boost self-awareness.

Marte Sheeran was a graduate student working on her goal of becoming a history teacher when she began to have doubts about her career choice. She even had doubts about the doubts. "It was a very difficult situation for me, trying to figure out what I was going to do," recalls Sheeran. The answer came, oddly enough, while she was asleep, in a series of vivid dreams.

"I was sinking into a bog, going down and down," Sheeran recalls. "And there was an enormous sense of being very afraid. That put me in touch with feelings that I was not really happy going into academia."

The feeling stirred by the dreams motivated Sheeran to change career plans. She got an MBA and went into business, working as a consultant and manager in several small companies. In 1992, she became an entrepreneur herself, beginning ShopFocus Inc., developer of employee-training products.

Now Sheeran says that without the dreams, she might be a frustrated history educator. She says, "The dreams released all these emotions and gave me the courage to finish my master's degree, and stop there."

prove ineffective. Let's say in one section you describe a mushrooming enterprise on a fast-growth track, then elsewhere endorse a strategy of slow and steady expansion. Any business plan reader worth his or her salt is going to be bothered seriously by inconsistencies like these. They strongly suggest that you haven't thought through your intentions. Avoid inconsistency by deciding in advance what your goals and objectives will be, and sticking to them.

Inconsistency is never a problem for some lucky people who are born knowing what they want to do. They have little or no trouble imagining precisely where their current endeavors will lead. But not everybody's like that. Some of us aren't sure what we'll be doing in the next minute, and most of us are likely to get a little fuzzy when talking about events as far off as a year. Unfortunately, "whatever" isn't going to be part of an acceptable business plan. You need to have some firm goals and objectives, no matter how difficult it is for you to pin your ambitions down.

Buzzword

Goals are short-term objectives, usually incorporating firm time deadlines and quantifiable measures. For instance, a goal may be to reach $1 million in sales within the first 12 months. Written, time-sensitive, quantifiable goals are essential parts of the business planning process.

Now is a good time to free-associate a little bit—to let your mind roam, exploring every avenue that you would like your business to go down. Try writing a personal essay on your business goals. It could take the form of a letter to yourself, written from five years in the future, describing all you have accomplished and how it came about.

As you read such a document, you may make a surprising discovery, such as that you don't really want to own a large, fast-growing enterprise but would be content with a stable small business. Even if you don't learn anything new, though, getting a firm handle on your goals and objectives is a big help in deciding how you'll plan your business.

FROM USHER TO TYCOON

From an early age, David Geffen knew he wanted to be part of Hollywood. This simple, uncomplicated desire was the spur that helped him create a billion-dollar entertainment empire built around music and movies. In fact, it's hard to identify any other advantages that the young Geffen possessed when he traveled from his New York City hometown to Los Angeles. He had only a high school education, no money and no contacts. His first job in Hollywood was as a studio usher.

But Geffen's pursuit of Hollywood success was unswerving. He went so far as to falsify his resume; he indicated he had a college degree to get a job at the William Morris talent agency. After working his way up to a position as an agent, he started his own record company and later sold it. Then he started Geffen Records, which he sold in 1990 for more than $550 million.

David Geffen's plan was nowhere near as sophisticated as even a modest business plan. But, backed by almost total certainty with regard to his ultimate objective, he succeeded on an incredible scale. Today, Geffen is a billionaire and one of the three visionaries, along with Steven Spielberg and Jeffrey Katzenberg, behind Dream-Works SKG.

GOALS AND OBJECTIVES WORK SHEET

If you're having trouble deciding what your goals and objectives are, here are some questions to ask yourself:

1. How determined am I to see this venture succeed?

2. Am I willing to invest my own money and to work long hours for no pay, sacrificing personal time and lifestyle, maybe for years?

3. What's going to happen to me if this venture doesn't work out?

4. If it does succeed, how many employees will this company eventually have?

5. What will be its annual revenues in a year? Five years?

6. What will be its market share in that time frame?

7. Will it be a niche marketer, or will it sell a broad spectrum of good and services?

(Cont'd. on next page)

GOALS AND OBJECTIVES WORK SHEET, CONT'D.

---

8. What are the plans for geographic expansion? Local? National? Global?

9. Am I going to be a hands-on manager, or will I delegate a large proportion of tasks to others?

10. If I delegate, what sorts of tasks will I share? Sales? Technical? Others?

11. How comfortable am I taking direction from others? Could I work with partners or investors who demand input into the company's management?

12. Is this venture going to remain independent and privately owned, or will it eventually be acquired or go public?

Financing

It doesn't necessarily take a lot of money to make a lot of money, but it does take some. That's especially true if, as part of examining your goals and objectives, you envision very rapid growth.

Energetic, optimistic entrepreneurs often tend to believe that sales growth will take care of everything, that they will be able to fund their own growth by generating profits. However, this is rarely the case, for one simple reason: You usually have to pay your own suppliers before your customers pay you. This cash flow conundrum is the reason so many fast-growing companies have to seek bank financing or equity sales to finance their growth. They are literally growing faster than they can afford.

Sometimes the cash flow gap is very large. Pharmaceutical companies, for instance, may spend tens or even hundreds of millions of dollars in a multi-year project to develop and bring to market a new drug. These companies must have large cash flows from other products to fill the gap or seek loans or other forms of financing to avoid running out of money before having a market-ready product.

Other companies require much smaller amounts of capital to finance their ongoing operations. Small service firms such as exterminators or carpet cleaners frequently operate on a cash basis, getting paid with cash, check or credit card at the time they perform their services after making only small outlays for supplies in advance. But as a general rule, your business will most likely have to consider some kind of financing. Now is the time to think about some of the issues that will surface.

Start by asking yourself what kinds of financing you are likely to need—and what you'd be willing to accept. It's easy when you're short of cash, or expect to be short of cash, to take the attitude that almost any source of funding is just fine. But each kind of financing has different characteristics that you should take into consideration when planning your plan. These characteristics take three primary forms:

First, there's the amount of control you'll have to surrender. An equal-equity partner may, quite naturally, demand approximately equal control. Venture capitalists very often demand significant input into management decisions by, for instance, placing one or more people on your board of directors. The wealthy individuals known as angel investors may be very involved or not involved at all, de-

Buzzword

Objectives are long-term aims. They frequently represent the ultimate level to which you aspire. For instance, you may have an objective to retire at 50, or to become the leading supplier in your industry. Neither of these will happen fast, but they help to guide the creation of shorter-term aims.

Plan Of Action

Many enterprises can be started with the help of only modest amounts of cash, no more than the contents of a small savings account. You'll find suggestions for hundreds of businesses you can start for amounts as little as nothing, plus general start-up suggestions, in *Start Your Own Business for $1,000* (Upstart), by Will Davis.

Buzzword

Cash conversion cycle is an arcane financial measure that is a powerful indicator of a business's health. It represents the time it takes to transform outlays into income. For a manufacturer, that means the number of days required to purchase raw material and turn it into inventory, then sales and, finally, collections. The shorter your cash conversion cycle, the better.

pending on personal style. Bankers, at the other end of the scale, are likely to offer no advice whatsoever as long as you make payments of principal and interest on time and are not in violation of any other terms of your loan. You can learn more about the characteristics of each of these financing sources in Chapter 2.

You should also consider the amount of money you are likely to need. Any amount less than several million dollars is too small to be considered for a standard initial public offering of stock, for example. Venture capital investors are most likely to invest amounts of $250,000 to $3 million. On the other hand, only the richest angel investor will be able to provide more than a few hundred thousand dollars, if that.

Almost any source of funds, from a bank to a factor, has some guidelines about the size of financing it prefers. Anticipating the size of your needs now will guide you in preparing your plan.

The third consideration is cost. This can be measured in terms of interest rates and shares of ownership as well as in time, paperwork and plain old hassle. At the top of the list are public offerings of stock, which may cost several hundred thousand dollars in legal and accounting fees to put together, besides requiring a great deal of your own time and attention.

PLANNING

Believe it or not, part of planning your plan is planning what you'll do with your plan. No, we haven't gone

Buzzword

Working capital is the amount of money a business has in cash, accounts receivable, inventory and other current assets. (Current assets are assets likely to be turned into cash within a year.) Net working capital, which is what this term usually refers to, is current assets minus current liabilities. (Current liabilities are things like accounts payable to suppliers and short-term loans due in less than a year.) The higher the amount of net working capital you require, the greater your financing needs are likely to be.

Financing Characteristics Comparison			
Financing Source	Control Issues	Funds Available	Cost
Bank Loan	Little	Varies	Varies
Partner	Large	Varies	Low
Government-backed Loan	Little	Usually Small	Low
Venture Capital	Large	Moderate to Large	Low
Angel Investor	Varies	Small to Moderate	Low
Stock Offering	Large	Large	Large

crazy—at least not yet. As you know from the previous chapter, a business plan can be used for several things, from monitoring your company's progress toward goals to enticing key employees to join your firm. Deciding how you intend to use yours is an important part of preparing to write it.

Do you intend to use your plan to help you raise money? In that case, you'll have to focus very carefully on the executive summary, management and marketing and financial aspects. You'll need to have a clearly focused vision of how your company is going to make money. If you're looking for a bank loan, you'll need to stress your ability to generate sufficient cash flow to service loans. Equity investors, especially venture capitalists, must be shown how they can cash out of your company and generate a rate of return they'll find acceptable.

Do you intend to use your plan to attract talented employees? Then you'll want to emphasize such things as stock options and other aspects of compensation as well as location, work environment, corporate culture and opportunities for growth and advancement. If you're a high-tech start-up, top employees are likely to ask to see your plans for attracting venture capital and later selling out to a bigger firm or going public so they can realize the value of their stock options.

Plan Of Action

Who you are has as much to do with how you prepare for writing your plan as what you hope to do with it. More than half the businesses started in the United States today are begun by women, a fact addressed in a book on business planning for women called *On Your Own: A Woman's Guide to Building a Business* (Upstart), by Laurie B. Zuckerman.

WHEN IS A NEGATIVE A POSITIVE?

Cash is one of the major constraints on the growth of any business. It's the reason why even highly profitable, fast-growing companies frequently have to go hat in hand to borrowers, seeking cash to allow them to fill their orders so they can turn sales into cash. There's one type of company, however, that doesn't have a problem with cash. It's one with a negative cash conversion cycle, and the best-known example in recent years has been Dell Computer Corp.

The rapidly growing Austin, Texas, computer company actually has a cash conversion cycle of minus four days. That means the company collects from its customers, on average, four days before it has to pay its suppliers. Here's how it works:

First, Dell sells direct to customers. This cuts out the typical 90-day wait for payment experienced by manufacturers who sell through retailers. Dell bills individual customers' credit cards immediately upon shipping their computers. Its corporate customers are asked to pay within 30 days.

The second part is the way Dell manages outlays of cash. It gets 30-day terms from suppliers and also asks that they bill for components only when the parts actually leave the trucks and enter the factory. There, in as little as a few hours, components are assembled into computers and shipped, and individual customers' credit cards are charged or corporate buyers are invoiced.

The result is that Dell collects cash faster than its operations are spending it. That frees Dell from the delay, distraction and cost of arranging and paying for loans or other external financing. It's one of the things that makes the company such a fearsome and successful competitor. It's estimated the company could grow at an annual rate of 500 percent using only internally generated cash.

Do you anticipate showing your plan to suppliers to demonstrate that you are a worthy customer? A solid business plan may convince a supplier of some precious commodity to favor you over your rivals. It may also help you to arrange supplier credit—one of the most useful forms of financing to a small business. You may want to stress your blue-ribbon customer list and spotless record of repaying trade debts in this plan.

Do you hope to convince big customers you will be a dependable supplier? Then you'll want to emphasize your staying power, innovation and special capabilities. And in this plan, unlike the supplier-targeted one, you may want to play down relationships with other big customers, especially if they are foes of the one you're wooing.

Do you expect to use your plan only for internal purposes? Then you'll want to build in many milestones, benchmarks and other tools for measuring and comparing your future performance against the plan. Such things may be of little interest to a banker evaluating your loan-worthiness but could make all the difference between a useful plan and one that's no good at all for monitoring corporate performance.

These distinctions are not merely academic. A plan that's well suited for internal purposes would probably be completely wrong for taking to a potential Fortune 500 customer. Actually, the marketplace of business plan consumers is even more finely segmented than that. A plan for a bank, for instance, wouldn't accomplish much by including a strategy for selling the company to a large conglomerate several years down the road, while a venture capitalist would look for your exit strategy very early on.

Think about all this and keep it in mind as you create your plan. Along the way, you'll have to make many decisions about what to include or leave out and what to stress or play down. Setting some direction now about how you intend to use your plan will make those later decisions faster and more accurate.

> **Buzzword**
>
> Trade credit is an important source of financing for many companies. It consists of your accounts payable, representing bills you owe to suppliers. Typical trade credit terms let you pay the bill in 30 days without penalty. You can learn more about trade credit in Chapter 2.

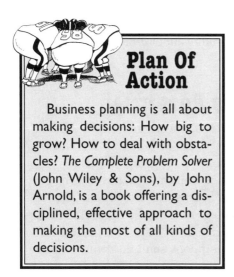

> **Plan Of Action**
>
> Business planning is all about making decisions: How big to grow? How to deal with obstacles? *The Complete Problem Solver* (John Wiley & Sons), by John Arnold, is a book offering a disciplined, effective approach to making the most of all kinds of decisions.

HIRING

One of the beauties of being an entrepreneur, as opposed to a solo practitioner or freelancer, is that you can leverage the activities and skills of all the people who are your em-

Fact Or Fiction?

Any business owner is an entrepreneur, right? Actually, most people define an entrepreneur as someone who started a business from scratch and intends to grow it to a large size. But that leaves out employees, even if they own a share, as well as people who bought existing businesses and those who started firms but, for various reasons, don't attempt to make them grow very much.

ployees. This is one of the secrets to building a huge personal fortune in business. And it's one you can use even if you didn't happen to be born with a silver spoon in your mouth, or an oil well in your backyard.

To use a simple example of the profit power of people, say you start a public relations firm. You bill clients $60 an hour, plus mailing and other office expenses, for services provided by your account executives. You pay your staff $30 an hour including benefits. Before expenses for rent and other overhead items, then, you clear $30 for every hour one of your AEs bills. If you can grow your AE staff very large (and generate enough business to keep them busy), it can leverage your earnings very rapidly indeed.

The flip side of all this is that, to earn the $30 gross margin on each employee's billable hour, you have to manage the employee. You may also have to generate the sales, issue the invoices, make the collections and otherwise run the company's functions. If you pay somebody else to do it, it costs you money and control.

So one of the questions you need to ask yourself when assessing your goals and objectives is: How many people do I plan to hire to work at my company?

The decision of how many people you want to manage is entirely up to you. But the decision of when to start thinking about it has been made for you. That time is now.

ASSESS YOUR COMPANY'S POTENTIAL

For most of us, unfortunately, our desires about where we would like to go are not as important as our businesses' ability to take us there. Put another way, if you choose the wrong business, you're going nowhere.

Luckily, one of the most valuable uses of a business plan is to help you decide whether the venture you have your heart set on is really likely to fulfill your dreams. Many, many business ideas never make it past the planning stage because their would-be founders, as part of a logical and coherent planning process, test their assumptions and find them wanting.

Test your idea against at least two variables. First, financial, to make sure this business makes economic sense. Second, lifestyle, because who wants a successful business that they hate?

Financial Potential

The main reason for businesses to be abandoned is failure to live up to financial expectations. Part of your planning process is to see if you can reasonably expect to actually turn a profit with your business. You'll also want to know when that's going to happen and, crucially, how much of an investment it will take to get you to that point.

Fact Or Fiction?

Must entrepreneurs always remain in control of their companies? Sometimes they have to let go. One case in point is when a company grows to more than 100 employees, and seat-of-the-pants management no longer works. The usual solution: Hire a professional manager as CEO.

Let's take a look at Madeline Fisher, a would-be newsletter publisher who's drafting a plan to see whether her dream business is going to fly. The would-be publisher envisions making a decent living (or maybe better) moonlighting part-time from her regular job producing a newsletter on a topic she knows and loves—namely, marketing coffee bars. She's done some research and made some assumptions about the market, how she'll reach it and the businesses' publishing operations. During the course of preparing her plan, she quickly finds out whether a business built around those assumptions is going to work.

Fact Or Fiction?

Beware the 1 Percent Fallacy. It occurs when a planner looks at a large market and thinks, "If I can just get 1 percent, this will work." The problem is, few markets lack tough competitors, and even a modest-sounding 1 percent is no gimme. Test share projections against reality and avoid the 1 Percent Fallacy.

Her market research tells her there are 10,000 people in the United States whose work largely or entirely involves marketing coffee bars. She guesses, based on rates she's paid for other professional newsletters, that they'd be willing to pay $200 for 12 annual issues of a 16-page newsletter packed with tips and tricks for getting people to come in and buy coffee and accessories. Reading up on newsletters, she learns that a well-designed direct-mail solicitation will generate subscriptions from 1 percent of recipients.

Checking with a local printer and

Plan Pointer

Every type of business has one or more key indicators that hint at its long-term viability. For newsletters, for example, it's the number of people who re-subscribe. For mail order sellers, it's the response rate to direct mail marketing efforts. Find your business's key indicators, describe them in your plan and monitor them carefully.

mailing service she learns that it will cost her around $1 to send a sales letter to each person on a rented mailing list. The same sources inform her that printing and mailing each copy of the 16-page newsletter will run her about $2. Since she works full-time in a retail marketing job, she'll have to hire a freelance or part-time editor to write and edit the contents, at around $100 a page, or $1,600 per issue.

The future publisher of *Coffee Bar Marketing News* has done a good research job. Now it's time to pull all this together to test its financial potential. She decides it would be reasonable to go for having 200 subscribers at the end of the first year. Then she'd like to double that annually until she has 1,600 subscribers. That represents 16 percent of the market today. But it's not ridiculous considering that she hasn't seen any competition and that the number of coffee bars and, presumably, coffee bar marketers, is growing at a healthy clip.

Punching a few numbers into her calculator, she comes up with a figure for gross annual sales with 1,600 subscribers each paying $200 annually. Wow! $320,000. Even after paying $28,800 to print and mail the issues, $19,200 for writing and editing and an estimated $4,200 in office costs, that still leaves . . .

Projected Subscribers	1,600
Revenues ($200 x 1,600)	$320,000
Costs (printing, labor and overhead)	$61,800
Gross Profit	$258,200

Double wow! This is more than decent. Madeline dives into the rest of her calculations, dizzy with excitement. She quickly regains her balance. The problem, she finds, is twofold.

First, there's the cost of getting those subscribers. Getting 200 subscribers will require mailing 20,000 pieces, based on her hoped-for 1 percent return rate. At approximately $1 per direct-mail piece, plus labor, printing, mailing and overhead, she loses money on each new subscriber the first year.

Annual Revenue Per Subscriber	$200
Marketing Costs Per Subscriber ($1 mailing with 1 percent return)	$100
Printing And Mailing For One Copy Of 12 Issues	$24
Fixed Costs (labor and overhead/200)	$117
Subtotal Costs Per Subscriber	$241
First Year Net Loss Per Subscriber	–$41

Madeline figures, correctly, that the key is to get some more subscribers, and to convince them to re-subscribe year after year. She does some more research and learns that a 50 percent re-subscription rate is doable. Then she does some more figuring. The results of her financial analysis show that she'll reach 1,600 subscribers, and a healthy profit, after four years.

First Year

Starting Number Of Subscribers	0
Re-subscribers (50 percent of starting number)	0
New Subscribers (to give 100 percent annual increase)	200
Total Subscribers	200
Annual Subscription Revenues	$40,000
Marketing Costs (new subs x $100)	$20,000
Printing And Mailing Costs (subs x $24)	$4,800
Labor And Overhead	$23,400
Total Costs	$48,200
Pretax Net Profit Or Loss	$8,200

Second Year

Starting Number Of Subscribers	200
Re-subscribers (50 percent of starting number)	100
New Subscribers (to give 100 percent annual increase)	300
Total Subscribers	400
Annual Subscription Revenues	$80,000
Marketing Costs (new subs x $100)	$30,000
Printing And Mailing Costs (subs x $24)	$9,600
Labor And Overhead	$23,400
Total Costs	$63,000
Pretax Net Profit Or Loss	$17,000

Third Year

Starting Number of Subscribers	400
Re-subscribers (50 percent of starting number)	200
New Subscribers (to give 100 percent annual increase)	600
Total Subscribers	800
Annual Subscription Revenues	$160,000
Marketing Costs (new subs x $100)	$60,000
Printing And Mailing Costs (subs x $24)	$19,200
Labor And Overhead	$23,400
Total Costs	$102,600
Pretax Net Profit Or Loss	$57,400

Fourth Year

Starting Number Of Subscribers	800
Re-subscribers (50 percent of starting number)	400
New Subscribers (to give 100 percent annual increase)	1,200
Total Subscribers	1,600
Annual Subscription Revenues	$320,000
Marketing Costs (new subs x $100)	$120,000
Printing And Mailing Costs (subs x $24)	$38,400
Labor And Overhead	$23,400
Total Costs	$181,800
Pretax Net Profit Or Loss	$138,200

Madeline's analysis shows her newsletter venture has definite financial potential, even if it's not quite as rosy as this quick forecast suggests. She should, for instance, apply an inflation factor—4 percent a year is a good figure—to expenses such as overhead. She has a more serious problem with her marketing plan, however. Is it really reasonable to mail 120,000 pieces of mail a year to a marketplace of just 10,000 people? Probably not, but Madeline left out positives as well. For instance, there are a number of other marketing tools, such as publicity, which she hasn't considered in her plan. And with a good product, she should be able to beat the 50 percent renewal rate, saving her a bundle on marketing.

We'll be talking in Chapter 12 about how to make detailed financial forecasts, as well as covering marketing plans comprehensively in Chapter 10. For now, Madeline's quick analysis shows that her venture does have the potential to be financially rewarding.

Assessing Your Company's Potential

Answer the following questions to help you outline your company's potential. There are no wrong answers. The objective is simply to help you decide how well your proposed venture is likely to match up with your goals and objectives.

Financial

1. What initial investment will the business require?

2. How much control are you willing to relinquish to investors?

3. When will the business turn a profit?

4. When can investors, including you, expect a return on their money?

5. What are the projected profits of the business over time?

6. Will you be able to devote yourself full-time to the business, financially?

7. What kind of salary or profit distribution can you expect to take home?

(Cont'd. on next page)

ASSESSING YOUR COMPANY'S POTENTIAL, CONT'D.

8. What are the chances the business will fail?

9. What will happen if it does?

Lifestyle

1. Where are you going to live?

2. What kind of work are you going to be doing?

3. How many hours will you be working?

4. Will you be able to take vacations?

5. What happens if you get sick?

6. Will you earn enough to maintain your lifestyle?

7. Does your family understand and agree with the sacrifices you envision?

Lifestyle Concerns

The decision to become an entrepreneur is as much a lifestyle choice as it is a business option. Entrepreneurs tend to work long hours, often for low pay in the beginning. As a natural consequence of their position as founders and owners, they bear a much greater burden of worry and pressure than other employees. The road to entrepreneurial success is frequently paved with 16-hour days and seven-day weeks. Now is the time to ask yourself if you really love what you plan to do that much, or if you'd be better taking on a less demanding project.

> **Buzzword**
>
> A lifestyle entrepreneur is one who starts a business not to dominate an industry or even to get rich, but because he or she thinks it will be more enjoyable to own a company than to work for one. Lifestyle entrepreneurs may want to live in a certain place, to work flexible hours, or simply to be able to make their own decisions.

You also may have to consider others' feelings about your proposed lifestyle changes. Entrepreneurship can be a great thing for a family because it provides flexibility and financial benefits that most employees can only dream about. Or it can represent considerable strain. Many entrepreneurs rarely take vacations, especially during the first years of getting their venture off the ground. Another issue has to do with how the business will accommodate the normal ups and downs of life. What happens if you get sick? Are you going to be able to take a few days off every now and then?

Lifestyle concerns are complex. They involve everything from where you are going to live to the kind and amount of work you'll be doing. Unlike the financial analysis of your company's potential, there are few hard-and-fast answers to lifestyle concerns and almost none that can be termed wrong or right. You simply have to think the matter over and decide whether you'll be happy with your venture.

A QUICK LOOK AT COMMON PLAN ELEMENTS

There are a few basic ingredients that almost all business plans include. They include an executive summary plus a description of management, a marketing plan, descriptions of products and services, operations background and financial data. We'll be going into all of these business plan elements in detail in later chapters. For now, though, here's a quick look at the major components of a business plan.

SUPER SUMMARY

Jimmy Treybig, the founder of Tandem Computers and now a venture capitalist in Austin, Texas, says that the executive summary is the most important part of the plans he reviews. "What I want is 20 sentences that tell me why someone who gives them money is going to get rich," says the veteran businessman.

Treybig's 20 sentences should contain information on how the business will address the market, the product idea, the competitive advantage, the amount of money that is needed, who is on the team, and how it will all come together. Most important of all, he says, the executive summary should convey urgency. Treybig wants to be told, "It's going to explode, and I'd better invest now or I'm going to miss out."

Executive Summary

One thing every plan has is an Executive Summary. It may be called something else, but there is sure to be a one- or two-page brief describing what the company's up to. The executive summary may contain things that aren't found elsewhere in the plan, such as a vision statement—a statement of corporate mission or an exploration of the company's ultimate business objective. But generally it will encapsulate other sections of the plan dealing with the market, features of the product or service, competition, management team and financial data. Many plans written for money-raising purposes also include here a statement of how much money the business is seeking to raise and how that money will be used.

Management

If you had a nickel for every financier who said, "I don't invest in products; I invest in people," you wouldn't need to raise money to fund your business. You wouldn't even need to be in business unless you simply enjoyed it, because you would already be rich. The point is that the people, especially the key managers in your company, are of great interest to potential investors, partners and employees.

The management section of your plan will consist of brief descriptions of your key managers, including their backgrounds and functions in your organization. You should cover pivotal positions, such as the vice president of research and development in a high-tech company, as well as more mundane functions, including CFO, controller and so on. Plan readers want to see evidence of a well-rounded management team that can deal with whatever comes up. You may want to include an organizational chart graphically depicting individual responsibilities and who reports to whom. If you want to provide detailed resumes on key managers, you may include them as appendices at the end of the plan.

Product Or Service

Your product or service is likely to be the thing you are most interested in. So it should be a pleasure to describe its features and benefits in this section of your plan. This is the place to explain all the key elements of the product or service, including its design, underlying technology and, especially, competitive advantages in the marketplace.

Plan Pointer

Are you the only manager you have? Then approach the management section of your plan as if you were writing a resume for a job. Put down anything that qualifies you to run this company, including prior work experience, school work, volunteer activities, homemaking experience and even hobbies. When you're all you have, people are going to want to know as much as possible about you.

Marketing

Ralph Waldo Emerson probably did countless small-business people a disservice when he proclaimed that the world will beat a path to the door of the inventor of a better mousetrap. The truth is, of course, without an effective marketing plan, you're unlikely to sell anything. This section of your plan is the place to tell readers about your plans for positioning, pricing, placing and promoting your product or service to potential customers.

Buzzword

Logistics is the science of moving objects from one location to another. For manufacturers and retailers, the logistics of supplies and products is crucial. For service firms, often the logistics of moving employees around is more important.

Operations

Many businesses succeed or fail on the basis of things that only people who work there ever notice. Wal-Mart didn't become the world's largest retailer because it snagged the best locations or hired the best ad agencies. It beat out Sears, Montgomery Ward and the rest because of its extremely efficient systems for stocking and distributing the most profitable products in the most profitable manner. Its likely that your business is based in large part on some aspect of its operations—manufacturing, logistics, customer service, etc.—that plan readers will want to know about.

Financial Data

In the financial section you'll provide your income statements, balance sheets, cash flow statement and other information on the money side of things. It's important, of course, that the final result be some kind of profit. But internal consistency is also imperative. If you don't stick to your assumptions about profit margins, selling prices, materials costs or other key measures throughout this section, it will show up immediately.

For some readers, such as bankers looking for balance sheet assets to collateralize a loan, the financial section may be the most important part of the plan. For others, such as employees looking for a great place to work, it's the least interesting. But it's actually of prime importance for everybody, because this section is where you'll distinguish a business from a mere hobby. If the numbers add up to a reasonable return on your investment, congratulations. Your plan—and your business—have at least a reasonable chance of succeeding.

CHAPTER 5

MATCH GAME

Finding the right plan for you

Business plans tend to have a lot of elements in common, like cash flow projections and marketing plans. And many of them share certain objectives as well, such as raising money, or persuading a partner to join the firm. But business plans are not all the same any more than all businesses are.

Depending on your business and what you intend to use your plan for, you may need a very different type of business plan from what another entrepreneur needs. Plans differ widely in their length, their appearance, the detail of their contents, and the varying emphases they place on different aspects of the business. "They come thick, they come thin, they come ugly, they come pretty," says Benjamin M. Rosen of venture capital firm Sevin Rosen Management Co. "Mostly, they just keep coming."

DIFFERENCES AMONG INDUSTRIES

One of the main reasons for differences among plans is that industries are different. A retailer isn't much like a manufacturer, and a professional services firm isn't much like a fast-food restaurant. Each of them requires certain critical components for success—components that may be irrelevant or even completely absent in the operations of another type of firm.

For instance, inventory is a key concern of both retailers and manufacturers. Expert, innovative management of inventory is a very important part of the success of Wal-Mart, one of the great all-time success stories of retail. And Dell Computer, with its direct-sales model, is another enterprise skyrocketing to global prominence with the help of, among other things, very savvy inventory management. Any business plan that purported to describe the important elements of these businesses would of necessity have to devote considerable space to telling how the managers planned to reduce inventory, increase turns and so on.

Now let's take a look at a professional services firm, such as a management consultant. The consultant has no inventory whatsoever. Her offerings consist entirely of the management analysis and advice she and her staff can provide. She doesn't have to pay now for goods to be sold later, or lay out cash to store products for eventual sale. The management consultant's business plan, therefore, wouldn't have any section on inventory or its management, control and reduction.

This is just one pretty obvious example of the differences among plans for different industries. Sometimes even companies in more closely related industries have significantly different business plans. For instance, a fine French restaurant's plan might need a section detailing how the management intended to attract and retain a distinguished chef. At another restaurant, one catering to the downtown lunchtime crowd, a great deal of plan space might be devoted to the critical concern of location, and very little to staffing issues.

PRESENTING YOURSELF IN THE BEST LIGHT

The reason that plan selection is so important is that it has a powerful effect on the overall impact of your plan. You want your plan to present yourself and your business in the best, most accurate light. That's true no matter what you intend to use your plan for, whether it's destined for presentation at a venture capital conference, or will never leave your own office or be seen outside internal strategy sessions.

When you select clothing for an important occasion, odds are you try to pick items that will play up your best features. Think about your plan the same way. You want to reveal any positives that your business may have and make sure they receive due consideration.

When you select your plan type, it's a lot like picking a dress or suit for a big interview or social outing. Flip through your closet carefully—this outfit may have an important bearing on how useful your plan eventually turns out to be.

TYPES OF PLANS

Business plans can be divided roughly into four separate types. There are very short plans, or miniplans. And there are working plans, presentation plans and even electronic plans. They require very different amounts of labor, and not always with proportionately different results. That is to say, a more elaborate plan is not guaranteed to be superior to an abbreviated one, depending on what you want to use it for.

The Miniplan

It's safe to say that almost every business idea starts out as a miniplan of some sort. It may be no more than a quick jotting down—even a mental scrawl—of some basic business formula or statement. A thought such as "I'm sure I can make one of those for less than he's selling them for!" could be considered a sort of business plan. Ideally, of course, even a miniplan will be more elaborate than that.

A miniplan may consist of one to 10 pages and should include at least cursory attention to such key matters as business concept, financing needs, marketing plan and financial statements, especially cash flow, income projection and balance sheet. It's a great way to quickly test a business concept or measure the interest of a potential partner or minor investor. It can also serve as a valuable prelude to a full-length plan later on.

Be careful about misusing a miniplan. It's not intended to substitute for a full-length plan. If you send a miniplan to an investor who's looking for a comprehensive one, you're only going to look foolish.

The Working Plan

A working plan is a tool to be used to operate your business. It has to be long on detail but may be short on presentation. As with a miniplan, you probably can afford a somewhat higher degree of candor and informality when preparing a working plan. In a plan you intend to present to a bank loan committee, you might describe a rival as "competing primarily on a price basis." In a working plan, your comment about the same competitor might be: "When is Jones ever going to stop this insane price-cutting!"

A plan intended strictly for internal use may also omit some elements that would be important in one aimed at someone outside the firm. You probably don't need to include an appendix with resumes of key executives, for example. Nor would a working plan especially benefit from, say, product photos.

Internal-policy considerations may guide the decision about whether to include or exclude certain information from a working plan. Many entrepreneurs, for instance, are sensitive about employees knowing the precise salary the owner takes home from the business. To the extent such information can be left out of a working plan without compromising its utility, you can feel free to protect your privacy.

Fit and finish are likely to be quite different in a working plan. It's not essential that a working plan be printed on high-quality paper and enclosed in a fancy binder. An old three-ring with "plan" scrawled across it with a felt-tip marker will serve quite well. That doesn't mean you should skimp on additions such as graphs and charts, however. These do more than look nice. They can be useful tools for communicating concepts and trends to other managers, as well as for reinforcing them in your own mind.

Internal consistency of facts and figures is just as crucial with a working plan as with one aimed at outsiders. You don't have to be as careful, however, about such things as typos in the text, perfectly conforming to business style, being consistent with date formats, etc. This document is like an old pair of khakis you wear into the office on Saturdays, or that one ancient delivery truck that never seems to break down. It's there to be used, not admired.

The Presentation Plan

If you take a working plan, with its low stress on cosmetics and impression, and twist the knob to boost the amount of attention paid to its looks, you'll wind up with a presentation plan. This plan is suitable for showing to bankers, investors and others outside the company.

Almost all the information in a presentation plan is going to be the same as your working plan, although it may be styled somewhat differently. For instance, you should use standard business vocabulary, omitting the informal jargon, slang and shorthand that's so useful in the workplace and is ap-

---

SLIDING BY

For Tod Loofbourrow, the presentation of his plan was everything—literally. The president and founder of Foundation Technologies, a human resources software company, grew his company to 70 employees without ever having a conventional plan written down on paper.

But that doesn't mean Loufbourrow didn't plan or use his plan wisely. Instead, he confined his planning to creating impressive presentations, primarily in the form of slides created in Microsoft PowerPoint, that conveyed the mission and promise of Foundation to investors. "We raised $8 million in venture capital with eight PowerPoint slides," he says.

"Our plan was really about presenting our story in the form of slides and oral discussion," explains Loofbourrow. The key task of a plan, he feels, is the ability to convey the company's story economically and convincingly rather than to amass a pile of detail.

propriate in a working plan. Remember, these readers won't be familiar with your operation. Unlike the working plan, this plan isn't being used as a reminder but as an introduction.

You'll also have to include some added elements. Among investors' requirements for due diligence is information on all competitive threats and risks. Even if you consider some to be of only peripheral significance, you need to address these concerns by providing the information. In the end, raising and dealing with such issues will only make your plan appear stronger.

Fact Or Fiction?

The first business plan a venture capitalist pulls from a pile will have the most impressive cover, loaded with color and eye-catching graphics, right? Actually, the deciding factor in drawing initial attention is usually the company name, followed by geographic location.

The big difference between the presentation and working plans is in the details of appearance and polish. A working plan may be run off on the office printer and stapled together at one corner. A presentation plan will be printed by a high-quality printer, probably using color. It will be bound expertly into a booklet that is durable and easy to read. It will include graphics such as charts, graphs, tables and illustrations.

It's crucial that you have your presentation plan proofread repeatedly, in addition to using spell-checking software. Typos, misspellings and grammatical errors will detract from the overall impression of smooth perfection that you want to impart and may suggest to readers that you are not as thorough as you should be.

It's also essential that a presentation plan be accurate and internally consistent. A mistake here could be construed as a misrepresentation by an unsympathetic outsider. At best, it will make you look less than careful. If the plan's summary describes a need for $40,000 in financing, but the cash flow projection shows $50,000 in financing coming in during the first year, you might think, "Oops! Forgot to update that summary to show the new numbers." The investor you're asking to pony up the cash, however, is unlikely to be so charitable.

The Electronic Plan

The majority of business plans are composed on a computer of some kind, then printed out and presented in hard copy. But more and more business information that once was transferred between parties only on paper is now sent electronically. And you may find it appropriate to have an electronic version of your plan available as well. An electronic plan can be

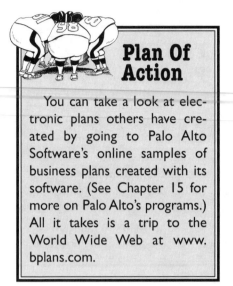

Plan Of Action

You can take a look at electronic plans others have created by going to Palo Alto Software's online samples of business plans created with its software. (See Chapter 15 for more on Palo Alto's programs.) All it takes is a trip to the World Wide Web at www. bplans.com.

handy for presentations to a group using a computer-driven overhead projector, for example, or for satisfying the demands of a discriminating investor who wants to be able to delve deeply into the underpinnings of complex spreadsheets.

An electronic plan may consist of a file on a floppy disk, or one sent by electronic mail via the Internet. It may be a document in the format of a popular word processing program, or a slideshow-type presentation.

One of the nice things about an electronic business plan is the speed with which you can transmit it. If you receive an expression of interest in your company from a financier or potential partner, you can electronically mail a plan to this person in minutes. Relying on express mail will require at least a day, and even a cross-town courier will take hours.

Another potential advantage of an electronic plan is that it lets a reader, by loading any spreadsheets it contains into his or her computer, see the underlying formulas you use for figuring important numbers. It's fairly easy to make spreadsheets with interlocking formulas that are so complicated that it's hard to tell exactly what is going on behind the scenes. Being able to view your calculations may give some readers an added comfort level that you're not trying to pull the wool over their eyes with your financial projections. This won't be the case, by the way, if your plan's spreadsheets consist of only the data copied into a grid format.

It's worth noting that an electronic plan is cheaper than a printed one. You can spend a bundle having a couple dozen copies of a long plan color-printed and professionally bound. Making a new copy of an electronic plan, on the other hand, is limited to the cost of a floppy disk.

There are some problems with electronic plans, however. The fact that they're easier to copy and disseminate makes it harder to control who sees your plan. The person you're sending it to has to have access to an appropriate computer and software to see it at all. Many people are not willing to look at electronic plans, preferring the convenience and familiarity of a paper plan. So despite some significant advantages to electronic plans, you aren't likely to be able to completely replace the paper version.

WHY YOU MAY WANT MORE THAN ONE PLAN

So you've looked over the different types of plans. Which one is for you? Actually, odds are good that you'll need more than one variety, perhaps even all these and more besides. That's because business plans have many uses and even more audiences. And if you want to get maximum impact from your plan, you'll need to tailor it to address the particular needs of your audience of the moment.

Target Audiences

The potential readers of a business plan are a varied bunch, ranging from venture capitalists to employees. While this is a diverse group, it is a finite one. And each type of reader does have certain typical interests. If you know these interests up front, you can be sure to take them into account when preparing a plan for that particular audience.

Active venture capitalists see hundreds of plans in the course of a year. Most plans probably receive no more than a glance from a given venture capitalist before being rejected, while others get just a cursory inspection prior to being mailed back. Even if your plan excites initial interest, it may receive only a few minutes of attention to begin with. It's essential with these harried investors that you make the right impression fast. Emphasize a cogent, succinct summary and explanation of the basic business concept, and do not stint on the details about the impressive backgrounds of your management team.

Bankers tend to be more formal than venture capitalists and more concerned with financial strength than with exciting concepts and impressive resumes. For these readers, you'll want to give extra attention to balance sheets and cash flow statements. Make sure they're fully detailed, and come with notes to explain any anomalies or possible points of confusion.

Angel investors may not insist on seeing a plan at all, but, as we pointed out in Chapter 3, your responsibilities as a businessperson require you to show them one anyway. For such an informal investor, prepare a less formal plan. Rather than going for impressive bulk, seek brevity. An angel

Fact Or Fiction?

Many entrepreneurs don't write plans, so if you do, that should place you in a select group, right? Actually, it's a pretty big group. Famed venture capitalist Frederick R. Adler estimates he's seen 3,000 plans cross his desk alone. But most, he says, "are pretty lousy."

investor used to playing her hunches might be put off by an imposing plan, rather than impressed with your thoroughness.

If you were thinking about becoming a partner in a firm, you'd no doubt be very concerned with the responsibilities you would have, the authority you would carry, and the ownership you would receive in the enterprise. Naturally, anyone who is considering partnering with you is going to have similar concerns. So make sure that any plan presented to a potential partner deals comprehensively with the ownership structure and clearly spells out matters of control and accountability.

Customers who are looking at your business plan are probably doing so because they contemplate building a long-term relationship with you. Also, they are certainly going to be more concerned about your relationships with your other customers and, possibly, suppliers, than most plan readers. So deal with these sections of your plan in depth. If your customer has special requirements, such as the ability to make hourly deliveries to a plant without variations of more than a few minutes, you'll want to talk about your record on these matters, which would probably be of little or no interest to other readers. On the other hand, customers presumably will already be familiar with trends in your industry, so you can probably skip or abbreviate these sections.

Suppliers have a lot of the same concerns as customers, except they're in the other direction on the supply chain. They'll want to make sure you can pay your bills, above all, so be sure to include adequate cash flow forecasts and other financial reports. Suppliers, who naturally would like their customers to order more and more, are likely to be quite interested in your growth prospects. In fact, if you can show you're probably going to be growing a lot, you may be in a better position to negotiate terms with your suppliers.

Strategic allies usually come to you for something specific—technology, distribution, complementary customer sets, etc. So naturally any plan you show to a potential ally will stress this aspect of your operation. Sometimes potential allies may also be potential competitors, of course. So you may want to present your plan in stages, saving sensitive information such as financials and marketing strategies for later in the process, when trust has been established.

Managers in your company are using the plan primarily to remind themselves of objectives, to keep strategies clear, and to monitor company performance and market conditions. You'll want to stress such things as corporate mission and vision statements and analyses of current industry and economic factors. The most important part of a plan intended for management consumption is probably in the financials. You'll want to take special care to make it easy for managers to compare sales revenue, profitability and other key financial measures against planned performance.

Employees in companies that use open-book management styles should receive a version of your plan edited for their understanding and needs, as well as your own comfort level. It's good to be frank and open, but if you're uncomfortable with, for instance, employees knowing exactly what all the managers earn, it's your option to leave this information out. As is the case with managers, an employee's plan should make it easy to compare actual production levels,

Plan Pointer

Instead of writing a whole new plan for each audience, construct a modular plan with interchangeable sections. Pull out the resume section for internal use, for example, and plug it back in for presentation to an investor. A modular, mix-and-match plan saves time and effort while preserving flexibility.

costs and other measures against prior projections. You may also include some data, such as rates of workplace accidents or absenteeism, that would be of only peripheral interest to investors.

There's one caution to the plan-customization exercise. Limit your alterations from one plan to another to modifying the emphasis of the information you present. Don't show one set of numbers to a banker you're trying to borrow from and another to a partner you're trying to lure on board. It's one thing to stress one aspect of your operation over another for presentation purposes and entirely another to distort the truth.

CHAPTER 6

SUM IT UP

Why the executive summary is the most important part of your plan

The first part of your plan that anybody will see, after the title page and table of contents, is the summary. Sometimes called the executive summary, it could also be considered sort of an expanded table of contents. That's because it's more than an introduction to the rest of the plan. It's supposed to be a brief look at the key elements of the whole plan.

The actual executive summary may be only a page or two. In it you may include your mission and vision statements, a brief of your plans and goals, a quick look at your company and its organization, an outline of your strategy, and highlights of your financial status and needs.

If you've ever read a *Cliffs Notes* version of a classic novel, you get the idea. Your executive summary is the *Cliffs Notes* to your business plan.

THE SUMMARY IS THE MOST CRITICAL PART

Labor over your summary. Polish it. Refine it. Ask friends and colleagues to take a look at it and take their suggestions to heart. If your plan isn't getting the response you want when you put it to work, suspect a flaw in the summary. If you get a chance to look at another plan that was used to successfully raise a pile of cash, give special scrutiny to the executive summary.

The summary is the most important part of your whole plan. Even though a plan is only 15 or 20 pages, it's difficult for most people to keep that much information in their minds at once. It's much easier to get your arms around the amount of information—just one or a few pages—in an executive summary. As a result, to a considerable extent your plan is going to be judged on what you include in the summary and on how well you present it.

A good rule of thumb for writing an effective and efficient business plan

Fact Or Fiction?

Since the executive summary comes first in your plan, you may think you should write it first as well. Actually, however, you should write it last, after you've spent considerable time mulling over every other part of your plan. Only then will you truly be able to produce a summary of all that is there.

is to avoid repeating information. Brief is better and clearer, and needless repetition may annoy some readers and confuse others. So the summary may be the only place in your plan where you intentionally do repeat yourself. But that doesn't make it any less valuable. Take extra care when writing your summary. You'll be glad you did.

PURPOSES OF THE EXECUTIVE SUMMARY

The executive summary has to perform a host of jobs. It has to briefly hit the high points of your plan. It should point readers with questions requiring detailed responses to the full-length sections of your plan where they can get answers. It should ease the task of anybody whose job it is to read it, and it should make that task enjoyable by presenting an interesting and compelling account of your company.

A lot of work for a short document? Sure. But that's why it comes first, and that's why you're spending so much time on it.

Simplify Scanning

One of the most important jobs of an executive summary is to simplify the work of investors reviewing your plan. Many investors will never get past the summary if they find that it contains enough information to let them know that this opportunity is not for them.

Ideally, of course, something quite different will happen when an investor scans your summary. He or she will become enthralled with your concept and excited about the opportunity to participate. And it could happen. But not without an executive summary. That's the first section people turn to to simplify the task of scanning your plan, and, if it's missing or seriously flawed, you might as well not have a plan at all.

Plan Pointer

Five minutes. This is how long an average reader will spend with your plan. If you can't convey the basics of your business in that time, your plan is in trouble. So make sure your summary, at least, can be read in that time and that it's as comprehensive as possible within that constraint.

Plan Pointer

Assessing your own strengths and weaknesses is a lot harder than assessing others' good and bad points, right? So when it comes time to select your best features, it's also time to solicit feedback from others. Ask people whose opinions you trust—colleagues, associates and peers—whether your assessment of your idea is off-base or on target.

Attract Readers

A lot of a business plan is dry material. It's inappropriate to use a lot of exclamation points in a marketing analysis, and it would definitely look odd if you put double-ruled lines printed in incandescent ink around the net cash flow figure for the first month you expect to be in the black. The rules are a little looser in the executive summary, however.

Here you're expected to put on something of a show, to try to attract readers into the rest of your plan. You'll emphasize your sexy concept and impeccable credentials. It's entirely appropriate to use a narrative style here, by the way, to recount the history of your company as if it were a thrilling saga. In fact, telling a great story is one of the best ways to fulfill a central function of the summary: attracting readers.

Put Your Best Foot Forward

If you do tell a story in the summary, give it a happy ending. That's because, while it's your duty in your plan to fully disclose to investors any significant risk factors, you can save that for later. The summary is the place to put your best foot forward, to talk up the upside and downplay the downside.

As always, accentuating the positive doesn't mean exaggeration or falsehood. If there is a really important, unusual risk factor in your plan—such as that one certain big customer has to make a huge order or the whole thing's kaput—then you will want to mention that in your summary. But run-of-the-mill risks like unexpected competition or simply customer reluctance can be ignored here.

Now's the time to use the higher end of the market estimates and profitability scales you've come up with. Try to paint a convincing portrait of an opportunity so compelling that only a dullard would not recognize it and desire to take part in it.

Select Your Best Features

In the executive summary you particularly want to summarize your strengths. That may seem obvious. But how do you know what your strengths are? And how do you select which ones to present here?

A lot of the answers to those two questions will depend on whom you're presenting your plan to. The special concerns of particular audiences were covered in the last chapter. For instance, if you're talking to a banker, you'd stress cash flow, management experience and balance-sheet strength. For a partner, the summary would select organizational flexibility and prospects for future growth. A venture capitalist will want very high growth rates, plus some hint that you'll be ready to go public or sell out in a few years.

Present Your Strong Points

Even if your best points aren't the kind of things normally included in executive summaries, try to include them. They may be your best friends. So don't neglect to invite them to the party.

There are several ways you can make sure your best points receive the lion's share of attention. You can mention them first and the rest last. You can soft-focus on the parts you like best. Or you can even just leave out the bad parts entirely until later on in your plan.

You can be completely candid without being unfair to your business's prospects if you present the good news first and the bad news last. People remember what they hear first. Tell them that "first-quarter sales were up strongly" and they'll more likely recall that more than what you said in the next sentence about "some deterioration in profit margins."

Soft-focusing on your strengths is mainly a matter of mentioning the

---

RAISING THE FUND-RAISING ROOF

Raising money for a business is ordinarily considered a pretty staid line of work. But not when Howard Getson gets involved. The president and co-founder of IntellAgent Control Corp. is famed for his brash but effective requests for money to grow his sales automation software manufacturing company.

How brash? In 1996, Getson sent a letter to prospective investors with outrageous lines like "Return this letter now! You may already have invested $10 million!" and "This is the most undervalued financing we've ever agreed to accept."

How effective? Getson raised $6.8 million from 70 investors over two years with similar pitches.

Why does it work? Getson melds his in-your-face style with solid financial acumen. "Really," he explains, "it is the perfect blend of direct-mail schlock and true business sense."

Plan Pointer

Every business needs a good corporate slogan, and the "Company Description" of your plan is a good place to work on one. Keep it short—six words or fewer—and make a specific quality statement or service promise. Top examples: "You're In Good Hands With Allstate" and Federal Express' "When It Absolutely, Positively Has To Be There Overnight."

more superficial, pleasant-sounding traits of your company without going into a lot of detail that may distract readers from the positive, powerful image you want to portray. For instance, you might say that your plant nursery is "dedicated to cultivating the finest landscaping vegetation in the five-county region." That sounds nice, so why go into a lot of detail right now about the fact that your plans require you to tackle a deeply entrenched, well-regarded competitor? You can talk about that later, after the executive summary has lured readers in.

Sometimes presenting your best features is a matter of not mentioning your weak points until later on in the plan. If, for instance, you have a great idea for a product but no idea where you'll have it manufactured, that's not the kind of thing you want to mention in the executive summary—although of course you have to bring up this important issue, and deal with it expertly, later on in your plan.

Company Description

If your company is complex, you'll need a separate section with a heading like "Company Description" to adequately describe its many product lines, locations, services or whatever else it is that makes it a little too complicated to deal with quickly. In any event, you will probably provide a brief description, amounting to a few sentences, of your company in the executive summary. And for many firms, this is an adequate basic description of their company. Here are some sample one- or two-sentence company descriptions:

- ◆ John's Handball Hut is the Hamish Valley's leading purveyor of handball equipment and clothing.

- ◆ Boxes Boxes Boxes Inc. will provide the people of the metropolitan area with a comprehensive source for packing materials, containers and other supplies for the do-it-yourself move.

- ◆ Johnny AppleCD buys, sells and trades used compact disc musical recordings through locations on the north and south side of town.

Legal Structure

Like your company description, if your firm isn't complicated in the way it splits up its ownership, responsibility, authority and liability, you can dispense with describing the legal structure in a sentence or two buried in the summary. But if you have two subsidiaries, a joint venture with another firm and dozens of owners spread across the country, you may want to have a special section detailing your company's legal structure.

Most small businesses are run as sole proprietorships. Solo businesses like these require little paperwork or expense to set up, are dissolved just as easily when debt-free, and have some significant advantages over other organizations. One of the best is clarity: You are your business and, to a large extent, your business is you. Anyone dealing with you in connection with this business knows he or she is talking to the top person.

Many small businesses are also partnerships. These require somewhat more paperwork, for legal and tax purposes. When you have a partner, you have to have clearly drawn areas of responsibility and accountability. Partners frequently argue about who is doing more work and taking less money, and similar issues. A partnership can be a great way to get expertise and other help for the price of a few shares of stock. Explaining the basic terms of your partnership in your business plan helps readers understand who's responsible for what.

Plan Of Action

The Small Business Administration publishes an inexpensive booklet called *Selecting the Legal Structure for Your Firm*, by Antonio M. Olmi. Write the Small Business Administration, 409 Third St. SW, Washington, DC, 20416, and ask for an order form.

Buzzword

Limited Liability Corporations, or LLCs, are relatively new business legal structures that many companies find attractive. An LLC resembles an S corporation but allows owners more flexibility in dividing up profits while still providing liability protection.

C corporations are the legal form of most big companies. Corporations pay taxes, just like people. They can also own things, get sued, etc. In fact, if you set up a corporation, you can let the corporation absorb much of the liability and other risk that would otherwise get passed to you. You are not necessarily responsible, for instance, for debts owed by the corporation, which isn't the case with a sole proprietorship. You do have to pay taxes on any after-tax profits you draw from the corporation, however. Issues of liability and responsibility for debts are crucial to lenders dealing with corporations, but banks often prefer dealing with corporate entities.

S corporations provide much the same legal shield as C corporations, but they're taxed differently. Instead of the corporation paying taxes on profits and then your having to pay taxes on them again, profits from an S corporation flow directly to you. Another benefit of a corporation, S or C, is that it will survive your death. Lenders like that security compared with a proprietorship, whose assets and debts simply become part of your estate when you die.

Deciding which legal form your business will take is an important move. It's also one that you need to explain in your business plan so that investors and others will know whom—legally—they're dealing with.

History And Corporate Milestones

How did your business get where it is today? Where did you get the idea for it? Everybody likes the feeling of accomplishment. Business plan readers like to hear about your business accomplishments. Don't disappoint them. If your company has enough of a history to have accomplished anything at all, provide a short list of major accomplishments or a time line to help readers get a quick feel for milestones you've passed.

You might include such things as the first day you opened for business, the month you hired your first employee, the quarter you passed 10 employees, the day you opened your second location, the date a patent or trademark was applied for and granted, and the like.

This is a good chance to show some of the human side of your company. For instance, you may want to include a photo of your first annual meeting, or employees toasting one another to celebrate the production of your millionth unit. There's nothing wrong, even in a business plan, with reminding potential investors that there are people behind the pages.

Financial Milestones

Milestones relating to money are naturally of special interest to investors. So while you're rattling off a list of all your nonfinancial accomplishments, don't forget to include

> **Plan Pointer**
>
> You may be modest and dislike bragging. But recall that companies sometimes become well-known as much for reaching more or less arbitrary financial milestones as for their excellent products and services. Compaq Computer won fame as the fastest at the time to reach $100 million in sales. Later, its rival Dell Computer won notice for its speed in joining the Fortune 500. Don't miss a chance to toot your own financial horn.

those of a purely mercenary nature as well.

Common financial milestones include the day you made your first sale, the month you first showed positive cash flow, and your first profitable quarter and year. Achievements relating to sales are especially popular: The month they passed $1 million in sales is one that many entrepreneurs will never forget.

Summarize Your Plans And Goals

It is likely to take a lot of steps to get where you want to go, and secondary and tertiary goals may lie between you and your ultimate goal. It's important to tell plan readers about many of these—breaking long-term objectives into short-term and intermediate-term goals shows you've thought things out. But you don't want to get too bogged down in the details.

> **Plan Pointer**
>
> Make your mission statement do double duty as a marketing slogan and employee motivator. Famous ones include Ford's (Quality Is Job One) and Avis (When You're Number Two, You Try Harder). Hint: Slogans are shorter—no more than six words—and more specific than most mission statements.

Mission Statement

A mission statement is a tool used for covering up stains on wallpaper—oops! The fact is, many mission statements get written, framed, hung and forgotten. But they do have use. They're supposed to communicate what you're about and should particularly include a description of what makes you different from everybody else in your field.

Mission statements get daily use, or at least exposure, to employees, customers and others. But they also have a place in a plan, where they help investors and other interested parties get a grip on what makes your company special.

A mission statement should be a clearly written sentence or two that tells what you sell and to whom, and why they buy from you. It may also summarize your goals and objectives. Here are some examples:

- ◆ River City Roadsters buys, restores and resells classic American cars from the 1950s and 1960s to antique auto buffs throughout Central Missouri.

- ◆ Captain Curio is the Jersey Shore's leading antique store, catering to high-quality interior decorators and collectors across the tri-state area.

- ◆ August Appleton, Esq., provides low-cost legal services to per-

Fact Or Fiction?

Must you have a mission statement? Not necessarily. Many entrepreneurs find it difficult to summarize their mission in a sentence. But people do pay attention to mission statements. Write one that steers them wrong, and they'll go wrong. So if you can't accurately describe your mission in a statement, do without.

sonal-injury, workers'-compensation and age-discrimination plaintiffs in Houston's Fifth Ward.

Corporate Vision

A vision statement differs from a mission statement in the way that a man's reach exceeds his grasp. That is to say, a mission statement should describe the goals and objectives you could "reasonably" expect to accomplish. A small software company whose mission statement included the goal of "putting Microsoft out of business" would be looked upon as foolishly naive.

In a vision statement, however, just those sorts of grandiose, galactic-scale images are perfectly appropriate. When you "vision"—to borrow the management consultant's trick of turning nouns into verbs—you imagine the loftiest heights you could scale, not the next step or several steps on the ladder.

Does a vision statement even have a place in a business plan? You could argue that it doesn't, especially since many include personal components such as "to love every minute of my work and always feel I'm doing my best." But many investors deeply respect visionary entrepreneurs. So if you feel you have a compelling vision, there's no reason not to share it in your plan.

SELECTING A STRATEGY

Probably the only thing worse than changing horses in the middle of the stream is never even reaching the middle of the stream because you're still standing on the bank, trying to decide which horse to attempt the crossing with. What's the point of this silly image? You need to select a strategy— some strategy—with which to guide future business decisions. Otherwise, you'll never get past knee deep before the current sweeps you away.

Veteran business plan readers know this. They've seen lots of businesses, many of them in the same industry but with different strategies. And they know that, while it's hard to tell in advance which strategies can succeed, companies that never settle on one are almost certain to make little headway.

So make it plain in your plan that you have firmly chosen a strategy. Don't be dogmatic; flexibility, paradoxically, is also considered a virtue. But do let people know how you plan to attack the market. Some will disagree, but others will agree and welcome your agreement with them.

Common Strategies

Conventional strategic thinking pigeonholes virtually all strategies into one of three categories. Companies try to become the low-cost producer, to differentiate themselves somehow or to become niche players. Here's a look at the three generic strategies:

Low-cost producers try to make a product or service at a lower cost than any competitor. It may then sell the product at the lowest price and thereby gain a large share of the market. Or, if quality is high enough, it may charge a higher price and enjoy the resulting robust profit margins. Most markets are somewhat price sensitive, but the low-cost producer strategy works best in markets where customers are highly price sensitive. Low-cost strat-

---

ONE BAD APPLE STRATEGY

The case of Apple Computer will be taught in business schools for years. The originator of the personal computer, innovator of enduring ideas in computing, owner of a fanatical fan base, and creator of many excellent products, Apple still managed to lose the personal computer market to the IBM clones, and nearly to lose itself along the way.

No doubt, Big Blue's marketing strength played a role. But many analysts guess that flawed strategy was the main reason Apple squandered its lead.

Essentially Apple differentiated itself with features that turned out to be not the most important with users. Easiest to use? Most durable? Least likely to crash? All were true of the Apple machines compared with IBM clones. But IBM's strategy of uncloaking the original PC's architecture and basically inviting the world to copy it was more valuable in the long run.

Apple refused to license hardware clones and attempted to sequester software development to itself as much as it could. As a result, PC clones got dramatically cheaper and more widely distributed. Their technology changed faster because there were more participants in its development. And programmers lined up to write software for the MS-DOS operating system and its descendent, Windows. In a few years, Apple held its secrets, but its strategy had lost the market.

Fact Or Fiction?

"If that's such a good idea, how come nobody else has done it?" You've heard that before. Here's the answer: Many good ideas are invented by big companies and discarded because they're not great. Frito-Lay, for instance, won't introduce a new chip flavor unless potential first-year sales exceed $100 million. A good product idea worth $10 million in sales to Frito-Lay is no idea at all.

egies are often difficult for small businesses to follow because the economies of scale possessed by larger competitors automatically put small firms at a handicap.

Differentiate your product from everything else—become the biggest, best, bluest, oldest or newest—and you may be able to charge more, have more loyal customers and discourage competitors all at the same time. You can differentiate by adding features or by cleverly promoting your product so that it merely seems somehow different. Take care to differentiate important features that will sway customers, however, or your efforts to follow a strategy of differentiation may be in vain.

"Nichemanship" is the realm of small companies. Surviving and prospering in markets too small to attract competitors is the one thing entrepreneurs can do far better than any big company. You can focus your company by creating a product or service that closely fits the needs of a small group of customers. The beauty of nichemanship is that you can find plenty to satisfy you without ever attracting the attention of bigger rivals. The ugly side is that, should your market ever grow big enough, you may get clobbered.

EXPLAINING HOW YOU'LL USE THE FINANCING

One of the key sections of your executive summery should be a quick explanation of how you'll use the proceeds of any financing you seek. Basically, you tell the banker exactly why you need the money, down to what you're going to buy with it.

It's not necessary to get into too much detail here. You don't have to justify every penny and wind up feeling obligated to ask for a loan of $23,558.36 because that's the exact price of everything you need. It's perfectly OK, alongside entries for "new pizza oven" and "three months' rent," to have in your sources and uses of funds section a catch-all category like "other business uses."

Round your asked-for number up from minimum needs, and put what's left over into some kind of "miscellaneous" grab bag. You'll almost certainly need it for some unexpected something, and most plan readers will appreciate that fact.

What Financiers Look For

We've already talked at some length about the characteristics of various financiers. However, in the context of your executive summary, you should consider the following:

♦ Venture capitalists look for ways to cash out, and for annual compound rates of return in the area of 50 percent.

♦ Bankers look for free cash flow to pay back loans, management experiences and collateral.

♦ Angel investors look for more moderate rates of return but may also want to be involved.

♦ Friends and family want to get their money back so they can remain your friends and family.

You may have special considerations to address in any given plan, depending on whom you're targeting it to. For instance, you may know or suspect that one of the conditions of getting a loan from your parents is that you employ your black-sheep sister. Be sure your summary of management has a slot—Director of Ephemera might work—for that unworthy individual.

Don't forget yourself: It's a rare company that doesn't have any investment from the entrepreneur or entrepreneurs who started it.

Using Money To Make Money

The best use of somebody else's money is to buy or build something that will make more money, both for you and for that somebody. No matter who your investor is, you'll look better if, in the summary, you can describe a use for borrowed or invested funds that will directly help to pay back the provider.

As the business manager, you have considerable discretion about what any given dollar is spent on. So make sure that in accounting for how you'll use funds, you don't apply borrowed money to, say, your salary or perks. Use operating income for those purposes. Investors like to feel they've purchased production tools, not country club memberships.

If you're in manufacturing, then, allocate invested funds to purchasing important equipment, the bigger the better. If you're in retail, use the cash for store fixtures or inventory. If you're in a service company, direct the infusion to a new marketing program that ought to boost sales.

Who'll Own What

When you're just getting started, ownership may seem more of a burden than a privilege, much less an asset. However, when a business gets going generating profits and plowing them back into the firm, it can build value quite rapidly. Even if you aren't in an industry likely to purchase buildings or patent valuable technology, the business derives value from the fact that it can generate profits into the future.

The point is that, given that your business is valuable, you'll need to spell out who owns what. If you have many equity investors, coupled with a pile of creditors, this can get pretty complicated.

For the summary section of your plan, a basic description such as "Ownership of the company will be divided so that each of the four original partners owns 25 percent" will suffice. If you have to negotiate details of exactly what any equity investors will get, there's time to do that later. For now, you just want to give people an idea of how the ownership is divided.

EXTRACTING THE ESSENCE

The key to the executive summary is to pick out the best parts of every part of your plan. In other words, you want to extract the essence. Instead of describing everyone in your company, tell only about your key managers. Instead of talking about all your products, mention only the major ones or discuss only product lines instead of individual products.

And when you talk about your company's purpose and mission, stick to the highlights. You have pages to come to get into the minutiae. But the executive summary is the first thing people read, so make sure it's interesting and to the point.

CHAPTER 7

TEAM WORK

Who's who on your team

The Management section of your plan is where you describe who will run the company. It may be no more than a simple paragraph noting that you'll be the only executive and describing your background. Or it may be a major section in the plan, consisting of an organizational chart describing interrelationships between every department and manager in the company, plus bios of all key executives.

For entrepreneur Bill Dunnam, his management experience really was the company. The basic idea behind Hanks Root Beer Co., the company he co-founded two years ago, was to compete in a soft drink industry dominated by Coke and Pepsi—not too promising. But Dunnam's 11 years' experience working for Coca-Cola had the power to convince everybody—well, almost everybody except former Coke colleagues. "They were like, 'You're nuts, Bill,'" he recalls. Investors didn't agree, and they helped him get Hanks off the ground and up to $2 million in sales the second year.

WHY MANAGEMENT MATTERS

Time and again, financiers utter some variation of the following statement: "I don't invest in ideas; I invest in people." While there's some question as to whether this is the whole story—investors certainly prefer good people with good ideas to bad people with good ideas—there's no doubt that the people who run your company will receive considerable scrutiny from financiers as well as customers, suppliers and anyone else with an interest in your plan. People are, after all, a company's most important asset in many cases. To not adequately address this issue in a plan is a serious failing. Luckily, it's one of the easiest parts of your plan.

WHO ARE YOUR MANAGERS?

Identifying your managers is more than a matter of giving their names. Plan readers want to know their qualifications to run your business. You can provide this by describing them in terms of the following characteristics.

◆ **Education:** Impressive educational credentials among company managers provide strong qualification for an investor or other plan reader to feel good about your company. Use your judgement in deciding what educational background to include and how to emphasize it. If you're starting a fine restaurant and your chef graduated at the top of her class from the Culinary Institute of America, play that front and center. If you're starting a courier service and your partner has an anthropology degree from a little-known school, mention it but don't make a big deal out of it.

◆ **Employment:** You can be proud to be an entrepreneur without being ashamed of having worked for somebody else. In fact, prior work experience in a related field is something many investors look for. If you've spent 10 years in management in the retail men's apparel business before opening a tuxedo outlet, an investor can feel confident that you know what you're doing. So describe any relevant jobs you've had in terms of job title, years of experience, names of employers, etc. But remember, this isn't a resume. You can feel free to skim over or omit any irrelevant experience, and you don't have to provide exact dates of employment.

◆ **Skills:** A title is one thing; what you learn while holding it is another. In addition to pointing out that you were a district sales manager for a stereo equipment wholesaler, you should describe your responsibilities and the skills you honed while fulfilling them. For instance, you'll note that you were responsible for hiring salespeople, planning and budgeting, working with key accounts, reporting to senior management and so on. Each time you mention skills that you or a member of your management team has spent years acquiring at another company, it will be another reason for an investor to believe you can do it at your own company.

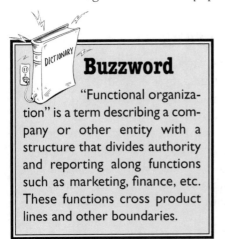

Buzzword

"Functional organization" is a term describing a company or other entity with a structure that divides authority and reporting along functions such as marketing, finance, etc. These functions cross product lines and other boundaries.

BEADING THE COMPETITION

Jerry Free had no experience as an inventor or manager of a product company when he came up with a better way to put up Sheetrock walls. What he did have was vast expertise and understanding of the issues involved in putting up Sheetrock developed through years of doing just that kind of work.

So when he went to a large company, U.S. Gypsum, asking for help marketing Speed Bead, an invention that makes corners easier to build in drywall construction jobs, they listened. Impressed by Free's grasp of drywall installation issues and the Speed Bead's well-thought-out design, U.S. Gypsum agreed to fund the patenting as well as marketing and distribution of the idea, in exchange for licensing rights.

"My idea was so simple, I couldn't believe it hadn't been done," Free says. "And if it hadn't, then why not?" The simple answer is, nobody else had the idea and the practical experience to make it workable. It also took several thousand dollars in advisors' fees, and five years of waiting. But now Free's Speed Bead expertise is starting to pay off—he's still installing drywall, but he's doing it from a new truck bought with licensing royalties.

◆ **Accomplishments:** Dust off your plaques and trot out your calculator for this one. If one of your team members has been awarded patents, achieved record sales gains, or once opened an unbelievable number of new stores in the space of a year, now's the time to tell about it.

Don't brag; just speak factually and remember to quantify. Say that you have 12 patents, your sales manager had five years of 30 percent annual sales gains and you personally oversaw the grand openings of 42 stores in 11 months. Investors are looking to back impressive winners, and quantifiable results speak strongly to businesspeople of all stripes.

Buzzword

Line organization describes an organization divided by product lines, means of production, industries served, etc. Each line may have its own support staff for the various functions.

◆ **Personal:** Who cares about personal stuff? Isn't this business? Sure, but investors want to know who they're dealing with in terms of the personal side too. Personal information on each member of your management team may include age, city of residence, notable charitable or community activities, any relevant health conditions, and, last but far from least, personal motivation for joining the company. Investors like to see vigorous, committed, involved people in the companies they back. Describing the relevant personal details of your key managers will help investors feel they know what they're getting into.

WHOM TO DESCRIBE IN YOUR PLAN?

If you're the only manager, this question is an easy one. But what if you have a pretty well-established organization already? Should you describe everyone down to shop foremen? Or stop with the people who are on your executive committee? The answer is, probably neither. Instead think about your managers in terms of the important functions of your business.

In deciding the scope of the management section of your plan, consider the following business functions and make sure you've explained who will handle those that are important to your enterprise:

❏ Accounting   ❏ Production

❏ Advertising   ❏ Purchasing

❏ Distribution   ❏ Sales

❏ Finance   ❏ Training

❏ Human Resources   ❏ Other _____

❏ Legal   ❏ Other _____

❏ Marketing   ❏ Other _____

❏ Operations

Many businesses contain unique functions. For example, only product companies such as software publishers have product-testing departments. Use the "other" category to list the functions that are unique to your company.

What Does Each Do?

There's more to a job than a title. A director in one organization is a high and mighty individual, while in another company a person bearing the same title is practically nobody. And many industries have unique job titles, such as managing editor, creative director and junior accountant level II, that have no counterparts in other industries.

So when you give your management team's background and describe their titles, don't stop there. Go on and tell the reader exactly what each member of the management team will be expected to do in the company. This may be especially important in a start-up, in which not every position is filled from the start. If your marketing work is going to be handled by the CFO until you get a little farther down the road, let readers know this up front. You certainly can't expect them to figure that out on their own.

Expanding Your Team

If you do have significant holes in your management team, you'll want to describe your plans for filling them. You may say, for example, "Marketing duties are being handled on a temporary basis by the vice president for finance. Once sales have reached the $500,000 per month level, approximately six months after start-up, a dedicated vice present of marketing will be retained to fulfill that function."

In some cases, particularly if you're in a really shaky start-up and you need really solid talent, you may have to describe in some detail your plans for luring a hotshot industry expert to your fledgling enterprise.

Buzzword

Line and staff organizations are hybrids in which staff managers, such as planners and accountants, act as advisors to support line managers, such as the operations vice president.

Making Hiring Projections

Work, they say, expands to fill time. Nobody knows that like a small-business owner. A job such as balancing the books or unpacking a new shipment of goods that should have taken an hour expands to fill a day. When quitting time comes, there's still a whole day's work to be done and only you to do it. This is one of the reasons small-business owners tend to have a slightly harried look all the time.

You can't increase the number of hours in the day, but you can add hands

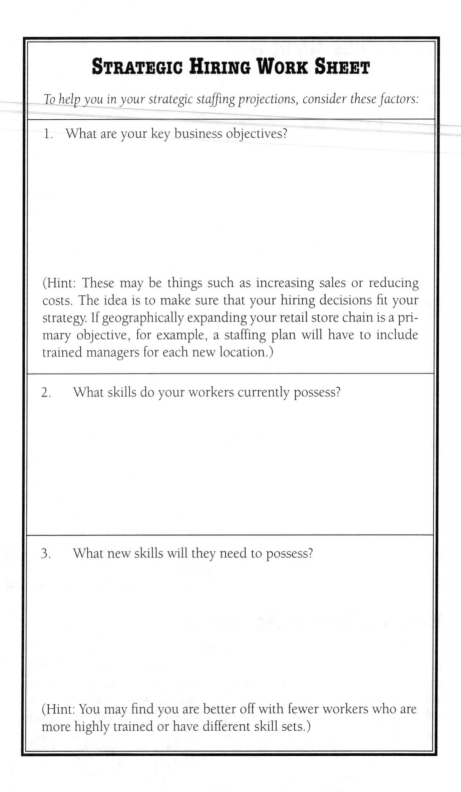

STRATEGIC HIRING WORK SHEET

To help you in your strategic staffing projections, consider these factors:

1. What are your key business objectives?

(Hint: These may be things such as increasing sales or reducing costs. The idea is to make sure that your hiring decisions fit your strategy. If geographically expanding your retail store chain is a primary objective, for example, a staffing plan will have to include trained managers for each new location.)

2. What skills do your workers currently possess?

3. What new skills will they need to possess?

(Hint: You may find you are better off with fewer workers who are more highly trained or have different skill sets.)

STRATEGIC HIRING WORK SHEET, CONT'D.

---

4. Which of these skills are central to your business—your core competencies?

(Hint: You may want to outsource peripheral functions. Accounting, legal and human resources are frequently outsourced by companies whose main business is elsewhere and who find it doesn't make sense to spend the effort to attract and retain skilled employees in these areas.)

---

5. List the jobs and job descriptions of the people it will take to provide these skills.

(Hint: The idea here is to identify the workers whose job titles may mask their true function in the organization so you can figure out how many and what type of people you really need to staff a job.)

Now you should be able to make an accurate projection of not only how many, but what kind of people you need to achieve your long-term objectives.

---

to do it. The question often becomes, How many hands do you need? After you ponder this one for a while, you'll find yourself wondering, When do I need them? How long do I need them for? Whom, exactly, do I need? And many other questions. Making staffing projections is a tricky yet essential part of business planning.

Let's say, for example, you wish to add a second shift at your small factory manufacturing storage cases for CD-ROMs. Your day shift employs 10 factory floor workers, plus a supervisor. Can you just hire 11 people and start running the swing shift? Not necessarily. It may be that two of those workers only work part-time on the production line, spending much of their day helping the shipping department process incoming materials and outgoing orders. Two more may devote several hours to routine maintenance procedures that won't to have be done twice a day even when a second shift is added. So your real needs may be for seven production workers and a supervisor—a savings of 20 percent in your projected staffing increase. It's decisions like this that easily can make the difference between a highly profitable operation and one barely scraping by.

Adding And Retaining Key Employees

As this book was being written, the U.S. economy was at a near-historical level of prosperity, including the lowest unemployment levels seen in decades. That's great for workers who find themselves in a seller's market of rare power. It's not so great for employers.

Finding and retaining employees of any kind in this type of job market is a serious difficulty for almost all businesses. Will it last? Not forever. Sooner or later the balance of power will shift back to employers, and as the number of help-wanted ads shrinks relative to the number of people reading them, it'll be easier to hire and hang on to employees.

Except for one kind of employee. Key employees, the people who are smart and hard-working and unafraid to take risks, are always in great demand. They can always write their own tickets, and a lot of employers are happy to go along because these employees are gold. Bill Gates has said that Microsoft, which employs 22,000, would become an unimportant company if it lost its 20 best people. And the importance of key employees is no secret. That's why you need to address the issue of how you will attract and retain key employees in any enterprise in which they are likely to be important.

Are you starting a software company? You'll need an ace programmer

> **Plan Pointer**
>
> An organizational chart graphically organizes your company into its major functional departments—finance, administration, marketing, production, etc. It's the quickest, clearest way to say who is in charge of what and who reports to whom.

or two. A gourmet restaurant? Then your executive chef becomes your key employee. An art gallery? Maybe you can pick great art, but a sales manager who knows how to close a deal will be essential. No matter what business you are in, unless you are one of the truly rare individuals who really can do it all, you are likely to find that one or more central tasks are really better farmed out to a key employee.

Plan Of Action

The Fast Forward MBA in Hiring (John Wiley & Sons), by Max Messmer, quickly, economically and precisely advises you on finding, hiring and keeping the best employees. It and others in the "fast forward" series are based on the *Portable MBA* in-depth guides.

The things that make employees want to come to work for you and stay vary. At bottom, choosing an employer is a highly personal decision. That's why it's crucial to understand the individual needs of your key employees so that you can give them exactly what they want. If you only offer a higher salary to an employee whose most important concern is that she work at a job offering flexible hours so she can care for an elderly parent, then you probably won't retain that employee.

Here are some common concerns that drive employment decisions:

♦ **Benefits:** Paid holidays and sick leave, health insurance, and retirement plans such as 401(k) plans are among the benefits most often listed as desirable by employees.

♦ **Compensation:** Salary, bonuses, stock options, profit sharing and auto mileage allowances are among the most important compensation issues to employees.

♦ **Miscellaneous:** On-site child care, flexible work hours, paid memberships to business groups and a personal day off on birthdays are hot buttons as well.

Your business plan should consider the above issues and describe the inducements you will offer key employees to encourage them to stay. Especially in a small company, an investor is likely to be very leery of a plan that appears to be based on the capabilities of a handful of employees unless the business owner has clearly given a lot of thought to keeping these important workers on board.

The above list is by no means comprehensive, however. Employee needs are as complex as humanity is. One worker may stay because she likes the view out her window on a high floor; somebody in an identical office may leave because heights make her nervous. One of the most important needs, especially for highly motivated employees, is maintaining a constant atmosphere of learning, challenge and advancement. If you can find a way to let your employees grow as your company does, they're likely to do just that.

OUTSIDE PROFESSIONALS

Some of the most important people who'll do work for you won't work for you. Your attorney, your accountant and your insurance broker are all crucial members of your team. A good professional in one of these slots can go a long way toward helping you succeed. The same may be true, to a lesser extent, for real estate brokers, management consultants, benefits consultants, computer consultants and trainers.

Your business plan should reassure readers that you have your bases covered in these important professional positions. Readers don't necessarily want to see an attorney on staff. It's fine that you merely state that you retain the services of an attorney in private practice on an as-needed basis.

Buzzword

Outsourcing is a 1990s trend among big firms, but entrepreneurs have known about it for years. If you've ever fired your bookkeeper and started sending payroll to a service, you've outsourced. Outsourcing can save time and money for support staff jobs, and add flexibility in production staffing.

You don't even need to name the firm you're retaining, although a prestigious name here may generate some reflected respect for you. For instance, if your firm is audited by a Big Six firm instead of a local one-man accounting shop, then by all means play it up. Few things are more comforting to an investor that the knowledge that this investment's disbursement will be monitored regularly and carefully by an expert.

Investors invest in companies for profit. They don't just give money to people they like or admire. But it's also true that if they don't like, admire or at least respect the people running your company, they're likely to look elsewhere. The management section of your plan is where you tell them about the human side of the equation. You can't control any reader's response to that, but you owe it to them and to yourself to provide the information.

CHAPTER 8

ANNOUNCING . . .

Your product or service

Every business has something to sell, and the product section (for simplicity's sake, we'll use the term "product" to refer to both products and services unless otherwise indicated) is where you tell readers what it is you're selling.

This is clearly a very important section of your plan. No matter how expert a team of managers you've assembled or how strong your financial underpinnings are, unless you have something to sell or at least plans to develop it, you don't really have a business at all.

While many businesses are founded to develop new, never-before-seen products, they're still built around a product, even though it may not exist at the moment. And even for these development-stage enterprises, it's just as important to describe the planned-for product. When Dan DaDalt went after investors to back his idea for a new red-colored rum liquor, he and his partner didn't bother with mixing up any booze. They spent $1,000 on a Lucite mockup of the dramatic red bottle, and showed that. Investors liked the flavor—to the tune of $800,000 for the two entrepreneurs. Now they're after $2 million, and even though the start-up, called Redrum, now has a real beverage, the main tool, says DaDalt, will be "an even cooler-looking bottle."

WHAT IS YOUR PRODUCT OR SERVICE?

It's easy to talk eloquently about a product you believe in. Some highly marketing-oriented businesses, in fact, are built as much on the ability to wax rhapsodic about a product as they are on the ability to buy or source compelling products to begin with. The example that comes to mind is

J. Peterman, a catalog operation that has become famous—and highly successful—by selling prosaic products with the help of romantic, overblown advertising copy.

It's very important in your plan to be able to build a convincing case for the product or service upon which your business will be built. The product description section is where you do that. In this section, you should describe your product in terms of several characteristics, including cost, features, distribution, target market, competition and production concerns. Here are some sample product descriptions:

♦ Street Beat is a new type of portable electronic rhythm machine used to create musical backgrounds for street dances, fairs, concerts, picnics, sporting events and other outdoor productions. The product is less costly than a live rhythm section and offers better sound quality than competing systems. Its combination of features will appeal to sports promoters, fair organizers and charitable and youth organizations.

♦ *Troubleshooting Times* is the only monthly magazine for the nation's 6,000 owners of electronics repair shops. It provides timely news of industry trends, service product reviews and consumer product service tips written in a language service shop owners can understand.

♦ HOBO, the Home Business Organization, provides business consulting services to entrepreneurs who work out of their homes. The group connects home business owners with experts who have extensive experience counseling home business owners in management, finance, marketing and lifestyle issues. Unlike entrepreneurial peer groups, which charge members for attending sessions whether or not they receive useful advice, HOBO will guarantee its services, asking home business owners to pay only if they derive solid benefit from the service.

Plan Pointer

No ideas to differentiate your product? Steal someone else's. That is, combine your product with another to create something new. Dry cleaners do this when they offer coupons for the neighborhood pizza parlor—which gives out cleaning coupons with each pie. It's called cooperative marketing.

A business plan product description has to be less image-conscious than an advertising brochure but more appealing than a simple spec sheet. You don't want to give the appearance of trying

NOTHING IF NOT NEW

Gary Hoover is a guy to watch. He almost single-handedly invented and proved the concept of the warehouse-sized bookstore by opening the first Bookstop in Austin, Texas, in 1982.

His product (or, in this case, service)? A business that would do for books what Toys "R" Us did for toys and Home Depot did for hardware, to create a category-killer superstore that stocked everything, had low prices and offered great service.

Hoover was more than a visionary with an idea. He had worked as a retail stock analyst for Citibank, a buyer for Federated Department Stores and vice president of marketing and planning for the shopping center arm of May Department Stores Co. So he could plan as well as dream.

His planning ability showed when he used his business plan to raise $350,000 from private investors to open the first Bookstop. Book superstores have since proved one of the great retailing innovations, with hundreds of Barnes & Noble and Borders superstores sprouting up nationwide.

Hoover, in fact, sold Bookstop to Barnes & Noble for $41.5 million in cash in 1989. Then he started an online information publisher, Hoover's Inc., and now he's moved onto a new idea—the travel superstore. There are just two TravelFest Superstores, both in Austin, Texas, now. But if Gary Hoover's track record indicates anything, his product will spawn imitators—if not acquirers—soon.

to snow readers with a glitzy product sales pitch. On the other hand, you want to give them a sampling of how you are going to position and promote the product.

You should also take note that a business plan product description is not necessarily only concerned with consumer appeal. Issues of manufacturability are of paramount concern to plan readers, who may have seen any number of plans describing exciting products that, in the end, proved impossible to design and build economically.

If your product or service has special features that will make it easy to build and distribute, say so. For instance, the portable rhythm machine maker should point out in the business plan that the devices will be constructed using new special-purpose integrated circuits, derived from military applications, which will vastly increase durability and quality while reducing costs.

UNIQUE SELLING PROPOSITION WORK SHEET

Following are potential unique selling propositions that any product or service may be able to provide. Look at the list and ask yourself what your product has to offer buyers in each category.

Features:

Price:

Service:

Financing:

Delivery:

Reputation:

UNIQUE SELLING PROPOSITION WORK SHEET, CONT'D.

Training:

Knowledge:

Experience:

Customers:

Other:

When you've explained the selling propositions associated with your product in each of these categories, give each one a score from 1 to 10 based on your evaluation of how convincing a case you can make for that being a unique selling proposition. The one or two strengths with the highest scores will be your candidates for inclusion in business plan product description.

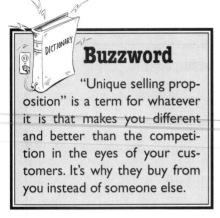

WHAT MAKES IT WORTHWHILE?

A product description is more than a mere listing of product features. You have to highlight your product's most compelling characteristics, such as low cost or uniquely high quality, that will make it stand out in the marketplace and attract buyers willing to pay your price. Even the simplest product has a number of unique potential selling strengths.

Many of the common unique selling strengths are seemingly contradictory. How can both mass popularity and exclusive distribution be strengths? The explanation is that it depends on your market and what its buyers want.

◆ **Features:** If your product is faster, bigger, smaller or comes in more colors, sizes and configurations than others on the market, you have a powerful selling strength. In fact, if you can't offer some combination of features that sets you apart, you'll have difficulty writing a convincing plan.

◆ **Price:** Everybody wants to pay less for a product. If you can position yourself as the low-cost provider (and make money at these rock-bottom prices), you have a powerful selling advantage. Conversely, high-priced products may appeal to many markets for their sheer snob value. One Amsterdam designer came out with a perfume that came in a sealed bottle that could not be opened. This "virtual perfume" was priced the same as Chanel No. 5 and found ready buyers.

◆ **Availability:** Ford Motor Co.'s F-series pickups and sedans such as the Taurus have been

Plan Pitfall

Don't count on getting your product into a major retailer on its own merits. The glut of tens of thousands of new products introduced annually, combined with the existing plethora of more than 30,000 products stocked by a typical supermarket, puts retailers in the driver's seat. They demand—and get from almost all new product makers—slotting fees, which are simply payments for the right to be on store shelves.

perennial bestsellers in the U.S. auto marketplace at least partly because there is a Ford dealership in every town in America. Similarly, if you can get your product into a major retailer such as Wal-Mart or Kmart, you create a powerful selling point by piggybacking on their redoubtable distribution powers.

> ## Plan Pointer
>
> It's easy and essential for Internet retailers to make information part of what they plan to give out. When pioneer online book retailer Amazon opened its music CD site, it included more than 750,000 pages of reviews, interviews and articles to encourage data-hungry Web surfers to visit and, more important, to buy.

◆ **Service:** Excellent service is perhaps the most important trait you can add to a plain-vanilla product to make it compelling. Many people look not for the best value or even the best product, but simply the one they can buy with the least hassle.

◆ **Financing:** Whether you "tote the note" and guarantee credit to anyone, offer innovative leasing, do buybacks or have other financing alternatives, you'll find that giving people different, more convenient ways to pay can lend your product a convincing strength.

◆ **Delivery:** Nobody wants to wait for anything anymore. If you can offer overnight shipping, on-site service or 24-hour availability, it can turn an otherwise unremarkable product or service into a very attractive one.

◆ **Reputation:** Why do people pay $10,000 for a Rolex watch that keeps worse time than a $10 Timex? The Rolex reputation is the reason. At its most extreme, reputation can literally keep you in business, as is the case with many companies, such as IBM and Sears, whose well-developed reputations have tided them over in hard times.

◆ **Training:** Training is a component of service that is becoming increasingly important in an era of high-technology products and services. For many sophisticated software products and electronic devices, a seller who couldn't provide training to buyers would have no chance at all of landing any orders.

◆ **Knowledge:** In the Information Age, your knowledge and the means you have of imparting that to customers is an important part of your total offering. Retailers of auto parts, home improvement supplies and all sorts of other goods have found that simply having knowledgeable salespeople who know how to replace the water pump in an '85 Chevy will lure customers in and encourage them to buy.

◆ **Experience:** "We've been there. We've done thousands of installations like yours, and there's no doubt we can make this one work as well." Nothing could be more soothing to a skeptical sales prospect than to learn that the seller has vast experience at what he's doing. If you have ample experience, make it part of your selling proposition.

◆ **Customers:** There's a reason Michael Jordan gets millions from Nike for endorsing Air basketball shoes—and it's not because shoe shoppers really think they'll be able to dunk if they just purchase new sneaks. The reason is that they want to be like Mike, even if it's just from the ankles down. If you have prestigious customers, mention it in your marketing materials and in your business plan.

HIGH FLIER

Today you can be a frequent shopper, frequent diner and frequent just-about-anything-else in addition to being the consumer that started it all, the frequent flier. The innovation that revolutionized airline marketing, and marketing of many other types of products and services, is credited to Robert Crandall, former CEO of American Airlines.

In the early 1980s, Crandall faced a difficult situation. He and other airlines flew the same passengers on the same planes, over the same routes and, since they were subject to the same economics, at about the same price. How to make travelers choose American over United, Delta and other rivals?

Crandall's solution was the now-ubiquitous frequent flier club. Passengers who chose American would accumulate points for each trip. When they had enough, they could redeem the points for free or discounted travel and, later, other awards.

The idea neatly solved the problem of how to differentiate nearly identical transportation services and also encouraged American passengers to become fiercely loyal to the airline. Today, travelers ponder the question of which frequent flier club to join almost as carefully as they used to pore over flight schedules and fare sheets.

◆ **Other factors:** There are many wild cards unique to particular products, or perhaps simply little used in particular industries, with which you can make your product stand out. For instance, consider a guarantee. When consumers know they can return a faulty product for free refund or repair, they're often more likely to buy it over otherwise superior competitors offering less powerful warranties.

> ## Fact Or Fiction?
>
> Don't assume too much when you're looking at a new product or service idea. For instance, you might think that horseshoers are an endangered breed in the automobile era. But actually there are more farriers active today than when horses were the main mode of transport. Just because something seems out of fashion doesn't mean you're out of luck.

The business world is always looking for a new idea that will influence buying behavior, especially if it adds value without costing a lot. Real estate companies offer a month's free rent to new tenants who sign two-year leases, auto dealers give a year's free car washes to the purchaser of a $30,000 vehicle, and entertainment restaurants catering to kids let parents eat free. Put your imagination and knowledge of a market and your own business's workings to the problem, and you may be able to come up with an innovative world-beater too.

WHO'S GOING TO BUY IT AND WHY?

The world's not going to beat a path to the door of the inventor of a passenger pigeon trap, because there are no passenger pigeons anymore. The point is, even the best product must meet a need in the market or it's a curio, not a foundation for a business plan. So make sure your plan identifies your markets and potential customers and tells why they're going to buy your product.

The first thing to do is identify the market you're going after. Talk about your market in terms of its characteristics, its needs and, if possible, its numbers.

A new Italian restaurant might say it's going for families on a budget eating out who live within a 5-mile radius of its location. It might quote Census Bureau figures showing there are 12,385 such families in its service area.

A bicycle seat manufacturer might have identified as its market casual middle-aged cyclists who find traditional bike seats uncomfortable. It may cite American College of Sports Medicine surveys, saying that sore buttocks due to uncomfortable seats is the chief complaint of recreational bicyclists.

It is important to quantify your market's size if possible. If you can point out that there are more than 6 million insulin-dependent diabetics in the United States, it will bolster your case for a new easy-to-use injection syringe your company has developed.

LIABILITY CONCERNS

To a typical consumer who's purchased her share of shoddy products from uncooperative manufacturers, it's cheering to hear of a multimillion-dollar settlement of a consumer's claim against some manufacturer. It provides proof that the high and mighty can be humbled and that some poor schmuck can be struck by lightning and receive a big fat check.

To manufacturers and distributors of products, however, the picture looks entirely different. Liability lawsuits have changed the landscape of a number of industries, from toy manufacturers to children's furniture retailers. If you visit public swimming pools these days, for instance, you don't see the diving boards that used to grace the deep ends of almost all such recreational facilities. The reason is that fear of lawsuits from injured divers, along with the allied increase in liability insurance premiums, has made these boards no longer financially feasible.

If you're going to come out with a diving board or offer diving board maintenance services, then you need to be prepared for this legal issue. Dealing with it may be as simple as merely including a statement to the effect that you foresee no significant liability issues arising from your sale of this product or service. If there is a liability issue, real or apparent, then you acknowledge it and describe in your plan how to deal with it. For instance, you may want to take note of the fact that, like all marketers of children's bedroom furniture, you attach warning labels and disclaimers to all your products and also carry a liability insurance policy.

Maybe it's obvious, but it bears taking notice of the fact that you must have an attorney's advice on this one. A layman's opinion on whether a product is more or less likely to generate lawsuits is not worth including in a plan.

On the subject of liability, here is a good place to deal with the question of whether you are already being sued for a product's perceived fail-

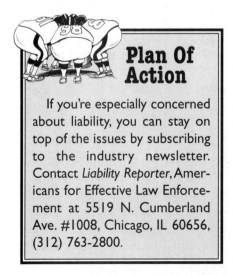

Plan Of Action

If you're especially concerned about liability, you can stay on top of the issues by subscribing to the industry newsletter. Contact *Liability Reporter*, Americans for Effective Law Enforcement at 5519 N. Cumberland Ave. #1008, Chicago, IL 60656, (312) 763-2800.

CHECKING IT TWICE

Here are some common licenses and certifications you may need. Check this list to see if there's anything you may have forgotten:

❏ Business license

❏ DBA (doing business as) or fictitious name statement

❏ Federal Employer ID Number

❏ Local tax forms

❏ Sales tax permit or seller's permit

❏ Health inspection certificate

❏ Fire inspection certificate

❏ Patent filing

❏ Trademark registration

❏ Zoning variance

Many of these forms and certificates will take days, weeks, months or longer to appear after you request them from the appropriate parties. So don't wait until the last minute to do so. Nothing is more frustrating than sitting in a ready-to-open store, with employees on the clock and interest charges on inventory and fixtures ticking away as well, but unable to serve customers because you don't have your sales tax permit.

ings and, if so, how you plan to deal with it. If you can't find an answer, you may wind up like private aircraft manufacturers, many of which were forced out of the business by increases in lawsuits following crashes.

It's often difficult to get an attorney to commit herself on paper about the prospects for winning or losing a lawsuit. Many times plans handle this with a sentence saying something along the lines of, "Our legal counsel advises us the plaintiff's claims are without merit."

LICENSES AND CERTIFICATIONS

Some paperwork is just paperwork, and some paperwork is essential. Every business must file tax returns, and most businesses have to have certain licenses and certifications to do business. Your plan should take notice, however briefly, of the fact that you have received or applied for any necessary licenses and certificates. If you don't mention the subject, some plan readers will assume all is hunky-dory. Others, however, may suspect the omission means you haven't thought about it or are having trouble getting the paperwork in order. Addressing those concerns now is a worthwhile idea.

Aside from the usual business licenses and tax forms, there are any number of certificates and notices you may require, depending on circumstances. Owners of buildings must have their elevators inspected regularly and, in some cities, post the safety inspection record in public. Plumbers must be licensed in many states. Even New York City hot dog vendors must be licensed by the city before they can unfurl their carts' colorful umbrellas.

For some businesses, their certification or occupational license essentially is what they sell. Think of a CPA. A lot of people sell accounting services. When you go to a CPA, you're paying for the probity and skill represented by the CPA designation, not just another accountant. You're basically buying those initials.

PRODUCT DESCRIPTION ROUNDUP

You explore a lot of aspects of your business in the process of writing a plan. It's easy to get confused about what's of central importance. But at bottom, a business isn't about financing or location or management's experience. It's about having something to sell that people want to buy. Always keep the importance of your product or service at the front of your mind and it will help make a lot of decisions easier.

FIELD NOTES

Inside info on your industry

A rising tide may not always lift all boats, but it tends to. And there's no doubt it's a lot harder to float when the tide is ebbing. These are truisms, certainly. But they're widely believed among the investment community, and that means it's important that you include an industry analysis in your business plan.

Readers of your business plan may want to see an industry on a fast-growth track with few established competitors and great potential. Or they may be more interested in a big, if somewhat slower-growing, market, with competitors who have lost touch with the market and are leaving the door open for rivals.

Whatever the facts are, you'll need to support them with a snapshot analysis of the state of your industry and any trends taking place. And this can't be mere off-the-cuff thinking. You'll need to buttress your opinions with market research that identifies competitors, their weaknesses and strengths and barriers to entry. Finally, and perhaps most important, you'll have to convincingly describe what makes you better and destined to succeed.

Convincing doesn't necessarily mean complex. Peter van Stolk, founder of Urban Juice & Soda, fulfills all desired functions of an industry description by merely pointing visitors to his bookcases full of the hundreds of new beverages he's been asked to distribute in his 10 years in business. Most are long gone, proving his main point: "The beverage industry is competitive, but there aren't a lot of smarts."

THE STATE OF YOUR INDUSTRY

In the early 1980s, all an entrepreneur needed was the word "energy" in the title of his company to draw the attention of financial backers. At other

Buzzword

Psychographics is the attempt to accurately measure lifestyle by classifying customers according to their activities, interests and opinions. While not perfect, a psychographic analysis of your marketplace can yield important marketing insights.

times, fields such as biotechnology, computer software or Internet commerce have been seen as gold fields waiting to be mined by gleeful investors. One of the things you will try to do with your plan is present a case for your industry being, if not the next big thing, at least an excellent opportunity. A section of your plan dealing with the state of your industry is the place to present this information.

When preparing the state of the industry section, you'll need to lift your eyes from your own company and your own issues and focus them on the outside world. Instead of looking at your business as a self-contained system, you'll describe the whole industry you operate in, and point to your position in that universe.

This part of your plan may take a little more legwork than other sections, since you'll be drawing together information from a number of outside sources. You may also be reporting on or even conducting your own original research into industry affairs.

MARKET RESEARCH

Successful entrepreneurs are famed for being able to seemingly feel a market's pulse intuitively, to project trends before anyone else detects them and to identify needs that even customers are hardly yet aware of. After you are famous, perhaps you can claim a similar psychic connection to the market. But for now, you'll need to buttress your claims to market insight by presenting solid research in your plan.

Market research aims to understand the reasons consumers will buy your product. It studies such things as consumer behavior, including how cultural, societal and personal factors influence that behavior. For instance, market research aiming to understand consumers who buy in-line skates

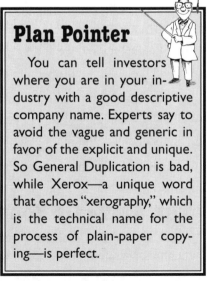

Plan Pointer

You can tell investors where you are in your industry with a good descriptive company name. Experts say to avoid the vague and generic in favor of the explicit and unique. So General Duplication is bad, while Xerox—a unique word that echoes "xerography," which is the technical name for the process of plain-paper copying—is perfect.

INDUSTRY ANALYSIS WORK SHEET

To start preparing your industry analysis and outlook, dig up the following facts about your field:

1. What is your total industrywide sales volume? Dollars? Units?

2. What are trends in industry sales volume?

3. Who are the major competitors? What are they like?

4. What does it take to compete? What are the barriers to entry?

5. What technological trends affect your industry?

(Cont'd. on next page)

INDUSTRY ANALYSIS WORK SHEET, CONT'D.

---

6. What are the main modes of marketing?

---

7. How does government regulation affect the industry?

---

8. How are consumer tastes changing in ways that affect your industry?

---

9. Identify recent demographic trends affecting the industry.

---

10. How sensitive is the industry to seasons and economic cycles?

---

11. What are key financial measures in your industry (average profit margins, sales commissions, etc.)?

might study the cultural importance of having a fit physique, the societal acceptability of marketing directed toward children and the effect of personal influences such as age, occupation and lifestyle in directing a skate purchase.

Market research is further split into two varieties: primary and secondary. Primary research studies customers directly, while secondary research studies information that others have gathered about customers. Primary research might be telephone interviews with randomly selected members of the target group, while secondary research might come from membership lists of clubs catering to the groups magazine subscription records and the like. For your plan, you can use either type.

The basic questions you'll try to answer with your market research include:

◆ **Who are your customers?** Describe them in terms of age, occupation, income, lifestyle, educational attainment, etc.

◆ **What do they buy now?** Describe their buying habits relating to your product or service, including how much they buy, their favored suppliers, the most popular features and the predominant price points.

◆ **Why do they buy?** This is the tricky one, attempting as it does to delve into consumers' heads. Answers will depend on the product and its uses. Cookware buyers may buy the products that offer the most effective nonstick surfaces, or those that give the most pans in a package for a given amount of money, or those that come in the most decorative colors.

Although some of these questions may seem very difficult, you'd be surprised at the detailed information about markets, sales figures and con-

Buzzword

Market research can be expensive. Here are some sources for inexpensive information that may be just as useful as the high-priced variety:

◆ Chamber of commerce

◆ Trade groups

◆ Department of Commerce

◆ Patent filings

◆ State and local economic development agencies

◆ Suppliers

◆ Customers

◆ Companies identical to yours but in different regions

◆ Competitors' annual reports, ads and news releases

◆ Industry trade journals

◆ Bankers

◆ Universities

sumer buying motivations that is available. Tapping these information sources to provide the answers to as many questions as you can will make your plan more convincing and your odds of success higher.

The industry of selling market research is a big one, and booming today. You can find companies that will sell you everything from industry studies to credit reports on individual companies. Market research is not cheap, however. It requires significant amounts of expertise, manpower and technology to develop solid research. Large companies routinely spend tens of thousands of dollars researching things they decide they're not interested in. Smaller firms can't afford to do that too often.

The best market research, however, you can't buy from any provider. It's the research you do on your own. In-house market research might take the form of original telephone interviews with consumers, customized crunching of numbers from published sources or perhaps competitive intelligence you've gathered on your rivals.

But the most likely source of in-house market research is information you already have. This information will come from analyzing sales records, gathering warranty cards containing the addresses and other information about purchasers, studying product return rates and customer complaint cards, and the like.

You can get in-house market research data from your own files, so it's

---

To Market, To Market

Following are some of the leading market research firms and their specialties:

◆ ACNielsen Corp., 177 Broad St., Stamford, CT 06901, (203) 961-3000, fax: (203) 961-3190, www.acnielsen.com. *Specialties:* TV-viewing habits, retail product sales

◆ Arbitron Co., 142 W. 57th St., New York, NY 10019-3300, (212) 887-1300. *Specialty:* Local broadcast audience measurement

◆ Burke Marketing Research Inc., 805 Central Ave, Cincinnati, OH 45202-5747, (513) 241-5663. *Specialties:* Various syndicated and custom research services

◆ Gallup Organization Inc., 47 Hulfish St., #200, Princeton, NJ 08542-3709, (609) 924-9600. *Specialty:* Public opinion polls

◆ Yankelovich Partners, 101 Merritt 7, Norwalk, CT 06851-6206, (203) 846-0100. *Specialty:* Social attitudes research

cheaper than buying it. It's also likely to be a lot fresher than third-party market research, which may have been moldering in some computer for years. Since it comes from your own operations, it will almost certainly be more precisely targeted than a packaged study, and probably better even than a custom survey you hire someone else to do.

One limitation of in-house market information is that it may not include exactly what you're looking for. For instance, if you'd like to consider offering consumers financing for their purchases, it's hard to tell how they'd like it since you don't already offer it. You can get around this limitation by conducting original research—interviewing customers who enter your store, for example, or counting cars that pass the intersection where you plan to open a new location—and combining it with existing data.

> **Plan Pointer**
>
> One of the most powerful trend-spotting tools available is the *Statistical Abstract of the United States*, published by the U.S. Census Bureau. It contains comparative data on everything from national average household food expenditures to what Anchorage, Alaska, residents pay in rent. And it's available on CD-ROM. For more information, call the Census Bureau at (301) 763-4100.

TRENDS

Timing, in business as in other areas of life, is everything. Marc Andreessen, founder of Netscape Communications, had the good fortune to develop software for browsing the World Wide Web just as the Internet, which had been around for 20 years, was coming to widespread popular attention. The timing of his move made him hundreds of millions of dollars, while most of those who came later fell by the wayside.

The best time to address a trend is before it is even beginning and certainly before it is widely recognized. If you can prepare a business that satisfies a soon-to-be popular need, you can generate growth that is practically off the scale. (This is, by the way, the combination that venture capitalists favor most.) The problem, of course, is spotting the trends first.

There are a couple of different techniques you can use to identify trends, and to present your identifications in your plan. A trend is basically a series of occurrences that indicate a pattern. So trend analysts look at past events (usually trends themselves) and project them forward. For example, a trend analyst would look at the aging U.S. population and project that in not too many more years, there will be far more old people than young. The problem with trend analysis is that it assumes the past is like the fu-

Soaking The Rich

Sometimes you don't need fancy market research to spot a customer need. Lonnie G. Paulson, an engineer for the Jet Propulsion Laboratory, was tinkering with a heat-pump design when he attached a nozzle to a piece of tubing and stuck it on his bathroom faucet. It made a lousy heat pump, he noticed, but a great water pistol.

Paulson made a portable prototype for his daughter, who promptly soaked every kid in the neighborhood. Faced with mounting demands for defensive armament, Paulson took his prototype to the offices of a toy maker called Larami Corp. When he squirted a jet of water across the meeting room, the executives were hooked.

Paulson's informal market research—and his dramatic presentation of his invention—led Larami to offer him a licensing agreement for the now-ubiquitous Super Soaker line of water pistols. The deal produces an estimated $10 million annually in licensing fees for Paulson, who has since started his own product-development company. There's no word on how he does his market research nowadays.

ture. Often, it's not and, to continue the aging population example, a lot of young immigrants may arrive and rear large families, throwing off the age curve.

Another good way to forecast trends is by test marketing. You try to sell something in a single store and see how it does before you roll it out in your whole chain. Keys to this technique are trying it in a well-selected test market, one that closely resembles the market you'll try to sell to later on.

Focus groups and surveys try to catch hold of trends by asking people what's hot. You can ask open-ended questions—What type of portable computer would you like to see?—or show them product samples and see how they react. This is also tricky because you are dealing with a small group of, you hope, representative people and extrapolating to a larger group. If your group isn't representative, your results may be misleading.

Some other ways you can try to nail a trend in advance include talking to salespeople who are in touch with customer needs, quizzing executives whose job is watching the big picture, reading a wide variety of periodicals and trying to spot connections, and hiring think tanks of experts to brainstorm over what the future might hold.

In most of these trend-forecasting techniques, statistics plays a big role. Mathematicians assign numerical values to variables such as loyalty to existing brands, then build a model that can indicate trends that are invisible to intuitive analysis. Providing some statistics in the trends section of your plan can make it more convincing.

BARRIERS
TO ENTRY

If you want to become a semiconductor manufacturer, you'll need a billion-dollar factory or two. If you want to have a TV network, you'll need programming and affiliate stations in at least the major markets. Want to sell personal computer operating systems? There's a little problem of 60 million customers who run Windows, and Windows only.

These problems are called barriers to entry, and they exist to some extent in all industries. The barriers may be monetary, technological, distribution- or market-related or simply consist of ownership of prime real estate. (This last is frequently cited as the real competitive advantage of McDonald's, Big Macs notwithstanding. "Whenever you see a good site, you find out McDonald's already owns it," groused one fast-food competitor.)

An important part of analyzing your market is determining what the barriers to entry are, and how high they stretch. If the barriers are high, as is the case with automobile manufacturing, then you can be assured that new competitors are likely to be slow in springing up. If they're low, as is the case with, say, screenwriting, where

Plan Pointer

Forecast Pro is software that runs on your Windows PC and lets nonstatisticians produce sophisticated business forecasts. Engineered for lay users, it automatically selects the best forecasting technique for the job you're doing. For more information on Forecast Pro 3.0, contact Business Forecast Systems at 68 Leonard St., Belmont MA 02748, (617) 484-5050, fax: (617) 484-9219.

Fact Or Fiction?

Nobody beats Microsoft, right? Not quite. Intuit's Quicken rules personal finance software, despite Microsoft's heavily promoted Money program. And an operating system for palmtop computers from tiny Palm Computing runs on nearly 2 million machines, 10 times as many as Microsoft's rival Windows CE. The conclusion? Pick the right niche, and you can beat anybody.

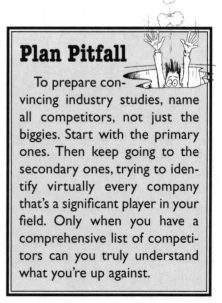

Plan Pitfall

Think twice before deciding barriers to entry are high for all potential competitors. For instance, you need billions of dollars to start a semiconductor company—but not if you contract out fabrication of the silicon chips to a manufacturer. Many semiconductor start-ups of the past few years do exactly that, providing serious competition for rivals who assumed the barrier was too high to allow many new entries.

anybody with a typewriter can play, then you know there will be an endless supply of competition lured by the low investment and chance of easy bucks.

Be alert for innovative competitors while writing the section of your plan where you analyze barriers to entry. It may save you from a disastrous error, and will certainly demonstrate to investors that you've thought your plan through and are not jumping to conclusions.

IDENTIFYING COMPETITORS

You're not alone, even if you have a one-person homebased company. You also have your competition to worry about. And your backers will worry about competition, too. Even if you truly are in the rare position of addressing a brand-new market where no competition exists, most experienced people reading your plan will have questions about companies they suspect may be competitors. For these reasons, you should devote a special section of your plan to identifying competitors.

If you had to name two competitors in the athletic shoe market, you'd quickly come up with Nike and Reebok. But these by far aren't the only competitors in the sneaker business. They're just the main ones and, depending on the business you're in, the other ones may be more important. If you sell soccer shoes, for instance, Adidas is a bigger player than either of the two American firms. And smaller firms such as Etonic, New Balance and Saucony also have niches where they are comparatively powerful.

Plan Pitfall

To prepare convincing industry studies, name all competitors, not just the biggies. Start with the primary ones. Then keep going to the secondary ones, trying to identify virtually every company that's a significant player in your field. Only when you have a comprehensive list of competitors can you truly understand what you're up against.

You can develop a list of competitors by talking to customers and suppliers, checking with industry groups and reading trade journals. But it's not enough to simply name your competitors. You need to know their manner of operation, how they compete.

Does a competitor stress a selective, low-volume, high-margin business, or does she emphasize sales growth at any cost, taking every job that comes along, whether or not it fits any coherent scheme or offers an attractive profit? Knowing this kind of information about competitors can help you identify their weaknesses as well as their names.

WHAT MAKES YOURS BETTER?

This is one of the most important sections of your plan. You need to convince anybody thinking of joining with your company, as an investor or in another way, that you offer something obviously different and better than what is already available. Sometimes this is called your distinctive competence or competitive advantage, but it's not too much to consider it your company's reason for being.

WHERE THE ELITE MEET TO EAT

The Elite Café in Waco, Texas, serves as a good case study of distinctive competence. The Elite has been near the campus of Baylor University, serving homestyle cooking for decades under the same ownership. Why do people stop there to eat instead of at one of the dozens of other restaurants along Interstate 35, many of them national chains with instantly recognizable names?

◆ *Convenience:* The Elite Café is near an exit ramp from both directions, and getting back onto the highway is also easy.

◆ *Visibility:* The Elite has a big sign that is easy to spot in plenty of time to get off the highway.

◆ *Customer base:* After decades in the same spot, the Elite is a familiar dining place for thousands of Central Texas residents and travelers.

◆ *Geography:* The main reason, however, is probably related to the fact that the Elite is located very near the midpoint of the drive between Dallas and Austin, the state capital. Anybody making that drive is likely to decide to stop halfway through to ease the job, and when they do, there will be the Elite Café.

Your distinctive competence may lie in any of the product features discussed in the last chapter, including cost, features, service, quality, distribution and so forth. Or it could be something totally different. The success of a retail convenience store located on an interstate highway, for instance, might depend almost entirely on how close it is to an exit ramp.

To figure out your competitive advantage, start by asking yourself:

1. Why do people buy from me instead of my competitors? Think about this question in terms of product characteristics. Ask your customers why they buy from you. Ask noncustomers why they don't. Ask suppliers, colleagues and anybody you can find.

2. What makes me different and, I hope, better? The answers, carefully analyzed, should spell out your distinctive competence.

Distinctive competence is not quite as important if your company operates in the beginning stages of a new industry. When interest and sales in a new field are growing fast, you can survive and prosper even if you aren't clearly better than the rest. If, however, you plan to take market share away from established competitors in a mature industry, then distinctive competence is all-important. Without a convincing case for being very different and much better than the rest, your business plan will have a hard time swaying anybody.

OVERALL OUTLOOK

As you set forth either to continue or to start up a business, it's important to take note of whether the tide is rising or ebbing. You may be confident that you can swim against the flow. Or you may be looking ahead to a time when the direction of the tide will change, and be preparing your business to take advantage of that sea change. Either way, you'll have to convince anybody reading your plan that you know how to read the tide charts, and use their power to help you reach your destination.

CHAPTER 10

MARKETING SMARTS

Your plan to promote your business

What are you selling? How are you selling it? Why would anybody want to buy from you? These are the kinds of questions that run through the minds of people reading business plans. The marketing section of your plan is where you politely but firmly answer them.

Let there be no misunderstanding: Your marketing strategy is a very important part of your plan. Lack of sales is a primary reason for business failure. The marketing section is the place where you tell how you are going to avoid that fate. Nobody knows that better than Fred Gratzon. After founding Telegroup in 1989, Gratzon couldn't afford to hire salespeople or do much marketing. In fact, he was literally begging friends and neighbors to try the discount long-distance telephone service—mostly with no success. "I was humiliated," admits Gratzon. "But I needed to support my family." It was only after he came up with the idea of using independent salespeople that Telegroup connected. He never raised a dime of capital, but thanks to the marketing solution, Telegroup grew to pull in an estimated $280 million a year in less than eight years.

For the marketing section of your plan, start by describing your strategy in terms of the traditional four P's of marketing: product, price, place and promotion.

DEFINING YOUR PRODUCT

Product, the first of the four P's, refers to the features and benefits of what you have to sell (as usual, we're using the term as shorthand for products and services). Many modern marketers have a problem with this "P," because it doesn't refer to customer service, which is an important part of the bundle of features and benefits you offer to customers. However, it's

TECH IT TO THE LIMIT

Sometimes merely applying technology to a product or service you're already offering can provide compelling marketing advantages. Timothy McCarthy founded Sales Building Systems in 1988 to help retail and restaurant chains boost individual store sales. But his business languished because he couldn't effectively teach or motivate store managers to do what he recommended.

In fact, the reverse happened. "Because I was creating additional work for them, the managers hated me," says McCarthy. The workbooks he wrote for them went unused, his advice went ignored, and his sales kept him barely scraping by.

Then a customer suggested he computerize his course material and, with the help of automation, ease the task of marketing for store managers instead of making it harder. "That's what I did," says McCarthy. The switch rapidly raised revenues, after nearly a decade of slow growth, to $4 million annually.

pretty easy to update "product" by simply redefining it to include whatever ancillary services are bundled into your offering.

There are a number of issues you need to address in your product section. You need to first break out the core product from the actual product. What does this mean? The core product is the nominal product. Say you're selling snow cones. A snow cone is your core product. But your actual product includes napkins, an air-conditioned seating area, parking spaces for customers and so forth. Similarly, a computer store nominally sells computers, but it also provides expert advice from salespeople, a service department for customers, opportunities to comparison shop, software and so on.

It's important to understand that the core product isn't the end of the story. Sometimes the things added to it are more valuable than the core product itself. That's not bad in itself, but failing to understand this is likely to lead to trouble.

In addition to fully defining your product, you may need to address other issues in your marketing plan. For instance, you may have to describe the process you're using for product development. Tell how you come up with ideas, screen them, test them, produce prototypes and so on.

You may need to discuss the life cycle of the product you're selling. This may be crucial in the case of quickly consumed products such as corn chips and in long-lived items like household appliances. You can market steadily to corn-chip buyers in the hopes they'll purchase from you frequently, but it makes less sense to bombard people with offers to sell refrigerators when they need one only every 10 or 20 years. Understanding the product's life cycle has a powerful effect on your marketing plan.

Other aspects of the product section may include a branding strategy, a plan for follow-up products or line extensions. Keeping these various angles on products in mind while writing this section will help you describe your product fully and persuasively.

> ## Buzzword
>
> A branding strategy is a marketing plan that calls for the creation of a name, symbol or design that identifies and differentiates a product from other products. Levi Strauss followed a branding strategy when it devised the Dockers brand for a new line of men's casual slacks.

THE PRICE CLUB

One of the most important decisions you have to make in a business plan is what price to charge for what you're selling. Pricing determines many things, from your profit margin per unit to your overall sales volume. It strongly influences decisions in other areas, such as what level of service you will provide and how much you will spend on marketing. Pricing has to be a process you conduct concurrently with other jobs, including estimating sales volume, determining market trends and calculating costs.

There are two basic methods you can use for selecting a price.

One way is to figure out what it costs you altogether to produce or obtain your product or service, then add in a suitable profit margin. This markup method is easy, straightforward and, assuming you can sell sufficient units at the suggested price, guarantees a profitable operation. It's widely used by retailers in particular. To use it effectively, you'll need to know your costs as well as standard markups applied by others in your industry.

The other way is more concerned with the competition and the customer

> ## Plan Pointer
>
> Product beauty may be only skin deep. Packaging, far from merely containing goods, is an important part of your product. Attractive packaging lures looks. Sturdy packaging ensures goods arrive intact. Environmental consciousness means recycled or organic packaging may be more important than the product inside. So attend to outer as well as inner product beauty.

SETTING PRICING OBJECTIVES

Before you can select a pricing approach, you need to know your pricing objectives. Following are questions to ask yourself about your pricing goals:

1. Which is more important: higher sales or higher profits?

2. Am I more interested in short-term results or long-term performance?

3. Am I trying to stabilize market prices or discourage price-cutting?

4. Do I want to discourage new competitors, or encourage existing ones to get out of the market?

5. Am I trying to quickly establish a market position, or am I willing to build slowly?

6. Do I have other concerns, such as boosting cash flow or recovering product development costs?

7. What will the impact of my price decision be on my image in the market? How does that fit the image I want?

Answer these questions first, then prioritize them to decide how each objective will weigh in setting your pricing strategy. That way, when you present your price objectives in your business plan, it will make sense and be supported by reasonable arguments integrated with your overall business goals.

than with your own internal processes. The competitive pricing approach looks at what your rivals in the marketplace charge, plus what customers are likely to be willing to pay, and sets prices accordingly. The second step of this process is tougher—now you have to adjust your own costs to yield a profit. Competitive pricing is effective at maintaining your market appeal and ensuring your enterprise's long life, assuming you can sell your goods at a profit.

Plan Of Action

Price Wars (St. Thomas Press), by Thomas J. Winninger, is a 275-page manual for avoiding or, if necessary, competing in and winning low-price competitions. The author provides many illuminating anecdotes of the dangers of price-cutting, as well as practical steps to follow.

FINDING YOUR PLACE

Place refers to channels of distribution, or the means you will use to put your product where people can buy it. Conventional distribution systems have three steps: producer, wholesaler and retailer. You may occupy or sell to members of any one of these steps. Some companies with vertically integrated distribution, such as Dell Computer, occupy all the steps themselves. Others, like franchisors, are parts of systems that orchestrate the activities among all channels. Still others, such as independent retailers, operate in one channel only.

Fact Or Fiction?

The best plan describes a business selling something everybody needs and yet that has no competition, right? Not quite. Business plan readers see so many plans claiming to have universal markets completely empty of competitors that they are highly skeptical of them. If you really are in such a position, you'll have to document it extra thoroughly.

Distribution tends to be treated as an afterthought by many manufacturers. However, your distribution scheme is often of critical importance. Say you have a mass-market consumer good such as a toy. Whether you plan effectively to get your product onto shelves in the major grocery, drug and discount store chains may make all the difference between success and failure.

If you're selling an informational product to a narrow market, such as political consulting services to candidates for elected office, physical distribution is of less importance. However, for just about all companies, an effective placement strategy is a big determinant of success.

Distribution Concerns

There are three main issues in deciding on a placement strategy: coverage, control and cost. Cost, it goes almost without saying, is an important part of any business decision, including distribution concerns. The other two issues, however, are unique to distribution and are trickier.

Coverage refers to the need to cover a large or small market. If you're selling laundry soap, you may feel the need to offer it to virtually every household in America. This will steer you toward a conventional distribution scheme running from your soap factory to a group of wholesalers serving particular regions or industries to retailers such as grocery stores and finally to the consumer.

What if you are reaching out to only a small group, such as chief information officers of Fortune 500 companies? In this case, the conventional, rather lengthy distribution scheme is clearly inappropriate. You're likely to do better by selling directly to the CIOs through a company sales staff, sales reps or perhaps an agreement with another company that already has sales access to the CIOs. In both these cases, coverage has a lot of say in the design of your distribution system.

Control is important for many products. Ever see any Armani suits at Target? The reason you haven't is that Armani works hard to control its distribution, keeping the costly apparel in high-end stores where its lofty prices can be sustained. Armani's need for control means that it deals only with distributors who sell to designer boutiques. Many manufacturers want similar control, for reasons of pricing, after-sale service, image and so forth. If you need control over your distribution, it will powerfully influence placement decisions.

Location Considerations

For retailers, the big place question involves real estate. Location commonly determines success or failure for many retailers. That doesn't necessarily mean the same location will work for all retailers. A low-rent but high-traffic space near a housing project may be a poor choice for a retailer stocking those Armani suits but will work fine for a fast-food restaurant or convenience store. Your location decision needs to be tied to your market, your product and your price.

Two of the most common tools for picking location are census data and

Fact Or Fiction?

Ever feel you're going to have to cut prices to stay in business? Don't trust that feeling! Studies show 16 out of 17 businesses that lower prices to compete eventually go out of business.

Plan Of Action

You can get mounds of economic and demographic marketing information—much of it free—from the U.S. Census Bureau. To learn more, contact the following office: Economic and Demographic Statistics, Bureau of the Census, U.S. Department of Commerce, Data User Service Division, Customer Service, Washington, DC 20233, (301) 763-4100.

traffic surveys. Retailers relying on walk-in traffic want to get a location that has a lot of people walking or driving past. You can usually get traffic data from local economic development agencies, or simply sit down with a clipboard and pencil and count people or cars yourself. Census data describing the number, income levels and other information about households in the nearby neighborhoods can be obtained from the same sources. An animal clinic, for example, wants to locate in an area with a lot of pet-owning households. This is the type of information you can get from census surveys.

PROMOTION NOTION

Promotion, in this context, is virtually everything you do to bring your company and your product in front of consumers. Promotional activities include picking your company name, going to trade shows, buying newspaper advertisements, making telemarketing calls, sending direct mail, using billboards, arranging co-op marketing, offering free giveaways and more. Not all promotions are suitable for all products, of course, so your plan should select the ones that will work best for you, explain why they were chosen, and tell how you're going to use them.

Promotion aims to inform, persuade and remind customers to buy your products. It uses a mix that includes four elements: advertising, personal selling, sales promotion and publicity or public relations.

Advertising Concerns

Advertising is what most people think of when they think of promotion. About two-thirds of ads use newspapers, magazines, broadcast media, direct mail and outdoor media or billboards to spread their message.

Buzzword

Co-op promotions are arrangements between two businesses to cross-promote their enterprises. When a soft drink can carries a coupon good for a discount on the price of entry to an amusement park, that's a co-op. Countless variations exist.

PROMOTIONAL BUDGET WORK SHEET

Select the advertising and promotional expenses you anticipate from the following list. Briefly describe the goal, such as "new leads" or "10 percent sales gain." Then estimate how frequently you'll insert an ad, run a spot, meet with a consultant and so forth. Finally, determine how much this will cost. The bottom line is the starting figure for your marketing budget.

Medium	Purpose/Goal	How Often?	Annual Budget
Ad Agencies			
Brochures			
Consultants			
Designers			
Direct Mail			
Displays			
Internet			
Magazines			
Newspapers			
Trade Journals			
Outdoor			
Public Relations			
Radio			
Sales calls			
Samples			
Specialties			
Telemarketing			
Television			
Trade Shows			
Yellow Pages			
Total			

The rest comes in the form of catalogs, specialty items such as pens and matchbooks, calendars and the like.

One of the first things to decide about your ad campaign is, What are we trying to do here? You may be advertising to raise your corporate profile, to improve a tarnished image, or simply to generate foot traffic. Whatever you're after, it's important to set specific goals in terms of such things as revenue increase, unit volume growth, inquiries and so forth. Without specific objectives, it's hard to tell what you can afford to do, and whether the campaign is living up to expectations.

Other Kinds Of Promotion

Personal selling is widely used in business-to-business models, when sales cycles are long, products are complex and the dollar amounts tend to be large. They are also used, however, by Avon beauty consultants, car dealers and barkers outside taverns on Bourbon Street in New Orleans. The key to effective personal selling is recruiting and training excellent salespeople.

Sales promotion is kind of a grab bag of promotional activities that don't fit elsewhere. If you offer free hot dogs to the first 100 people who come to your store on Saturday morning, that's a sales promotion. This category also includes in-store displays, trade shows, off-site demonstrations and just about anything else that could increase sales and isn't included in the other categories.

Publicity is the darling of small businesses because it lets them get major exposure at minimal cost. If you volunteer to write a gardening column for your local newspaper, it can generate significant public awareness of your plant nursery and position you as a leading expert in the field, all for the price of a few hours a week spent jotting down some thoughts on a subject you know very well already. To buy comparable exposure might cost many thousands of dollars. Press releases announcing favorable news about your company are one tool of publicity; similar releases downplaying bad news are the flip side.

"Public relations" is a somewhat broader term that refers to the image

Plan Of Action

Not sure where to send a press release or whom to address it to? *Bacon's Media Information Directories* give names, addresses and other contact information for virtually every newspaper, magazine, radio and TV station in the United States and abroad. Directories come in various editions and cost $250 and up. For more details, contact Bacon's Information Inc. at 332 S. Michigan Ave., Chicago, IL 60604, (800) 621-0561.

ONE-HIT WONDER

Back in 1986, all any kid wanted for Christmas was a Teddy Ruxpin. Manic demand for the $80 talking toy bear pushed its maker, a start-up called Worlds of Wonder Inc. (WOW), to sales of $327 million in just its second year in business. WOW went public and was valued at more than half a billion dollars.

What happened next was a lesson in the need to maintain a ceaseless stream of new ideas. First, competitors flooded the market with talking dolls that were often cheaper and of higher quality. Then overall demand declined as the fad faded.

WOW tried, to be sure. It came out with a game called Lazer Tag. Next was a gadget dubbed "the world's most intelligent doll." But they never found an understudy to Teddy. Within two years, the company was bankrupt, and soon it vanished from the scene.

It's hard to say that WOW would have done better if it had never had the Ruxpin doll. But there's little doubt that its failure to follow up meant that even its blazing initial success amounted to little.

---

you present to the public at large, government entities, shareholders and employees. You may work at public relations through such tools as company newsletters, legislative lobbying efforts, your annual report and the like.

Whatever you do, don't neglect public relations and publicity. There is no cheaper or more powerful tool for promotion.

FOLLOW-UP PLAN

Customers may ask, "What have you done for me lately?" Investors and others reading your business plan want to know, "What are you going to do for me tomorrow?" Any serious business plan has to take note of the fact that every product has a life cycle, that pricing pressures change over time, that promotions need to stay fresh and that new distribution opportunities are opening up all the time. So the portion of your plan where you describe how you'll continue your success is a vital one.

The annals of business are full of companies that turned out to be one-trick ponies that introduced a product or service that zoomed to stardom, but failed to follow it up with another winner. In the best cases, these companies survive but fade back into obscurity. In the worst, they fail to negotiate the switch from booming sales to declining sales and disappear completely.

You can reduce your chances of winding up as a one-trick pony by obtaining patents, registering trademarks, copyrighting slogans, and otherwise forestalling competition. Diversifying into more than one product is another good way to reduce the risk. It's a good idea to divert part of any boost in revenues to studying market trends and developing new products.

Investors looking at a plan, especially those contemplating long-term involvement, are alert to the risk of backing a one-trick entrepreneur. Showing competitive barriers you've erected and systems for developing new products is an important part of calming their fears.

There's one caveat when it comes to learning new tricks, however. Very simple concepts are the easiest to communicate, and extremely focused companies usually show the fastest growth—although not always over the long term. So you don't want to appear, in the process of reducing risk, that you've lost sight of the answers to the key questions: What are you selling? How are you selling it? And why would anybody want to buy from you?

CHAPTER 11

THE WORKS

Detailing your operations

"**O**perations" is the term used to describe how you buy, build and prepare your product or service for sale. That covers a lot of ground, including sourcing raw materials, hiring labor, acquiring facilities and equipment, and shipping off the finished goods. And it's different ground depending on whether you're a manufacturer or a service firm.

Not surprisingly, investors and other plan readers pay careful attention to the part of your plan describing your operations. The good news is that few entrepreneurs skimp on this section. They usually are highly expert and interested in operations and love to talk about it—in fact, one risk is that you'll go into too much detail here and wind up with what amounts to a technical treatise in which the essential marketing element seems lost. David Wheeler recognized that risk when seeking investors for his software start-up called InfoGlide Inc. So one of his first hires was someone to take on the job of CEO, to interface directly with investors and high-profile prospects, so Wheeler could get back to the operations he loved. "That's what I like," he says, "working with database code, not doing product demos."

The basic rule for your operations section is to cover just the major areas—materials, labor, facilities, equipment and processes—and provide the major details—things that are critical to operations or that give you competitive advantage. If you do that, you'll answer investors' questions about operations without overwhelming them.

OPERATIONS FOR MANUFACTURERS

Companies that make things have certain characteristics in common that set them apart from others, including retailers and service firms. The big difference is that manufacturers are far more complex. Rather than simply buying, transporting and selling goods, they have to take raw materials and labor and transform them into sellable products.

Process Points

The lead actor in manufacturing is the process of production. While product development, marketing and distribution all play important roles, it's the production process that sets manufacturers apart from all other enterprises. And the better your production process, the better a manufacturer you will be. It's the star that leads to your company's success.

A manufacturing production process consists of several components. One step is usually fabrication, or the making of products from raw materials. There is also assembly of components, testing and inspection of finished goods.

Manufacturing processes can become extremely detailed, down to calculating the number of seconds allowed for a sewing machine operator to complete the inseam on a pair of men's slacks. If you're an operations-minded entrepreneur, you may revel in these details. But control your enthusiasm for minutiae when it comes to writing a business plan. Stick to the important processes, those essential to your production or that give you a special competitive advantage.

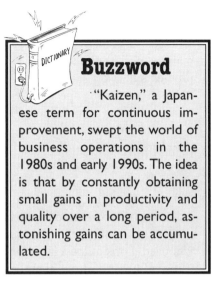

Buzzword

"Kaizen," a Japanese term for continuous improvement, swept the world of business operations in the 1980s and early 1990s. The idea is that by constantly obtaining small gains in productivity and quality over a long period, astonishing gains can be accumulated.

Plan Pointer

How much detail should you give about the technology you employ? A plan for internal use only can tell all, but be careful not to let it reach the wrong hands. A plan for venture capitalists should contain fewer details. Venture investors are often expert in their fields but can't guarantee confidentiality. Bankers care less about details, so a basic outline should do.

Personnel And Materials

Manufacturers combine labor and materials to produce products. Problems with either one of these critical inputs spell trouble for your business and for its backers. So plan readers look for strong systems in place to make sure that personnel and materials are appropriately abundant.

You should show in your plan that you have adequate, reliable sources of supply for the materials you need to build your products. Estimate your needs for materials and describe the agreements with suppliers, including their length and terms, that you have arranged to fulfill those needs. You may also give the backgrounds of your major suppliers and show that you have backup sources available should problems develop.

It's an interesting spectacle, every now and then, to watch an industrial giant such as an automaker or railroad paralyzed by a labor strike. It illustrates the importance of ensuring a reliable supply of adequately trained people to run your processes.

You'll first need to estimate the number and type of people you will require to run your plan. Start-ups can do this by looking at competitors' plants or by relying on the founders' prior experience at other companies. Existing firms can extrapolate what they'll need to expand from current operations. Then show that you can reasonably expect to be able to hire what you need. Look at local labor pools, unemployment rates and wage levels, using information from chambers of commerce or similar entities. If you plan to import sizable numbers of workers, check out housing availability and build an expense for moving costs into your budget.

Getting Equipped

Manufacturing a product naturally requires equipment. A manufacturer is likely to need all sorts of equipment such as cars, trucks, computers, telephone systems and, of course, machinery of every description for bending

---

THE MAKING OF A BARON

The person most famous for building an empire based on ownership of capital equipment is Andrew Carnegie. In the 19th century, this Scottish immigrant to America rose from beginnings as a textile-plant worker to become a baron of steel and oil.

Carnegie was always a hard worker—as a teenage delivery boy he was his family's primary source of income. But it was his savvy in acquiring capital equipment that made him a business legend.

At the age of 21, Carnegie borrowed to buy shares in a new railroad being built near his Pennsylvania home. A few years later, he acquired oilfield assets in Titusville, Pennsylvania. In railroad car manufacturing, bridge-building and, finally, iron and steel mills, Carnegie followed the same strategy: Control the means of production.

Shortly after 1900, Carnegie sold out to J.P. Morgan. Those holdings became U.S. Steel, today known as USX Corp.

Facilities Work Sheet

Use this work sheet to analyze your facilities requirements. Fill out the sections, then test available facilities against your requirements.

Space Requirements:

Initial Space _____

Expansion Space _____

Total Space _____

Location Requirements:

Proximity to Labor Pool _____

Proximity to Suppliers _____

Transportation Availability _____

_____

Layout Requirements: _____

_____

Cost Requirements (Dollar Amounts of Estimated Expenses):

Purchase/Lease Costs _____

Brokerage Costs _____

Moving Costs _____

Improvements Costs _____

Operating Costs _____

Total Cost _____

Plan Pitfall

Stay up on technology if you're in a so-called software industry—including books, movies and music as well as computer programs. New tools for ripping off intellectual property—like copying recorded music with digital technology—make catching copycats tougher than ever. Increasingly, your secrets are only safe if you keep up with the high-tech highwaymen.

metal, milling wood, forming plastic, or otherwise making a product out of raw materials.

Much of this equipment is very expensive and hard to move or sell once purchased. Naturally, investors are very interested in your plans for purchasing equipment. Many plans devote a separate section to describing the ovens, drill presses, forklifts, printing presses and other equipment they'll require.

This part of your plan doesn't have to be long, but it does have to be complete. Make a list of every sizable piece of equipment you anticipate needing. Include a description of its features, functions and, of course, its cost.

Be ready to defend the need to own the more expensive items. Bankers and other investors are loath to plunk down money for capital equipment that can only be resold for far less than its purchase price.

The Facilities Section

Everybody has to be somewhere. Unless you're a homebased businessperson or a globe-trotting consultant whose office is his suitcase, your plan will need to describe the facilities in which your business will be housed.

Land and buildings are often the largest capital items on any company's balance sheet. So it makes sense to go into detail about what you have and what you need.

Decide first how much space you require in square feet. Don't forget to include room for expansion if you anticipate growth.

Now consider the location. You may need to be close to a labor force and materials suppliers. Transportation needs such as proximity to rail, interstate highways or airports can also be important.

Next ask whether there is any specific layout that you need. Draw up a floor plan to see if your factory floor can fit into the space you have in mind.

To figure the cost of facilities, you'll first have to decide whether you will lease or buy space and what your rent or mortgage payments will be for the chosen option. Don't forget to include brokerage fees, moving costs and the cost of any leasehold improvements you'll need. Finally, take a look at operating costs. Utilities including phone, electric, gas, water and trash pickup are concerns; also consider such things as maintenance and general upkeep.

These aren't the only operations concerns of manufacturers. You should also consider your need to acquire or protect such valuable operations assets as proprietary processes and patented technologies. For many businesses—Coca Cola, with its secret soft drink formula, comes to mind—intellectual property is more valuable than their sizable accumulations of plants and equipment. Investors should be warned if they're going to have to pay to acquire intellectual property. If you already have it, they will be happy to learn they'll be purchasing an interest in a valuable technology.

SCALING SUCCESS BY THE CENTURY

Would you like to create a company that will last 150 years? The solid foundation provided by a secure, broad-based patent could be just what you need. Take the case of Fairbanks Scale.

More than 150 years ago, a Massachusetts entrepreneur named Thaddeus Fairbanks grew dissatisfied with the scales available to weigh hemp processed by a company he'd started with his brother. Fairbanks had already invented a couple of modestly successful contraptions, including a stove and an iron plow, and felt he could improve on the inaccurate and ponderous steelyard scales then in wide usage.

After a spell in his invention shop, Thaddeus emerged with a new type of scale that used a system of levers and could be buried in the ground, allowing wagonloads of hemp and other materials to be easily, quickly and accurately weighed. He obtained a patent on the invention and then, backed with $4,000, he and brothers Joseph and Erastus formed Fairbanks Platform Scale in 1830.

From that humble beginning, with the help of Thaddeus' patented scale technology, Fairbanks Scale would dominate the business of weighing everything from postal letters to canal barges for the next century. After a merger with its largest distributor in 1916, the company became known as Fairbanks Morse, and it survives today as a major division of a $1.5 billion sales company, Coltec Industries.

OPERATIONS FOR RETAIL AND SERVICE FIRMS

Service firms naturally have different operations requirements from manufacturers. Companies that maintain or repair things, sell consulting, or provide health care or other services generally have higher labor content and lower investments in plants and equipment.

Another important difference is that service and retail firms tend to have much simpler operational plans than manufacturers. In the process of turning raw materials into finished goods, manufacturers may employ sophisticated techniques in a complex series of operations. By comparison, it's pretty simple for a retailer to buy something, ship it to his store and sell it to a customer who walks in.

That's not to say operations are any less important for retailers and service firms. But most people already understand the basics of processes such as buying and reselling merchandise or giving haircuts or preparing tax returns. So you don't have to do as much explaining as, say, someone who's manufacturing computer chips.

The Importance Of People

For many service and retail firms, people are the main engines of production. The cost of providing a service is largely driven by the cost of the labor it entails. And retail employees' skills and service attitude drive their employers' productivity and market acceptance to a great degree.

A service firm plan, then, has to devote considerable attention to staffing. You should include figures on the local labor market for low-skilled employees such as counter clerks. Regional educational attainment data will help readers understand why you think you can hire sufficient semi- and higher-skilled workers for a service or repair operation. You'll want to include background information and, if possible, describe employment contracts for key employees such as designers, marketing experts, buyers and the like.

Buzzword

E-commerce is short for electronic commerce and basically refers to selling things through sites on the World Wide Web. E-shoppers ordered books, software, computers, flowers and even pizza online, to the tune of $3.3 billion in 1997, a number that will double by the year 2000.

Big-Time Buying

The ability to obtain reliable, timely and reasonably priced supplies of easily saleable merchandise is perhaps the prime skill of any retailer. If you have what consumers want when few others do, you're almost guaranteed to have strong sales. If you run out of a hot item, on the other hand, disappointed consumers may leave your store, never to return.

Operations plans for retailers, therefore, may devote considerable attention to sourcing desirable products. They may describe the background and accomplishments of key buyers. They may detail long-term supply agreements with manufacturers of in-demand branded merchandise. They may even discuss techniques for obtaining on the gray market desirable products from manufacturers who try to restrict the flow of goods to their stores.

Fact Or Fiction?

Is success a matter of buying low or selling high? Retailers say that, contrary to popular opinion, they really make their money when they buy, not sell, goods. The trick, mastered by successful retailers like Wal-Mart and Toys "R" Us, is to buy goods for a price low enough that you can sell them at a profit while still attracting customers and discouraging competitors.

Site Sensitivity

Manufacturers require certain basic conditions for their sites, but retailers and some service firms are exquisitely sensitive to a wide variety of location factors. In some cases, a difference of a few feet can make the difference between a location that is viable and one that is not.

Site selection plans for retailers should include traffic data, demographics of nearby populations, estimated sales per square foot, rental rates and other important economic indicators. Service firms such as restaurants will want many of the same things. Service firms such as travel agencies, pest control services and bookkeeping businesses will want to provide information about local income levels, housing and business activity.

Store design also must be addressed. Retailing can be as much about entertaining shoppers as it is about displaying goods. So store design becomes very important, especially for high-fashion retailers. Floor plans are probably not enough here. Retailers may want to include photos or illustrations of striking displays, in-store boutiques and the like.

INFORMATION TECHNOLOGY

No matter what business you are in, information technology probably looms larger all the time. Manufacturers link computers to speed orders directly from their customers' computers to their production control software. Retailers place their orders faster and more accurately using the same systems. Many service firms, such as travel agents, accountants and Web site designers, are also heavily dependent on technology.

If you use or anticipate using a promising new technology, whether it's a Web site for online commerce or an interactive computer training course to improve customer service, include it in your description of operations. Investors are always looking for an operations edge, and if you have it, you should tell them about it in your business plan.

Buzzword

Electronic Data Interchange, or EDI, is a computer-to-computer linkup of ordering and inventory systems between manufacturers and retailers. The hookup helps retailers maintain higher inventories of hot-selling products and lower inventories overall, while reducing return rates of unsaleable merchandise for manufacturers.

CHAPTER 12

STATE YOUR CASE

How to prepare your financial statements

Financial data is always at the back of the business plan, but that doesn't mean it's any less important than up-front material such as the description of the business concept and the management team. Astute investors look carefully at the charts, tables, formulas and spreadsheets in the financial section, because they know that this information is like the pulse, respiration rate and blood pressure in a human—it shows whether the patient is alive and what the odds are for continued survival.

Financial statements, like bad news, come in threes. The news in financial statements isn't always bad, of course, but taken together they provide an accurate picture of a company's current value, plus its ability to pay its bills today and earn a profit going forward. And this news is very important to business plan readers.

The three common statements are a cash flow statement, an income statement and a balance sheet. Most entrepreneurs should provide them and leave it at that. But not all do. Robert Crowley, vice president of Massachusetts Technology Development Corp., a state-owned venture firm, once described it as "this horrible disease . . . called spreadsheet-itis. It's the most common ailment in business plans today." Crowley says electronic spreadsheet software allows business plan writers to easily crank out many pages and many varieties of financial documents. But this is a case of the more, the less merry. As a rule, stick with the big three: income, balance sheet and cash flow statements.

These three statements are interlinked, with changes in one necessarily altering the others, but they measure quite different aspects of a company's financial health. It's hard to say that one of these is more important than another. But of the three, the income statement may be the best place to start.

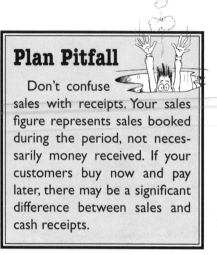

Plan Pitfall

Don't confuse sales with receipts. Your sales figure represents sales booked during the period, not necessarily money received. If your customers buy now and pay later, there may be a significant difference between sales and cash receipts.

INCOME STATEMENT

An income statement shows you whether you are making any money. It adds up all your revenues from sales and other sources, subtracts all your costs, and comes up with the fabled net income figure, also known as the bottom line.

Income statements are called various names—profit and loss statement, or P&L, and earnings statement are two common alternatives. And they can get pretty complicated in their attempt to capture sources of income such as interest and expenses such as depreciation. But the basic idea is pretty simple: If you take costs away from income, what you have left is profit.

To figure your income statement, you need to gather a bunch of numbers, most of which are easily obtainable. They include your gross revenue, which is made up of sales and any income from interest or sales of assets; your sales, general and administrative (SG&A) expenses; what you paid out in interest and dividends, if any; and your corporate tax rate. If you have those, you're ready to go.

Sales And Revenues

Revenue is all the income you receive from selling your products or services as well as from other sources such as interest income and sales of assets.

Gross Sales

Your sales figure is the income you receive from selling your product or service. Gross sales includes sales, minus any returns. It doesn't include interest or income from sales of assets.

Interest And Dividends

Most businesses have a little reserve fund they keep in an interest-bearing bank or money market account. Income from this fund, as well as from any other interest-paying or dividend-paying securities they

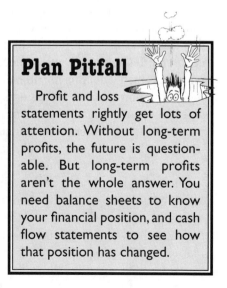

Plan Pitfall

Profit and loss statements rightly get lots of attention. Without long-term profits, the future is questionable. But long-term profits aren't the whole answer. You need balance sheets to know your financial position, and cash flow statements to see how that position has changed.

Buzzword

What sounds like Elmer Fudd is actually a common acronym used on many financial statements. EBIT stands for earnings before interest and taxes—an admirably descriptive accounting term that probably needs no further clarification.

own, shows up on the income statement just below the sales figure.

Other Income

If you finally decide that the branch office out on County Line Road isn't ever going to turn a decent profit, and you sell the land, building and fixtures, the income from that sale will show up on your income statement as "other income." Other income may include sales of unused or obsolete equipment or any income-generating activity that's not part of your main line of business.

Costs

Costs come in all varieties—that's no secret. You'll record variable costs, such as the cost of goods sold, as well as fixed costs—rent, insurance, maintenance and so forth. You'll also record costs that are a little trickier, the prime example being depreciation.

Cost Of Goods Sold

Cost of goods sold, or COGS, includes expenses associated directly with generating the product or service you're selling. If you buy computer components and assemble them, your COGS will include the price of the chips, disk drives and other parts, as well as the wages of the assembly workers. You'll also include supervisor salaries and utilities for your factory. If you're a solo professional service provider, on the other hand, your COGS may amount to little more than whatever salary you pay yourself.

Sales, General And Administrative Costs

You have some expenses that aren't closely tied to sales volume, including

Plan Pitfall

Acronyms are handy for those who know what they mean. But they can easily get out of hand in the financial data section of a business plan. SG&A, for sales, general and administrative expense, and COGS, for cost of goods sold, are commonly understood. But when you start throwing around NOPAT (net operating profit after taxes) and other obscure terms, you're likely to confuse rather than clarify.

salaries for office personnel, salespeople compensation, rent, insurance and the like. These are split out from the sales-sensitive COGS figure and included on a separate line.

Depreciation

Depreciation is one of the most baffling pieces of accounting wizardwork. It's a paper loss, a way of subtracting over time the cost of a piece of equipment or a building that lasts many years even though it may get paid for immediately.

Depreciation isn't an expense that involves cash coming out of your pocket. Yet it's a real expense in an accounting sense, and most income statements will have an entry for depreciation coming off the top of pretax earnings.

If you have capital items that you are depreciating, such as an office in your home or a large piece of machinery, your accountant will be able to set up a schedule for depreciation. Each year, you'll take a portion of the purchase price of that item off your earnings statement. While it hurts profits, depreciation can, it should be noted, reduce future taxes.

Interest

Paying the interest on loans is another expense that gets a line all to itself and comes out of earnings just before taxes are subtracted. This line doesn't include payments against principal, it should be noted. Because these payments result in a reduction of liabilities—which we'll talk about in a few pages in connection with your balance sheet—they're not regarded as expenses on the income statement.

Taxes

The best thing about taxes is that they're figured last, on the profits that are left after every other thing has been taken out. Tax rates vary widely according to where your company is located, how and whether state and local taxes are figured, and your special tax situation.

The best way to figure taxes is to have your accountant do a projection of your tax rate based on past years' filings and this year's projected results. Then multiply that percentage times your earnings before tax. We've used an estimated effective tax rate of 30 percent, which is not usually too far off the mark, for this section. Whatever you use, you'll have your net income—the much talked-about bottom line—after you take out taxes.

SAMPLE INCOME STATEMENT

In the following income statement for NetKnowledge Internet Training Center, total receipts from tuition charged to students came to $23,568. The company got an extra $115 from interest on bank accounts.

Sales Receipts	$23,568
Interest Income	115
COGS	12,615
Gross Margin	11,068
Expenses	4,835
Depreciation	1,125
Operating Earnings	5,108
Interest Expense	1,410
Pretax Earnings	3,698
Income Tax	1,109
Net Income	**$2,589**

Cost of goods sold amounted to $12,615. Subtracting COGS from sales gives the gross margin of $11,068. Subtracting expenses and depreciation from that returns a figure of $5,108 for operating earnings.

NetKnowledge racked up interest charges of $1,410. When this is removed from operating earnings, the resulting net income before taxes is $3,698. With income taxes calculated at $1,109, that leaves a net income of $2,589.

BALANCE SHEET

If the income sheet shows what you're earning, the balance sheet shows what you're worth. A balance sheet can help an investor see that a company owns valuable assets that don't show up on the income statement, or that it may be profitable but is heavily in debt. It adds up everything your business owns, subtracts everything the business owes and shows the difference as the net worth of the business.

Actually, accountants put it differently and, of course, use different names. The things you own are called assets. The things you owe on are called liabilities. And net worth is referred to as equity.

> ## Plan Pointer
>
> Legendary investor Warren Buffett reads thousands of financial statements describing businesses every year. He says that, in most cases, the first thing he goes to is the balance sheet to check a company's strength. So if you'd like to attract an investor of Buffett's stature, spend time on the balance sheet.

The three elements are governed by a simple equation:

Liabilities + Equity = Total Assets

It can also be useful to look at it another way:

Assets – Liabilities = Net Worth

Both formulas mean the same thing.

A balance sheet shows your condition on a given date, usually the end of your fiscal year. Sometimes balance sheets are compared. That is, next to the figures for the end of the most recent year, you place the entries for the end of the prior period. This gives you a snapshot of how and where your financial position has changed.

A balance sheet also places a value on the owner's equity in the business. When you subtract liabilities from assets, what's left is the value of the equity in the business owned by you and any partners. Tracking changes in this number will tell you whether you're getting richer or poorer.

> ## Plan Pointer
>
> The two sides of a balance sheet—assets and liabilities—can be presented side by side or one on top of the other. The first is called columnar format; the second report format. There's no rule about which is best. Do whatever looks or feels natural.

Assets

An asset is basically anything you own of value. It gets a little more complicated in practice, but that's the working definition.

Assets come in two main varieties: current assets and fixed assets. Current assets are anything that is easily liquidated or turned into cash. They include cash, accounts receivables, inventory, marketable securities and the like.

Fixed assets include stuff that is harder to turn into cash. Examples are land, buildings, improvements, equipment, furniture and vehicles.

> ## Plan Pointer
>
> One of the key characteristics of a balance sheet is that it . . . balances. The bottom lines of both halves of the balance sheet, assets in one half and liabilities in the other, are always equal. They balance.

The fixed asset part of the balance sheet sometimes includes a negative value—that is, a number you subtract from the other fixed asset values. This number is depreciation, and it's an accountant's way of slowly deducting the cost of a long-lived asset such as a building or piece of machinery from your fixed asset value.

Intangibles are another asset category. They include such things as patents, long-term contracts and that ephemeral something called goodwill. Goodwill consists of such things as the value of your reputation, which is not really susceptible to valuation. Probably the best way to think of goodwill is like this: If you sell your company, the IRS says the part of the sales price that exceeds the value of the assets is goodwill. As a result of its slipperiness, some planners never include an entry for goodwill, although its value may in fact be substantial.

Patents, trademarks, copyrights, exclusive distributorships, protected franchise agreements and the like do have somewhat more accessible value. They may never be turned into cash, but you can estimate their worth, or at least figure out what you paid for them and use that.

> ## Plan Pointer
>
> Many people are uncomfortable with figuring any value at all for goodwill but don't want to ignore it completely. One common alternative is to just enter $1 for intangibles and leave it at that.

Liabilities

Liabilities are the debts your business owes. They come in two classes: short-term and long-term.

Short-term liabilities are also called current liabilities. Any debt that is going to be paid off within 12 months is considered current. That includes accounts payable you owe suppliers, short-term bank loans (shown as

SAMPLE BALANCE SHEET

December 31, 1999

ASSETS		LIABILITIES	
Cash	$4,387	Notes Payable	$11,388
Accounts Receivable	12,385	Accounts Payable	2,379
Inventory	1,254	Interest Payable	1,125
Prepaid Expenses	3,548	Taxes Payable	3,684
Other Current Assets	986	Other Current Liabilities	986
Total Current Assets	22,560	Total Current Liabilities	19,562
Fixed Assets	27,358	Long-term Debt	4,896
Intangibles	500	Other Noncurrent Liabilities	1,156
Other Noncurrent Assets	0	**Total Liabilities**	**$25,614**
		Net Worth	24,804
Total Assets	**$50,418**	**Total Liabilities & Net Worth**	**$46,031**

notes payable) and accrued liabilities you have built up for such things as wages, taxes and interest.

Any debt that you won't pay off in a year is long-term. Mortgages and bank loans with more than a one-year term are considered in this class.

CASH FLOW STATEMENT

Where did the money go? The cash flow statement tells you the answer to that. It monitors the flow of cash over a period of time such as a year, a quarter or a month and shows you how much cash you have on hand at the moment.

The cash flow statement, also called the statement of changes in financial position, probes and analyzes changes that have occurred on the balance sheet. It's different from the income statement, which describes sales and profits but doesn't necessarily tell you where your cash came from or how it's being used.

A cash flow statement consists of two parts. One follows the flow of cash into and out of the company. The other shows how the funds were spent. The two parts are called, respectively, sources of funds and uses of funds. At the bottom is, naturally, the bottom line, called net changes in cash position. It shows whether and by how much you improved your cash on hand during the period.

SOURCES OF FUNDS

Sources of funds usually has two main sections in it. The first shows cash from sales or other operations. In the cash flow statement, this figure represents all the money you collected from accounts during this period. It may include all the sales you booked during the period, plus some collections on sales that actually closed earlier.

The other category of sources of funds includes interest income, if any, plus the proceeds from any loans, line of credit drawdowns or capital received from investors during the period. Again, these figures represent money actually received during the period. If you arranged for a $100,000 line of credit but only used $10,000 during this period, then your sources of funds would show $10,000.

PENNY'S LACK OF PENNIES

When Penny McConnell's dreams came true, her cash flow fell short. The owner of an eight-person cookie bakery, McConnell had been making a living selling low volumes of fresh Penny's Pastries brand cookies to local stores. Then a buyer from Southwest Airlines called and said the airline wanted to serve her new cookies on all its flights. It would be a year's worth of sales—every month.

Inexperienced at planning for such volume, McConnell made crucial mistakes. She cut prices to meet Southwest's budget, which reduced profits. Then she borrowed heavily to buy equipment, order supplies, hire employees and rent a new facility, increasing expenses sharply.

When costs rose after a technical problem cropped up, profits vanished completely. Then losses mounted. Within six months Penny's Pastries filed for bankruptcy. What happened? Too much spending, too much discounting and too little planning doomed her from the start. Now in business with another venture, McConnell says a well-thought-out plan might have confirmed what her instincts suggested. "It was such a tremendous increase in volume," she says, "that I had a gut feeling from the beginning it wasn't going to work."

Fact Or Fiction?

Is it possible to have too much cash? In fact, it is. If your cash is simply sitting in a bank account, it may be drawing little or no interest. In a typical inflation environment, it will often lose purchasing power from one day to the next. If you have large amounts of cash and nothing to do with it, consider reinvesting in your company—or perhaps another.

Uses Of Funds

The sources of funds section often has only one or two entries, although some cash statements break out sources of funds by businesses and product lines. But even simple statements show several uses of funds. A cash flow statement will normally show uses such as cost of goods sold; SG&A, or sales, general and administrative expense; and also any equipment purchases, interest payments, payments on principal amounts of loans, and dividends or draws taken by the owners.

Net Change In Cash

Few things feel better for a start-up businessperson than to have plenty of cash in the bank. And few things tell better what's going on with cash on hand than the net change in cash line on your business plan. Net change in cash is the difference between total funds in and total funds out. If you bring in $1 million and send out $900,000, your net change in cash is $100,000. Ideally, you want this number to be positive and, if possible, showing an upward trend.

OTHER FINANCIAL INFORMATION

If you're seeking investors for your company, you'll probably need to provide quite a bit more financial information than what is in the income statement, balance sheet and cash flow statements. For instance, a personal finance statement may be needed if you're guaranteeing loans yourself. Applying business data to other ratios and formulas will yield important information on what your profit margin is and what level of sales it will take for you to reach profitability. Still other figures, such as the various ratios, will help predict whether you'll be able to

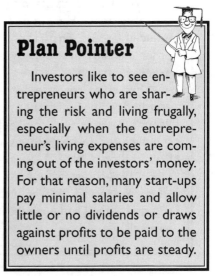

Plan Pointer

Investors like to see entrepreneurs who are sharing the risk and living frugally, especially when the entrepreneur's living expenses are coming out of the investors' money. For that reason, many start-ups pay minimal salaries and allow little or no dividends or draws against profits to be paid to the owners until profits are steady.

SAMPLE CASH FLOW STATEMENT

The following sample one-month cash flow statement for Net-Knowledge Internet Training Centers reflects $23,568 in sales receipts. That includes sales booked and collected during the period and accounts receivable that were collected. The interest entry reflects interest received on NetKnowledge's cash reserves account at the bank. The $10,000 was an injection of capital by one of the firm's partners.

Sources Of Cash	
Sales	$23,568
Other Sources	0
Interest	115
Invested Capital	10,000
Total Cash In	**$33,683**
Uses Of Cash	
COGS	$12,615
SG&A	4,835
Interest	1,410
Taxes	1,109
Equipment Purchase	8,354
Debt Principal Payments	2,000
Dividends	0
Total Cash Out	**$30,323**
NET CHANGE IN CASH	**$3,360**
Beginning Cash On Hand	**$4,387**
Ending Cash On Hand	**$7,747**

COGS stands for cost of goods sold and includes primarily salaries paid to NetKnowledge's educators and staff. Sales, general and administrative, or SG&A, expenses include the base salary for NetKnowledge's single salesperson. The interest outlay is for interest on NetKnowledge's line of credit. The $8,354 entry is for a new computerized presentation projector. NetKnowledge paid its credit line down by $2,000 during the same period, and the owners took no draw out of the business.

The net result, equal to total cash in minus total cash out, comes to $5,903, and that is NetKnowledge's net cash flow for the month.

The bottom two entries sum up NetKnowledge's current cash position. You add the amount of cash on hand from the prior period's cash flow statement to the net cash flow figure on this statement.

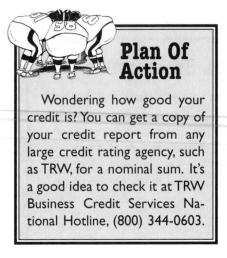

Plan Of Action

Wondering how good your credit is? You can get a copy of your credit report from any large credit rating agency, such as TRW, for a nominal sum. It's a good idea to check it at TRW Business Credit Services National Hotline, (800) 344-0603.

pay your bills for long. These bits of information are helpful to you, as well as to investors, it should be noted. Understanding and, if possible, mastering them, will help you run your business more smoothly.

PERSONAL FINANCIAL STATEMENT

Investors and lenders like to see business plans with substantial investments by the entrepreneur, or with an entrepreneur who is personally guaranteeing any loans and who has the personal financial strength to back those guarantees. Your personal financial statement is where you show plan readers how you stack up financially as an individual.

The personal financial statement comes in two parts. One is similar to a company balance sheet and lists your liabilities and assets. A net worth figure at the bottom, like the net worth figure on a company balance sheet, equals total assets minus total liabilities.

A second statement covers your personal income. It is similar to a company profit and loss statement, listing all your personal expenses, such as rent or mortgage payments, utilities, food, clothing and entertainment. It also shows your sources of income, including earnings from a job, income from another business you own, child support or alimony, interest and dividends, and the like.

The figure at the bottom is your net income; it equals total income minus total expenses. If you've ever had to fill out a personal financial statement to borrow money for a car loan or home mortgage, you've had experience with a personal financial statement. You should, in fact, be able to simply update figures from a previous personal financial statement.

FINANCIAL RATIOS

Everything in business is relative. The numbers for your profits, sales and net worth need to be compared with other components of your business for them to make sense. For instance, a $1 million net profit sounds great. But what if it took sales of $1 billion to achieve those profits? That would be a modest performance indeed.

To help understand the relative significance of your financial numbers, analysts use financial ratios. These ratios compare various elements of your financial reports to see if the relationships between the numbers make sense based on prior experience in your industry.

Some of the common ratios and other calculations analysts perform include your company's break-even point, current ratio, debt-to-equity ratio, return on investment and return on equity. You may not need to calculate all these; depending on your industry you may find it useful to calculate various others, such as inventory turnover, a useful figure for many manufacturers and retailers. But ratios are highly useful tools for managing, and most are quick and easy to figure. Becoming familiar with them, and presenting the relevant ones in your plan, will help you manage your company better and convince investors you are on the right track.

Break-Even Point

One of the most important calculations you can make is figuring your break-even point. This is the point at which revenues equal costs. Another way to figure it is to say it's the level of sales you need to get to for gross margin or gross profit to cover all your fixed expenses. Knowing your break-even point is important because when your sales are over this point, they begin to produce profits. When your sales are under this point, you're still losing money. This information is handy for all kinds of things, from deciding how to price your produce or service to figuring whether a new marketing campaign is worth the investment.

The process of figuring your break-even point is called break-even analysis. It may sound complicated, and if you were to watch an accountant figure your break-even point, it would seem like a lot of mumbo-jumbo. Accountants calculate figures with all sorts of arcane-sounding labels, such as variable cost percentage and semifixed expenses. These numbers may be strictly accurate, but given all the uncertainty there is with projecting your break-even point, there's some question as to whether extra accuracy is worth all that much.

There is, however, a quicker if somewhat dirtier method of figuring break-even. It is described on the work sheet at left. While this approach

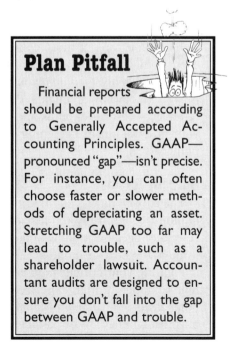

Plan Pitfall

Financial reports should be prepared according to Generally Accepted Accounting Principles. GAAP—pronounced "gap"—isn't precise. For instance, you can often choose faster or slower methods of depreciating an asset. Stretching GAAP too far may lead to trouble, such as a shareholder lawsuit. Accountant audits are designed to ensure you don't fall into the gap between GAAP and trouble.

ACCOUNTING THROUGH THE AGES

If you don't understand accounting as well as you should, you can't blame it on being a recent innovation. Double-entry accounting dates at least from 1340, and the first book on accounting, by a monk named Luca Pacioli, was published in 1494.

Surprisingly, a medieval accountant would feel quite comfortable with much of what goes on today in an accounting department. But accountants haven't been sitting back and relaxing during the intervening centuries. They've thought up all kinds of ways to measure the health and wealth of businesses (and businesspeople).

There are more ratios, analyses and calculations than you can shake a green eye-shade at. And wary investors are prone to use a wide variety of those tests to make sure they're not investing in something that went out of style around the time Columbus set sail. So although accounting may not be your favorite subject, it's a good idea to learn what you can. Otherwise, you're likely to be seen as not much more advanced than a 14th-century monk.

may not be up to accounting-school standards, is highly useful for entrepreneurs and, more important, it can be done quickly, easily and frequently, as conditions change.

Once you get comfortable with working break-even figures in a simple fashion, you can get more complicated. You may want to figure break-even points for individual products and services. Or you may apply break-even analysis to help you decide whether an advertising campaign is likely to pay any dividends. Perform break-even analyses regularly and often, especially as circumstances change. Hiring more people, changing your product mix or becoming more efficient all change your break-even point.

Current Ratio

The current ratio is an important measure of your company's short-term liquidity. It's probably the first ratio anyone looking at your business will compute, because it shows the likelihood that you'll be able to make it through the next 12 months.

Figuring your current ratio is simple. You divide current assets by current liabilities. Current assets consist of cash, receivables, inventory and other assets likely to be sold for cash in a year. Current liabilities consist of bills that will have to be paid before 12 months pass, including short-term

BREAK-EVEN ANALYSIS WORK SHEET

To determine your break-even point, start by collecting these two pieces of information:

1. **Fixed costs:** These are inflexible expenses you'll have to make independently of sales volume. Add up your rent, insurance, administrative expenses, interest, office supply costs, maintenance fees, etc. to get this number. Put your fixed costs here: _____.

2. **Average gross profit margin:** This will be the average estimated gross profit margin, expressed as a percentage, you generate from sales of your products and services. Put your average gross profit margin here: _____.

Now divide the costs by profit margin, and you have your break-even point. Here's the formula:

$$\frac{\text{Fixed Costs}}{\text{Profit Margin}} = \text{Break-even Point}$$

If, for instance, your fixed costs were $10,000 a month and your average gross profit margin 60 percent, the formula would look like this:

$$\frac{\$10,000}{0.6} = \$16,667$$

So in this case, your break-even point is $16,667. When sales are running at $16,667 a month, your gross profits are covering expenses. Fill your own numbers into the following template to figure your break-even point:

$$\frac{\$ _____}{_____} = \$ _____$$

notes, trade accounts payable and the portion of long-term debt due in a year or less. Here's the formula:

$$\frac{\text{Current Assets}}{\text{Current Liabilities}} = \text{Current Ratio}$$

For example, say you have $50,000 in current assets and $20,000 in current liabilities. Your current ratio would be:

$$\frac{\$50,000}{\$20,000} = 2.5$$

The current ratio is expressed as a ratio, that is, the above example shows a current ratio of 2.5 to 1 or 2.5:1. That's an acceptable current ratio for many businesses. Anything less than 2:1 is likely to raise questions.

Quick Ratio

This ratio has the best name—it's also called the acid-test ratio. The quick ratio is a more conservative version of the current ratio. It works the same but leaves out inventory and any other current assets that may be a little harder to turn into cash. You'll normally get a lower number with this one than with the current ratio—1:1 is acceptable in many industries.

Buzzword

Liquidity measures your company's ability to convert its noncash assets, such as inventory and accounts receivable, into cash. Essentially, it measures your ability to pay your bills.

Sales/Receivables Ratio

This ratio shows how long it takes you to get the money owed you. It's also called the average collection period and receivables cycle, among other names. Like most of these ratios, there are various ways of calculating your sales/receivables cycle, but the simplest is to divide your average accounts receivable by your annual sales figure and multiply it by 360, which is considered to be the number of days in the year for many business purposes. Like this:

$$\frac{\text{Receivables}}{\text{Sales}} \times 360$$

If your one-person computer consulting business had an average of

$10,000 in outstanding receivables and was doing about $120,000 a year in sales, here's how you'd calculate your receivables cycle:

$$\frac{\$10,000}{\$120,000} = 1/12$$

$$1/12 \times 360 = 30$$

If you divide 1 by 12 on a calculator, you'll get .08333, which gives you the same answer, accounting for rounding. Either way, your average collection period is 30 days. This will tell you how long, on average, you'll have to wait to get the check after sending out your invoice. Receivables will vary by customer, of course. You should also check the receivables cycle number against the terms under which you sell. If you sell on 30-day terms and your average collection period is 40 days, there may be a problem, such as customer dissatisfaction, poor industry conditions or simply lax collection efforts on your part, that you need to attend to.

Buzzword

Leverage refers to the use of borrowed funds to increase your purchasing power. Used wisely, leverage can boost your profitability. Overused, however, borrowing costs can eradicate operating earnings and produce devastating net losses.

Inventory Turnover

Retailers and manufacturers need to hold inventory, but they don't want to hold any more than they have to because interest, taxes, obsolescence and other costs eat up profits relentlessly. To find out how good they are at turning inventory into sales, they look at inventory turnovers.

The inventory-turnover ratio takes cost of goods sold and divides it by inventory. The COGS figure is a total for a set period, usually a year. The inventory is also an average for the year; it represents what that inventory costs you to obtain, whether by building it or by buying it.

$$\frac{\text{Average COGS}}{\text{Average Inventory}} = \text{Inventory Turnover}$$

An example:

$$\frac{\$500,000}{\$125,000} = 4$$

In this example, the company turns over inventory four times a year. You can divide that number into 360 to find out how many days it takes you to turn over inventory. In this case, it would be every 90 days.

It's hard to say what is a good inventory-turnover figure. A low figure suggests you may have too much money sitting around in the form of inventory. You may have slow-moving inventory that should be marked down and sold. A high number for inventory turnover is generally better.

Debt-To-Equity Ratio

This ratio is one that investors will scrutinize carefully. It shows how heavily in debt you are compared with your total assets. It's figured by dividing total debt, both long- and short-term liabilities, by total assets.

$$\frac{\text{Total Debt}}{\text{Total Assets}} = \text{Debt-To-Equity Ratio}$$

Here's a sample calculation:

$$\frac{\$50,000}{\$100,000} = 1{:}2$$

You want this number to be low to impress investors, especially lenders. A debt-to-equity ratio of 1:2 would be comforting for most lenders. One way to raise your debt-to-equity ratio is by investing more of your own cash in the venture.

Profit On Sales

This is your ground-level profitability indicator. Take your net profit before taxes figure and divide it by sales.

$$\frac{\text{Profit}}{\text{Sales}} = \text{Return On Sales}$$

For example, if your restaurant earned $100,000 last year on sales of $750,000, this is how your POS calculation would look:

$$\frac{\$100,000}{\$750,000} = 0.133$$

Is 0.133 good? That depends. Like most of these ratios, a good number in one industry may be lousy in another. You need to compare POS figures for other restaurants to see how you did.

Return On Equity

Return on equity, often abbreviated as ROE, shows you how much you're getting out of the company as its owner. You figure it by dividing net profit, from your income statement, by the owner's equity figure—the net worth figure if you're the only owner—from your balance sheet.

$$\frac{\text{Net Profit}}{\text{Net Worth}} = \text{Return On Equity}$$

Take a look at the ROE for NetKnowledge, the company's sample income statement and balance sheet looked at earlier in this chapter.

$$\frac{\$2,589}{\$21,403} = 12\%$$

NetKnowledge's owners are getting a 12 percent return on their equity. To decide whether this is acceptable, compare it with what you could earn elsewhere, such as in a bank certificate of deposit, stock mutual fund or the like, as well as with other companies in your industry.

Return On Investment

Your investors are interested in the return on investment, or ROI, that your company generates. This number, figured by dividing net profit by total assets, shows how much profit the company is returning based on the total investment in it.

Plan Of Action

Making sense of financial ratios requires knowing the normal ratios for your industry. Check these two books: *Industry Norms and Key Business Ratios* (Dun & Bradstreet) and *Statement Studies* (Robert Morris Associates) to compare your apples with other people's apples. Both reference works are available in many libraries.

$$\frac{\text{Net Profit}}{\text{Total Assets}} = \text{Return On Investment}$$

For NetKnowledge, this would be:

$$\frac{\$2,589}{\$47,017} = 5.5\%$$

Notice that the ROE, which reflects the return on the owners' equity

---

EVA Sigh Of Relief

EVA is an acronym standing for economic value added, and it's one of the most interesting new financial management tools available to business owners. The aim of EVA is to find out whether you're doing better with the money you have than you could by, say, investing in U.S. Treasury bills.

EVA has been pioneered by consulting firm Stern Stewart, which has counseled hundreds of companies on how to apply EVA. And experts say that entrepreneurs, in particular, already understand EVA on a gut level. In any event, the basic concept is fairly simple—you measure EVA by taking net operating earnings before taxes and subtracting a reasonable cost of capital, say, 12 percent.

In practice, however, it's complicated. Stern Stewart has identified more than 160 potentially needed adjustments to a company's accounting procedures before EVA can be effectively implemented.

---

alone, is a lot higher than the ROI. This is because NetKnowledge's leverage—the fact that it has borrowed against its assets—increases the ROE.

Forecasts

Where you've been is of interest in business, but it's a lot more intriguing to contemplate where you're going. Figuring out where you're going is what financial forecasting is all about. You can forecast financial statements such as balance sheets, income statements and cash flow statements to project where you'll be at some point in the future.

Forecasts are necessities for start-ups, which have no past history to report on. Existing businesses find them useful, too, for planning purposes. Forecasts help firms foresee trouble, such as a cash flow shortfall, that is likely to occur several months down the road, as well as give them benchmarks to which they can compare actual performance.

Projected Income Statement

Business planning starts with sales projections. No sales, no business. It's that simple. Even if you're in a long-range development project that won't produce a marketable product for years, you have to be able to look ahead and figure out how much you'll be able to sell before you can do any planning that makes sense.

Now that the pressure's on, making a sales projection and the associated income projection may look a little tricky. So let's do it step-by-step.

First pick a period to project for. You should start with a projection for the first year. Then make projections for the next two years as well.

Next, come up with some baseline figures. If you're an existing business, what were last year's sales? The prior years'? What's the trend? You may be able to simply project out the 10 percent annual sales you've averaged the past three years for the next three.

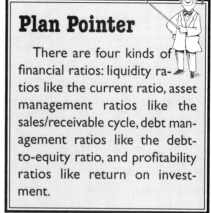

Plan Pointer

There are four kinds of financial ratios: liquidity ratios like the current ratio, asset management ratios like the sales/receivable cycle, debt management ratios like the debt-to-equity ratio, and profitability ratios like return on investment.

If you're a start-up and don't have any prior years' figures to look at, look at some other things. The most important question to ask is, What has been the experience of similar companies? If you know that car dealers across the nation have averaged 12 percent annual sales gains, that's a good starting point for figuring your dealership's projections.

Sometimes conditions are expected to change so much that past experience isn't helpful. Internet retailing has been around for more than three years, for instance, but that doesn't really mean much for where sales in this revolutionary new channel will be in several years. In these circumstances, you can look at constraints, such as your business's production capacity. Your restaurant is unlikely to sell more meals than its kitchen can cook, for example. Now you can take that high-end limit and adjust it to reflect economic conditions such as interest rate trends, the expected emergence of competitors and any other important factors. Don't forget to include very specific future factors of which you may be aware, such as the well-publicized fact that the highway department is going to tear up the road in front of your restaurant for several months next year. When you add up all these past experiences, sales constraints and modifiers, you should be able to come up with a forecast you can have some confidence in.

Forecasting expenses is your next step, and it's much easier. You can of-

Plan Pitfall

Pro forma and projected financial statements are based on the future and, as such, are imprecise. You need to make them as realistic and reasonable as possible but not believe in them too explicitly. Be extra-sure not to overstate revenues or understate expenses.

Plan Pointer

When making forecasts it's useful to change dollar amounts into percentages. So if you figure sales will rise 20 percent next year, you'll enter 120 percent on the top line of the projection. Using percentages helps highlight overoptimistic sales projections and suggest areas, especially costs, for improvement.

ten take your prior year's cost of goods sold, adjust it either up or down based on trends in costs, and go with that. The same goes for rent, wages and other expenses. Even start-ups can often find good numbers on which to forecast expenses, since they can just go to the suppliers they plan to deal with and ask for current price quotes plus anticipated price increases. You'll hope, of course, to uncover good news with regard to expenses. You may find that unit costs go down thanks to economies of scale, for instance. And fixed costs, as the name suggests, are not likely to change significantly.

Projected Balance Sheet

Balance sheets can also be projected into the future, and the projections can serve as targets to aim for or benchmarks to compare against actual results. Balance sheets are affected by sales, too. If your accounts receivable or inventory go up, your balance sheet reflects this. And, of course, increases in cash show up on the balance sheet. So it's important to look ahead to see how your balance sheet will appear given your sales forecast.

When you sit down to prepare a projected balance sheet, it will be helpful to take a look at past years' balance sheets and figure out the relationship of certain assets and liabilities that vary according to sales. These include cash, receivables, inventory, accounts payables and tax liabilities.

If you have any operating history, you can calculate the average percentages of sales for each of these figures for the past few years and use that for your balance sheet projection. You can simply take last year's figures, if you don't think they'll change that much. Or you can adjust the percentage to fit some special knowledge you have about the coming year—you're changing your credit terms, for instance, so you expect receivables to shrink, or you're taking out a loan for an expensive new piece of equipment. Firms without operating history can look at one of the books describing industry norms referred to earlier to get guidance about what's typical for their type of company.

Cash Flow Forecast

Businesses are very sensitive to cash. Even if your operation is profitable and you have plenty of capital assets, you can easily go broke if you

SAMPLE PROJECTED INCOME STATEMENT

The following projected income statement for Small Bites, a catering service specializing in children's birthday parties, shows that the planner expects year 2000 revenues to follow the steady trend of 25 percent increases annually; it also shows the effect of opening a second operation in a nearby city.

The expenses section generally tracks expense trends as well, with many costs showing sharp jumps associated with opening the new location. The result is that depressed earnings are projected for the first year of the expanded operation, despite higher revenues.

INCOME PROJECTION

	1997	1998	1999	2000 (projected)
INCOME				
Net Sales	$138,899	$173,624	$217,030	$271,287
Cost Of Sales	69,450	83,339	99,834	135,644
Gross Profit	$69,449	$90,285	$117,196	$135,643
OPERATING EXPENSES				
General And Administrative Expenses				
Salaries And Wages	$13,890	$17,362	$21,703	$27,129
Sales Commissions	6,945	8,681	10,851	13,564
Rent	5,400	5,670	5,954	11,252
Maintenance	1,389	1,458	1,531	2,894
Equipment Rental	2,452	2,575	2,703	5,109
Furniture And Equipment Purchase	3,232	3,394	3,563	6,735
Insurance	1,207	1,267	1,331	1,999
Interest Expenses	3,008	3,158	3,316	6,268
Utilities	1,250	1,563	1,953	3,692
Office Supplies	776	750	899	977
Marketing And Advertising	6,256	6,805	7,150	9,204
Travel	550	750	1,000	1,000
Entertainment	323	301	426	555
Bad Debt	139	174	217	323
Depreciation And Amortization	1,800	2,700	4,050	6,075
TOTAL OPERATING EXPENSES	$48,617	$56,608	$66,647	$96,776
Net Income Before Taxes	$20,832	$33,677	$50,549	$38,867
Provision For Taxes On Income	3,125	5,051	7,582	5,830
NET INCOME AFTER TAXES	$17,707	$28,626	$42,967	$33,037

run out of cash and can't pay your taxes, wages, rent, utilities and other essentials. Similarly, a strong flow of cash covers up a multitude of other sins, including a short-term lack of profitability. A cash flow forecast or cash budget is your attempt to spot future cash shortfalls in time to take action.

SAMPLE PROJECTED BALANCE SHEET

The following balance sheet projects variable expenses and liabilities by taking each item's percentage of the previous year's sales and multiplying that by the estimated sales for the coming year. This generates numbers for all but long-term debt, which the owner knows will rise slightly, and other noncurrent debt, consisting of a note to the owner.

	2000	% Sales	2001 (projected)
Sales	$87,740		$110,000
ASSETS			
Cash	$4,387	5.0%	$5,500
Accounts Receivable	12,385	14.1%	15,510
Inventory	1,254	1.4%	1,540
Other Current Assets	986	1.1%	1,210
Total Current Assets	$19,012	21.7%	$23,870
Fixed Assets	27,358	31.2%	34,320
Intangibles	500	0.6%	660
Other Noncurrent Assets	0	0.0%	0
Total Assets	**$46,870**		**$58,850**
LIABILITIES			
Notes Payable	$11,388	13.0%	$14,300
Accounts Payable	2,379	2.7%	2,970
Interest Payable	1,125	1.3%	1,430
Taxes Payable	3,684	4.2%	4,620
Other Current Liabilities	986	1.1%	1,210
Total Current Liabilities	$19,562		$24,530
Long-term Debt	4,896		5,200
Other Noncurrent Liabilities	1,156		1,156
Total Liabilities	**$25,614**		**$30,866**
Net Worth	**$21,256**		**$27,964**
Total Liabilities & Net Worth	**$46,870**		**$58,850**

A cash budget is different from a cash flow statement in that it's generally broken down into periods of less than a year. This is especially true during start-up, when the company is especially sensitive to cash shortages and management is still fine-tuning its controls. Start-ups, highly seasonal businesses and others whose sales may fluctuate widely should do monthly cash flow projections for a year ahead, or even two. Any business would do well to project quarterly cash flow for three years ahead.

The added detail makes monthly cash flow forecasts somewhat more complicated than figuring annual cash flow, since revenues and expenses should be recorded when they will be paid out. Sales and cost of goods sold should be allotted to the months in which they can be expected to actually occur. Other variable expenses can be allocated as percentages of sales for the month. Expenses paid other than monthly, such as insurance and estimated taxes, are recorded when they occur.

As with the balance sheet projection, one way to project cash flow is to figure out what percentage of sales historically occurs in each month. Then you can use your overall sales forecast for the year to generate monthly

THE UNREAL THING

If you're having trouble envisioning how you could run out of cash while experiencing strong and profitable sales growth, take a peek at the iThink business-simulation software from High Performance Systems. It runs on your PC and uses just six variables to give you a new appreciation for the importance of cash.

You're a start-up business owner. You have $30,000 and access to lenders if you need it. You can set your selling prices, hire and lay off workers, and order raw materials. Competitors will affect the outcome of some decisions.

You have only two years of simulated time while making money and capturing significant market share. Easy? Sure, once you figure out the interlocking variables. For instance, you can lower prices to boost sales—until back orders pile up and poor service drives away business. Raise prices to slow sales, and competitors jump in.

High Performance's simulation isn't quite like being there. But it will give you a feel for the real thing.

For more information, contact High Performance Systems Inc. at 45 Lyme Rd., #200, Hanover, NH 03755, (603) 643-9636, ext. 110, fax: (603) 643-9502, www.hps-inc.com.

estimates. If you don't have prior history, you'll need to produce estimates of such things as profit margins, expenses and financing activities, using your best guesses of how things will turn out.

The cash flow forecast also takes into account sources of cash other than sales, such as proceeds from loans and investments by owners.

SAMPLE CASH FLOW FORECAST

Following is a cash flow forecast for The Boardroom, a sailboard rental shop. The forecast begins by calculating what percentage of sales occurs in each month, as in the following table. Note that the percentages do not add up to exactly 100 because of rounding. This is still adequately accurate for our purposes. The sales by month portray a tolerably seasonal business, with close to half the annual sales occurring in the late spring and summer months. All the sales are for cash.

Month	% Of Sales
Jan.	5.0%
Feb.	6.1%
Mar.	7.5%
Apr.	10.5%
May	11.9%
Jun.	13.8%
Jul.	12.2%
Aug.	9.0%
Sep.	7.6%
Oct.	5.5%
Nov.	4.8%
Dec.	6.2%

Translating these monthly percentages of sales to the cash flow projection provides us with our beginning figures. The rest of the figures, for the most part, flow from these sales forecasts.

SAMPLE CASH FLOW FORECAST, CONT'D.

Projected Cash Flow: 2000

	Jan.	Feb.	Mar.	Apr.	May	Jun.	Jul.	Aug.	Sep.	Oct.	Nov.	Dec.	TOTAL
CASH RECEIPTS													
Income From Sales													
Cash Sales	$6,550	$7,991	$9,825	$13,755	$15,589	$18,078	$15,982	$11,790	$9,956	$7,205	$6,288	$8,122	$131,131
Total Cash From Sales	6,550	7,991	9,825	13,755	15,589	18,078	15,982	11,790	9,956	7,205	6,288	8,122	$131,131
Income From Financing													
Loan Proceeds	5,000	0	0	2,500	0	0	0	0	0	0	0	0	$7,500
Other Cash Receipts	10,000	0	0	0	0	0	0	0	0	0	0	0	$10,000
Total Cash Receipts	21,550	7,991	9,825	16,255	15,589	18,078	15,982	11,790	9,956	7,205	6,288	8,122	148,631
CASH DISBURSEMENTS													
Expenses													
COGS	2,948	3,596	4,421	6,190	7,015	8,135	7,192	5,306	4,480	3,242	2,830	3,655	$59,010
SG&A	11,555	2,507	3,083	4,316	4,891	5,672	5,014	3,699	3,124	2,261	1,973	2,548	$50,643
Interest	0	80	80	80	80	80	80	80	80	80	80	80	$880
Taxes	0	0	0	1,500	0	1,500	0	0	1,500	0	0	0	$4,500
Equipment Purchase	5,000	0	0	5,000	0	0	0	0	0	0	0	0	$10,000
Debt Principal Payments	0	0	0	0	0	0	0	0	0	0	0	7,500	$7,500
Dividends	0	0	0	0	0	0	0	0	0	0	0	0	$0
Total Cash Disbursements	19,503	6,183	7,584	17,086	11,986	15,387	12,286	9,085	9,184	5,583	4,883	13,783	$132,533
Net Cash Flow	2,047	1,808	2,241	-831	3,603	2,691	3,696	2,705	772	1,622	1,405	-5,661	$16,098
Opening Cash Balance	0	2,047	3,855	6,096	5,265	8,868	11,559	15,255	17,960	18,732	20,354	21,759	$0
Cash Receipts	21,550	7,991	9,825	16,255	15,589	18,078	15,982	11,790	9,956	7,205	6,288	8,122	$148,631
Cash Disbursements	-19,503	-6,183	-7,584	-17,086	-11,986	-15,387	-12,286	-9,085	-9,184	-5,583	-4,883	-13,783	-$132,533
Ending Cash Balance	$2,047	$3,855	$6,096	$5,265	$8,868	$11,559	$15,255	$17,960	$18,732	$20,354	$21,759	$16,098	$16,098

SAMPLE CASH FLOW FORECAST, CONT'D.

Notice that there are two nonsales sources of cash: $7,500 in proceeds from a bank loan and $10,000 in a loan from the owner. At the end of the year, after steady payments of interest on the bank loan, the principal is paid in a balloon payment. The loan proceeds are used at the beginning of the year to purchase a new mobile surfboard display stand. Additional personnel are trained during this period to be ready when the busy season starts up. Another equipment purchase occurs just as the busy season gets under way.

The forecast for The Boardroom shows a company that will wind the year up in a strong cash position. It will probably be able to not only pay its bills but to also finance further growth internally. As far as its financial vital signs are shown in the cash flow statement, this patient is alive and well.

CHAPTER 13

EXTRA, EXTRA

How to design the appendices

A business plan is a story, the narrative of your enterprise, and you want to maintain a certain amount of flow as you lead readers from concept to management, through marketing and on to financials. Some material that you'd probably like to fit into your plan somewhere just doesn't fit well into any of those sections. For instance, you may want to include resumes of some of your management team, product samples, product photos, advertising samples, press clippings, facility photos or site plans.

For these and other items that the plan writer wants in the plan but that don't seem to belong anywhere, many plans include appendices and attachments. This is material that may be optional and that many plan readers may not need to refer to. However, for those readers who want to delve deeper into the workings of the company, appendices provide additional answers.

KEY EMPLOYEE RESUMES

The management section of your business plan will contain a listing and brief descriptions of the senior managers and other key employees on your team. However, many investors and lenders are going to want to know more about you and your important associates than you give them in this section. For that purpose, you can include full resumes in an appendix.

PRODUCT SAMPLES

If your products are portable enough, you may be able to include samples in your appendix. Some examples of products that are suitable for inclusion in a plan are fabric swatches, stationery samples, printing samples, software screenshots or even floppy disks.

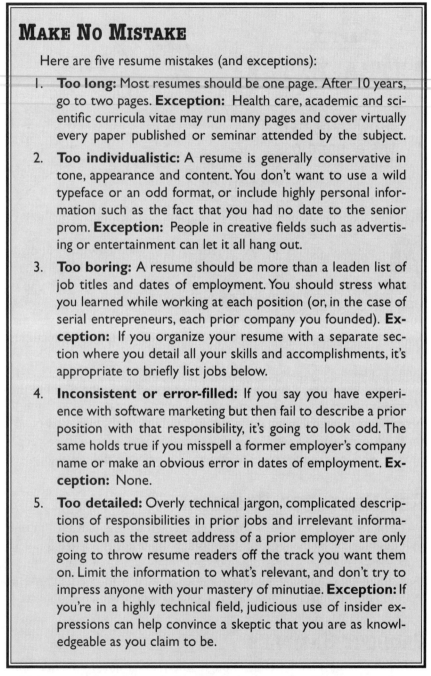

MAKE NO MISTAKE

Here are five resume mistakes (and exceptions):

1. **Too long:** Most resumes should be one page. After 10 years, go to two pages. **Exception:** Health care, academic and scientific curricula vitae may run many pages and cover virtually every paper published or seminar attended by the subject.

2. **Too individualistic:** A resume is generally conservative in tone, appearance and content. You don't want to use a wild typeface or an odd format, or include highly personal information such as the fact that you had no date to the senior prom. **Exception:** People in creative fields such as advertising or entertainment can let it all hang out.

3. **Too boring:** A resume should be more than a leaden list of job titles and dates of employment. You should stress what you learned while working at each position (or, in the case of serial entrepreneurs, each prior company you founded). **Exception:** If you organize your resume with a separate section where you detail all your skills and accomplishments, it's appropriate to briefly list jobs below.

4. **Inconsistent or error-filled:** If you say you have experience with software marketing but then fail to describe a prior position with that responsibility, it's going to look odd. The same holds true if you misspell a former employer's company name or make an obvious error in dates of employment. **Exception:** None.

5. **Too detailed:** Overly technical jargon, complicated descriptions of responsibilities in prior jobs and irrelevant information such as the street address of a prior employer are only going to throw resume readers off the track you want them on. Limit the information to what's relevant, and don't try to impress anyone with your mastery of minutiae. **Exception:** If you're in a highly technical field, judicious use of insider expressions can help convince a skeptic that you are as knowledgeable as you claim to be.

It's important not to overdo it with product samples. Investors tend to regard many entrepreneurs as being somewhat more product-focused than operations- or marketing-minded. By all means, provide samples if it's feasible and helpful. But don't expect appealing samples to overcome deficiencies in the concept, management, marketing, operations or financing schemes presented in your plan.

PRODUCT PHOTOS

Appendices are good places to include photographs of products whose appearances are important or whose features are difficult to explain in words. It's normal and acceptable to include line drawings of products in the main sections of your plan. But again, most investors are more interested in such items as your balance sheet, management experience and cash flow projections than they are in glossy product photos.

> ### Plan Pointer
>
> Don't draw the line at two dimensions when considering illustrations of products and other key features of your plan. Three-dimensional models, mock-ups and prototypes let investors get a hands-on feel for what you're proposing. If you've prepared a 3-D sample or model, you can use it to give your plan a high degree of physical reality.

ADVERTISING SAMPLES

It may be advisable to include examples of the advertising you intend to use to market your products or services. For many companies, innovative and persuasive advertising approaches are essential to the success of the firm. Without actual examples of the ads, it may be difficult for readers to grasp the appeal and power of your marketing ideas.

Copies of newspaper and magazine ads, photos of billboards, still photos from TV spots, Web site banner ads and transcripts of radio spots are all acceptable. However, keep in mind that this information is optional. If you have an unimpressive advertising campaign, it won't help you to expose investors to the fact.

PRESS CLIPPINGS

Reviews and articles in influential publications and broadcast shows drive many product sales. If your new software program got rave reviews in a major computer magazine, by all means include it here. Readers knowledgeable about the industry will recognize the value that such intangible assets as favorable press notice can provide.

Generating favorable publicity is one of the more valuable things you can do for your business. To learn how to do it on your own, consult one

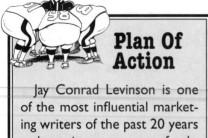

Plan Of Action

Jay Conrad Levinson is one of the most influential marketing writers of the past 20 years and a major proponent of publicity. His low-cost marketing manuals, beginning with *Guerrilla Marketing* (Houghton Mifflin) in 1985 and continuing with books focusing on topics from online marketing to marketing homebased businesses, provide countless tips for generating and capitalizing publicity.

of the many excellent manuals that have been written.

You may also want to include complimentary ratings, certifications or other endorsements by entities such as travel guides, associations, and watchdog groups. If your hotel got an impressive number of stars from the Mobil or Michelin guides, you'll probably want to mention it more prominently in your plan, such as in you main marketing or concept sections. And it might not be a bad idea to include a copy of the actual certificate bearing the seal.

FACILITY PHOTOS

Few real estate investors will buy a property without firsthand knowledge of its appearance, state of repair and general impression. When an investor is being asked to put money into your company, perhaps in exchange for partial ownership of your plan or, often, for the specific purpose of purchasing a building, then it's a good idea to calm any concerns about the facility's condition by providing a few photos.

Make sure any facility photos you provide are more informative than glitzy. Skip over the sculpture at the entrance in favor of an outside shot illustrating that the property is in overall good repair.

SITE PLANS

You may want to include basic factory layouts and store floor plans in the operations section of your plan. If your site plan is complex and you feel some readers would benefit from seeing some of the additional details, provide them here rather than cluttering up the main part of the plan with them. If you have a number of store locations with varying layouts, for instance, you could give an idea of how several of them look.

CREDIT REPORTS

Credit reports could be included in the financial statements section of your plan. However, since bankers are the main ones who will be interested in credit reports, you may want to place them in a separate appendix to make it easier to customize your plan.

LEASES

The devil is in the details when it comes to leases. It's not appropriate to discuss every last clause of even an important lease in the main section of your plan. However, there's a chance that diligent readers will have questions about any especially significant leases that can only be answered by reading the actual documents. For these discriminating plan readers, you can include here the actual leases, or at least the more important sections.

CUSTOMER CONTRACTS

Few things are better to include in a plan than a long-term contract to supply an established customer. If you're lucky enough have such a powerfully appealing deal in your pocket, you'll surely want to refer to it early on in your plan.

Like leases, however, the value of a contract may lie in its details. So it might be a good idea to include copies of relevant sections of any really significant contracts as appendices. If the deal is as good as you think (it had better be—otherwise, you wouldn't highlight it in your plan), then exposing potential investors to the beneficial details can only do you good.

There's no hard-and-fast rule about the overall length of a plan. Most new-venture plans should be under 20 pages. And though plans for complicated enterprises can legitimately run much longer, it's probably a good idea to exercise restraint when it comes to packing things into an appendix. Recall the idea of diminishing returns, and make sure that anything you put in your plan contributes significantly to presenting a clear, compelling picture of your business.

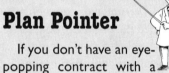

Plan Pointer

If you don't have an eye-popping contract with a marquee client, but you have a lot of lesser arrangements with more or less impressive customers, use the laundry list approach. Many plans effectively devote a page or so to a dense roster of all existing clients, conveying a positive impression of having a robust customer base.

CHAPTER 14

LOOKING GOOD

Creating a great impression with your plan

You wouldn't show up for a meeting with an investor wearing the clothes you normally wear for cleaning out the warehouse. Don't send your business plan out improperly clothed, either. You spend a lot of time and energy on your plan. It would be a shame to have it marred by spelling and typographical errors and a poor general appearance.

Stationery, Printing And Design

A three-ring binder is the ideal container for a business plan you're using only for internal management purposes. You'll find it easy to remove and replace pages with updated figures. And the plan will lie flat on a conference table for easy reference when you're discussing strategy, forecasts and other issues with your team.

For sending out to bankers or other investors, you'll want to use something different, however. The most common approach is to copy the plan onto good-quality white paper, using both sides of the paper, then bind it together permanently into a booklet. Any copy shop or printer can do such a binding for you, or you may purchase a do-it-yourself binding kit at an office supply store. Cover your plan with a clear plastic binder so that the cover page shows, or print your cover page information on a heavy piece of paper to serve as a cover for the binder.

Permanent binding helps plan readers keep all the pages of your plan together and makes it easier to read. It's important to keep these reasons for permanent binding in mind—it's a decision that improves the functionality of the plan, not its looks. Spending a lot of money creating a beautiful perfectly bound plan is not a wise investment. Plan readers are interested in information, not entertainment.

The same thing goes for choosing the paper and typeface you'll use in

Plan Pitfall

It's easy to go wild with fonts these days. Every computer comes with dozens of more or less standard fonts, and you can get on the Internet and download almost any number of crazy, unique software typefaces. But don't do it. Stick to a standard—Courier or Times Roman or perhaps Arial on a Windows PC, Palatino or another standard on a Macintosh.

your plan. Pick white paper, perhaps gray or cream or some shade of off-white. But leave the colored paper to fliers from the pizza place down the street. To make a businesslike impression, use businesslike stationery.

Your general guide to selecting paper is the fact that investors tend to be conservative. Don't be less conservative than they are if you want to win a hearing.

CHARTS, GRAPHS AND TABLES

Graphs and charts are invaluable tools for conveying certain types of information. Common visuals in business plans include organizational charts, product illustrations, sales trends, break-even points, market trends, competitor market shares and the like. If you are including such information in your plan, consider using graphs or charts to help get the message across.

Many computer software programs, including general-purpose spreadsheets and word processors, can easily be used to construct serviceable charts. Be sure to use a good-quality printer to create the charts. Often small type is unreadable on a chart that has to be compressed to fit on a page and is then output from a low-quality printer. This type of chart isn't going to help your case.

Not all plan readers are comfortable with charts, just as not all are comfortable with endless columns of numbers. So use charts and graphs to supplement, not replace, information presented in text or report form. A visual is a way to emphasize and ease the communication of detailed material. But it can't replace the actual detail.

Fact Or Fiction?

If a plan is used for internal purposes only, it doesn't matter what it looks like as long as it's functional, right? That's true to some extent, but it's also true that part of a plan's functionality is to convince and persuade. A plan that looks shabby and casually thrown together won't command as much respect among other managers and employees as one that's polished and professional looking.

MULTIMEDIA PRESENTATIONS

Some plans have to be more than paper. If your plan is going to be presented at a venture capital conference, before a company planning meeting, to a conclave of potential suppliers, at an industry conference, or in a similar group setting, you'll need slides instead of simple sheets of paper. Be prepared to talk attendees through the plan instead of relying on them to navigate it on their own.

> ### Plan Pointer
>
> Use as many charts, tables and other graphic elements as it takes to get your point across. But don't count on lavish visuals to sway a skeptical reader. Some readers actually are put off by plans that seem to be trying to wow them with presentation.

You can use a variety of presentation programs to quickly generate slides or transparencies suitable for an overhead projector, sometimes with nothing more than the outline or text of your original plan. Remember to keep the amount of information presented on each page of a multimedia presentation brief and to give people time to read and absorb it before moving on to the next page of your presentation.

You'll also have to choose carefully what and when to present details culled from your full-length plan. One reason for the need for careful editing is the fact that a presentation plan is a lot shorter than a printed plan. People aren't going to sit while you read through 30 pages of text. Nor can they control the pace or direction of a presentation the way they can in a written plan they peruse on their own. You'll have to ask yourself such questions as, "Will this group be more interested in the marketing or financial aspects of the plan?" and present accordingly.

> ### Plan Of Action
>
> The standard software for presentations these days is PowerPoint from Microsoft. It's included in most versions of the Microsoft Office suite and is available as a stand-alone package as well. For more information, visit Microsoft's Web site at www.microsoft.com.

COVER SHEETS

The first thing anyone looking at your business plan will see is the cover page. After that, they may never look at it again, to be sure. But the fact is, your plan's cover page will contribute strongly to the first impression you make. Take care in how you present it, and make sure it fits with the overall image you want to portray.

A few cover-page components are essential. You should definitely have your company name, address, phone number and other contact information. Another good item to include is the date, as well as perhaps a notice that this is, indeed, a business plan. Format this information in large, black, easily readable type and place it toward the top of the page. You want, above all else, for a plan reader to know which business this plan is for and how to contact you.

If you have a striking, well-designed corporate logo, it's also a good idea to include that on the cover page. A corporate slogan, as long as it's not too long, is also a good identifying mark that does something to communicate your strategy as well.

Some plans include a confidentiality notice or nondisclosure request on the cover page. For your own tracking purposes, if your plan contains highly sensitive information, you may want to number the copies of your plans and include the number of this copy on the cover page.

It's tempting to put all kinds of stuff on the cover page, but you should probably resist it. Your business concept, the amount you're trying to raise and other details can go on the inside. The cover page must identify the company. Very much more than that is likely to be too much.

COVER LETTERS

A cover letter is a brief missive introducing your plan to the person you have sent it to. In some cases it may never be read; in others it may be the only part of your plan that is read. But in any event, it serves several important functions.

First, the cover letter serves as an introduction to the plan. It should briefly explain why you've contacted this person—basically, to get him to look at your plan. You should also explain generally what you're looking for—an investor, a loan, a long-term supplier relationship, etc. Often this will be obvious from the circumstances. A banker, for instance, is going to recognize a business plan package immediately and guess why he's received it. But if there's any question, the cover letter is the place to resolve it.

The cover letter provides a valuable

Plan Pointer

Remove "To Whom It May Concern" from your vocabulary. Program your computer to explode if this phrase is typed into it. Never address a plan cover letter to something as vague as "Loan Department" if you can help it. And strive to get the name of an actual person, whom you can identify as a "Mr." or "Ms." and use the proper honorific. "To Whom It May Concern" is off-putting. Don't use it.

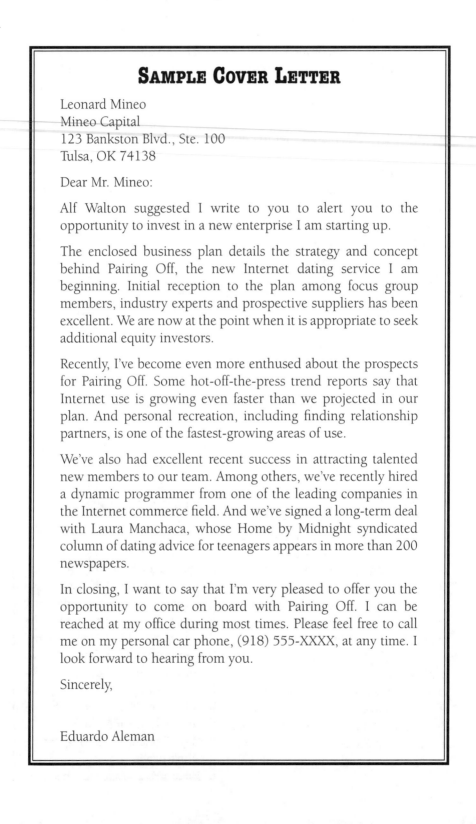

SAMPLE COVER LETTER

Leonard Mineo
Mineo Capital
123 Bankston Blvd., Ste. 100
Tulsa, OK 74138

Dear Mr. Mineo:

Alf Walton suggested I write to you to alert you to the opportunity to invest in a new enterprise I am starting up.

The enclosed business plan details the strategy and concept behind Pairing Off, the new Internet dating service I am beginning. Initial reception to the plan among focus group members, industry experts and prospective suppliers has been excellent. We are now at the point when it is appropriate to seek additional equity investors.

Recently, I've become even more enthused about the prospects for Pairing Off. Some hot-off-the-press trend reports say that Internet use is growing even faster than we projected in our plan. And personal recreation, including finding relationship partners, is one of the fastest-growing areas of use.

We've also had excellent recent success in attracting talented new members to our team. Among others, we've recently hired a dynamic programmer from one of the leading companies in the Internet commerce field. And we've signed a long-term deal with Laura Manchaca, whose Home by Midnight syndicated column of dating advice for teenagers appears in more than 200 newspapers.

In closing, I want to say that I'm very pleased to offer you the opportunity to come on board with Pairing Off. I can be reached at my office during most times. Please feel free to call me on my personal car phone, (918) 555-XXXX, at any time. I look forward to hearing from you.

Sincerely,

Eduardo Aleman

forum for you to explain why you're contacting this particular person. If you've received a personal referral, you'll want to say who gave you the referral very early on, probably in the first sentence following the salutation. Never underestimate the power of a personal referral from a friend, colleague or acquaintance of the person you're writing to. It may not land you an investor, but it gets your foot well in the door.

You may have some personal connection to the person other than a referral. For instance, perhaps you once met the person. Perhaps you even worked together at a company or communication organization. A shared interest, such as a hobby, is of less value, but it may be worth mentioning if your shared interest is unusual or marked by a close degree of identification among those who share it. For instance, it may not mean much to

---

PRESENTING—YOUR BUSINESS PLAN!

Once you've prepared your plan for presentation, put it in front of the right people. There are five steps:

1. **Obtain leads and referrals.** Find names, addresses and telephone numbers of investors of the type you wish to target. Ask people you know for referrals.

2. **Research your target.** Learn as much as possible about how much money people have to invest, industries they're interested in and other requirements. Search venture capital directories, *Who's Who*, news articles and similar sources.

3. **Make your pitch.** First, mail or messenger your plan to the target. Assuming you don't hear immediately, follow up with a letter or telephone call in a few weeks. If this doesn't produce a meeting, look elsewhere.

4. **Defuse objections.** Although you may think you've answered everything in your plan, you haven't. Prepare a list of possible objections—potential competitors, hard-to-buttress assumptions, etc.—that your investor may raise. Then prepare cogent answers.

5. **Get a commitment.** You won't get an investment unless you ask for it. When all objections have been answered, be ready to offer one last concession—"If I give your representative a board seat, can we do this today?"—and go for the close.

point out that you, like the reader, are a fan of professional basketball. However, if you both have competed as crewmembers on long-distance ocean racing sailboats, this might be worth mentioning. In any case, the cover letter, not the plan, is obviously the place to bring up this type of personal connection.

Finally, the cover letter may detail the terms under which you are presenting your plan. You may, for instance, say that you are not submitting the plan to any other investor. You may explicitly point out that you are currently seeking financing from a number of sources, including this one. If there is a deadline for responding to your plan, if you wish to stress that the plan is confidential and must be returned to you, or if you would like to ask the recipient to pass it on to someone else who may be interested, this is the place to do so.

The cover letter is also an opportunity to expand upon any concerns that you didn't include in your plan. Perhaps a late-breaking development, such as the hiring of a new key employee, occurred too late to be included in the finished plan. Or perhaps you have come across a brand-new market research report that validates some of the assumptions you made in your marketing section. The cover letter gives you a chance to provide updated, expanded or other important information that isn't in your plan.

WHEN YOU GET TURNED DOWN

Some people have lots of success in presenting business plans, and some people have less. But nobody is always successful. Even a talented entrepreneur with a long track record of starting up winners will frequently run up against an investor who doesn't want to play. Investors may not be interested in your particular industry, may not have any funds to invest at the moment, may need a larger or smaller amount to invest or may have any of a hundred other reasons for turning you down.

So the question is not, Will you get turned down? The question is, What do you do you when it happens?

The first thing you should do is try to find out why, really, you got the thumbs-down. Is it truly because the person is out of the country, or is it something else?

Your purpose is not to uncover someone's evasion or white lie. An investor has the right to turn you down for any reason whatsoever (unless, of course, you're dealing with an institution such as bank that must abide by equal opportunity lending guidelines). Instead of pointing fingers at the investors, you should really be interested in pointing fingers at your plan.

If there is a problem with your plan, you want to know about it. If the projected return to investors is so low that nobody is going to take you seriously, now's the time to find out, not after you've presented it unsuccessfully dozens of times.

So gently probe, asking questions that focus on your plan, to find out whether you've made a mistake or just hit an unreceptive audience. If you identify a failing, of course, fix it before submitting your plan to another party.

Get A Referral

Even a total refusal to consider your plan is helpful if the person suggests another place where you might be successful. You should always ask for a referral from anyone who turns your proposal down. It can't hurt—you've already been nixed. And a referral from a knowledgeable, respected investor can carry a lot of weight when you use it as an introduction (even if he or she is just trying to get rid of you.)

Venture investing, in particular, is very much a network-driven business. Venture capitalists are always asking for referrals, and they're usually willing to give them as well.

Keep The Door Open

Leigh Steinberg, the well-known sports agent who has negotiated more than $2 billion worth of contracts for many star athletes, says you should always keep in mind that one negotiation leads to the next. Keep that next negotiation in mind while working toward and planning for the one at hand. What that means in a business plan context is don't burn any bridges.

If an investor doesn't respond to your plan, brushes you off or even rudely tells you to get lost, your response should still be unfailingly courteous and professional. If you let your frustration, disappointment, hurt feelings and anger show, it could cost you plenty. That investor may be having a bad day and change her mind tomorrow. She may recall your name and the way you behaved so well under pressure, and mention it to a more open-minded associate the next week. Or perhaps next year, when you're promoting a more exciting concept, she'll be willing to back the improved idea.

None of these scenarios is certain or even probable in any individual instance. But considering the aggregate potential to help or hurt you that all the people you'll present your plan to will possess, any of these scenarios is quite likely. And they're only possible if you keep the door open for the future.

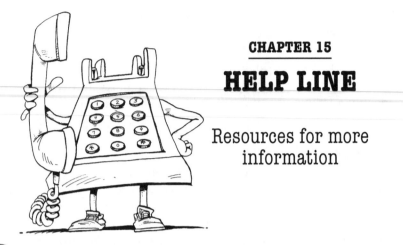

CHAPTER 15

HELP LINE

Resources for more information

By the time you've read this book, completed the work sheets and tried your hand at a few of the various components of a plan, you should be ready to go ahead and complete your own. However, there's always room for improvement, and there are a number of resources you can tap into for the purpose of increasing your expertise in plan writing.

SOFTWARE FOR WRITING BUSINESS PLANS

We should make it clear: you don't have to have any particular software or even have access to a computer to write a plan. You can do all the calculations and draft all the text using nothing more than a calculator or even pencil and paper for the figuring, and a typewriter for the writing. Until computers came into wide use 15 or 20 years ago, of course, that's the way all plans were done. Yours may look old-fashioned if it comes in with the telltale traits of manual typewriting, but if the information in it is compelling enough, that shouldn't matter.

Be that as it may, computers are very handy when it comes to writing a plan. Numerous computer programs of various descriptions ease the creation of business plans. They range from word processing software such as WordPerfect to electronic spreadsheets such as Lotus 1-2-3 and even software for tapping into the Internet for research and data-gathering jobs. If you plan to present your plan to a group of people, you may want to use a program such as Microsoft PowerPoint to create slides or an electronic version of your plan.

However, these are general-purpose software programs, only incidentally of use for creating business plans. The Microsoft Excel spreadsheet program may be chock-full of useful formulas you can use for such otherwise tricky tasks as figuring the depreciation of an asset, but it won't help you with business plan-specific questions such as How should I format the Executive Summary?

For these questions, you can go to software specially made for writing business plans. Numerous such products exist, and the category has been around for a while.

Business Plan Pro

This program from Palo Alto Software is one of the best business plan programs on the market. It's full-featured, helping you write a plan with complete text, financial tables for forecasts and analysis, and even charts for illustrating points graphically.

Business Plan Pro's split-screen interface is one of its most useful features. The two-screen setup splits your display in half, showing one thing, such as instructions, in one window, while you see another, such as the material you're entering, in the second window. A click of the mouse takes you from one window to the other. This feature helps you simultaneously view and move easily between different sections of the program.

Business Plan Pro also has a complex set of menu commands to do such jobs as select a chart for display, go to the outline and print the plan. A number of always-visible buttons help you navigate between previous and next tasks or steps you've worked on.

Using Business Plan Pro requires you to work in three modes: Text Mode, Table Mode and Chart Mode. Respectively, they roughly correspond to a word processor, a spreadsheet and a chart program. However, they're specially set up for making business plans. For instance, the chart program has ready-made charts to show such things as cash flow projections and break-even analyses.

You use the Text Mode in Business Plan Pro to write the words. Before you start typing, however, take a look at the outline, always available by clicking the big Plan Outline button at the bottom of the screen. This is your command center for navigation throughout your plan, as well as for understanding the organization of it. The outline, recognizing that not all businesses or business plans are the same, adjusts its topics to whatever type of business you're planning for. For instance, it will

Plan Pitfall

Thanks to plan-writing software's built-in financial formulas, you just have to plug in the data. Since you don't enter the formulas yourself, however, you won't have the same understanding of your financial statements as if you had to think about and manually enter them. So if you use plan-writing software, look under the hood and see what is going on inside all those spreadsheets.

Buzzword

Rich Text Format (RTF) is a standard word processing format in which most plan-writing software lets you export your work. RTF will convert into almost any word processing program.

include an inventory section for a bicycle manufacturer but not for an architect.

Table Mode is preprogrammed for preformatted financial statements. The tables are linked to one another to help provide consistency in your business analysis. That's something you can do with any decent general-purpose electronic spreadsheet program, but it's nice that it's done for you. It makes it harder to be inconsistent, which is only too likely when you change a number in one table, say, the income projection, but neglect to do the same in another, like the cash flow plan.

Chart Mode plugs you into a set of business charts that are developed from the data entered in your financial statements. This makes it easy to include attractive and informative charts in your plan. And if you change the data, the charts are automatically updated.

Business Plan Pro formats and prints plans with page headings and numbers, and various styles for topic headings, table titles and chart titles. You can print text, tables and charts individually or do the whole plan all at once. Individually printed tables and charts may be useful for appendices or special presentations.

Business Plan Pro comes with several sample plans, along with an outline that it will automatically customize to fit the needs of the type of business you specify. Business Plan Pro 3.0 comes in versions for Windows 95 and Windows NT computers. You can get another version, Business Plan Pro 6.0, for the Macintosh. Finally, one other nice thing about Business Plan Pro 3.0 is that you can download a free demo program from Palo Alto Software's Web site at www.pasware.com.

BizPlanBuilder

Jian Software's BizPlanBuilder is consistently one of the top-rated business planning software packages. Reviewers give it high marks for being easy to use and flexible. Two of its distinguishing characteristics are the question-and-answer process, which you use to enter information about your company, and an interactive document creator that

Plan Pointer

Built-in spreadsheet templates in plan-writing software ease the task of computing financials considerably. They come with preprogrammed formulas and are often linked so you only have to enter information once to have it appear in several places—a real time-saver.

Plan Of Action

For more information on Business Plan Pro 3.0, contact Palo Alto Software at 144 E. 14th Ave., Eugene, OR 97401, (541) 683-6162 or (800) 229-7256, www.pasware.com

leads you through the writing and organization of your plan. These are powerful aids if you are building a plan from scratch.

You don't have to start at square one, however. BizPlanBuilder comes with a robust selection of more than 90 typed pages of templates and sample text. One of the coolest features is that the data entry blanks in the templates are hot linked. That means, for example, you can type your company name into the correct spot on one of the templates, and have it appear automatically in scores of other appropriate spots throughout your plan.

BizPlanBuilder comes with built-in word processing and spreadsheet software so you don't have to purchase these programs separately. However, if you already have a favorite word processing or spreadsheet program, BizPlanBuilder will let you use those instead of its integrated applications.

If you're trying to compare the results you can expect using several different scenarios, it can be a real pain to prepare complete projections for each of them. BizPlanBuilder has a much simpler approach. A tool called Sensitivity Analysis lets you compare best- and worst-case scenarios to your plan on a single page.

The program disk also has a number of supporting documents. There's an exhaustive description of various funding methods and contact information for resources such as the Small Business Administration and other government agencies. It also has ideas for presenting your plan and suggestions for cover sheets and nondisclosure agreements.

To sum up, BizPlanBuilder is a powerful and easy-to-use program with the sophistication and flexibility to help you with planning even complex businesses. It is available in versions for Windows 95, Windows 3.1 and Macintosh systems.

Plan Of Action

Small Business Development Centers are one-stop shops set up by the Small Business Administration to give entrepreneurs free to low-cost advice, training and technical assistance. There are more than 50 centers, at least one in each state and territory. Learn more online at www.sbaonline.sba.gov or by calling (800) 8-ASK-SBA.

Books And How-To Manuals

Scores of books have been written on how to write a business plan. Most provide skimpy treatment of the issues while devoting many pages to sample plans. Sample plans are useful, but unless planners understand the principles of the planning process, they can't really create sophisticated, one-of-a-kind plans. The following books will help you with the details of various sections in your plan.

Dictionary of Business Terms (Barons): This compact, 650-page dictionary is a cure for jargon overexposure. It provides concise definitions of business terms from "abandonment" to "zoning ordinance." Appendices explain common business acronyms, provide tables of compounded interest rate factors and more. It's the kind of book you'll turn to again and again.

Encyclopedia of Entrepreneurs (John Wiley & Sons), by Anthony and Diane Hallett: This reference profiles the lives and enterprises of hundreds of famous entrepreneurs, from Wallace Abbott of Abbott Laboratories to Ziebart International's Kurt Ziebart. The stories are inspiring and provide a rich trove of real-life business strategies that worked.

Finance for the Non-Financial Manager (John Wiley & Sons), by Herbert T. Spiro: If you're puzzled about any aspect of finance, this book contains the answers. Although intended for nonfinancial professionals, it does not compromise, providing great detail about financial analysis, planning and decision-making.

Guerrilla Marketing (Houghton Mifflin), by Jay Conrad Levinson: The most recent release of this marketing classic provides updated marketing techniques for those with little cash but high hopes. Levinson's insistence on the central role of planning, and his simple but effective explanations of how to do it, will serve business planners well.

Guts & Borrowed Money (Bard Publishing), by Tom Gillis: This practical guide is organized like an encyclopedia so you can quickly and easily look up detailed explanations of everything from arbitration to vision statements.

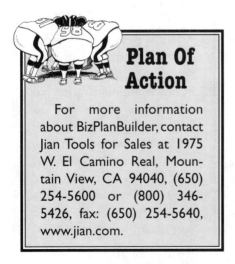

Plan Of Action

For more information about BizPlanBuilder, contact Jian Tools for Sales at 1975 W. El Camino Real, Mountain View, CA 94040, (650) 254-5600 or (800) 346-5426, fax: (650) 254-5640, www.jian.com.

Web Sites

The World Wide Web provides a virtually inexhaustible source of information for and about small business, including numerous sites with substantial databases of tips and ideas concerning business planning. Some of the best include the following:

Entrepreneur Magazine's Small Business Square (**www.entrepreneur mag.com**): This is the Web site of the business monthly with the nation's largest readership and also the parent corporation of the publisher of this book. It contains a vast array of information resources, practical advice, interviews with experts, profiles of successful entrepreneurs, product and service reviews, and more. One you won't find anywhere else is the Franchise 500, a computer-searchable directory of franchise opportunities.

Plan Pointer

Lack time and budget to buy and learn a business plan software program? Try Adarus Business Plan. This shareware consists of Visual Basic wizards that use Microsoft Office applications to build a plan in Word. If you know Office, it saves time. At $40, it saves money too.

In addition to articles from past and present issues of the print magazine, sections of the site pull from the resources of *Business Start-Ups*, a publication for brand-new enterprises, *Entrepreneur International*, a sister publication dedicated to global entrepreneurs, and *Entrepreneur's Home Office*, for homebased business owners.

The *Entrepreneur* Web site also hosts *Entrepreneur* magazine's smallbizbooks. com, a source for books—including this one—that offer expert advice on starting, running and growing a small business. These include business start-up guides, step-by-step start-up guides to specific businesses, and business management guides, which offer in-depth information on financing, marketing and more.

Small Business Administration (**www.sba.gov** or **www.sbaonline. sba.gov**): The SBA's Web site is a vast directory to services provided by the federal agency devoted to helping small businesses. These include special lending programs, electronic databases of minority- and disadvantaged-owned businesses, directories of government contracting opportunities and more.

There is also a generous selection of answers to frequently asked questions, tip sheets and other advice. You can get a list of questions to ask yourself to see if you have the personality of an entrepreneur, find help with selecting a business and browse an entire area devoted to help with your business plan.

Two things are of particular interest. First, the vast collection of nearly 3,000 links to other small-business-related sites. Second, the online library to publications contained on the SBA site. The library provides on-

HOMEMADE, BUT NOT HALF-BAKED

Lindsay Frucci created a fat-free brownie mix and built it into a homebased business success. No Pudge! Foods Inc. began in January 1995 with Frucci baking in her home kitchen in Elkins, New Hampshire. The start-up notched just $6,000 in first-year revenues and reached $42,000 the second year but exploded to $253,000 the third year.

Frucci's secret ingredient was a pair of SCORE (Service Core of Retired Executives) counselors who told her to find outside manufacturing and get No Pudge! out of her kitchen. The flexibility and increased capacity allowed Frucci to handle large orders, package products with UPC codes, and devote her own energy to product development and marketing.

Frucci had faith in the SCORE counselors' advice because they'd already helped her draft a business plan when she needed more money to expand the homebased firm. They had faith in her, as they showed when they advised her to turn down a bank's offer of a loan because the bank required her husband to co-sign. Insisting the business should be financed on its own merits, without personal guarantees, they went to a second bank, which saw the light.

Frucci says flexibility is her watchword, and it's reflected in the way she runs and plans her business. "Sometimes businesses fail because they have a business plan that says 'This is the way I'm going,' and they don't consider changing midstream," she says. "Allow your business plan to change. It's not set in stone."

line access to dozens of forms, legislation, regulations, reports, studies, FAQ (frequently asked questions) lists and more. There are even hundreds of downloadable shareware and freeware computer programs for managing time, preparing invoices, tracking inventory, calculating loan payments and many other business activities.

American Express Small Business Exchange (www.americanexpress. com/smallbusiness): This site, sponsored by American Express, has a broad array of well-organized files providing advice and tips about all kinds of business problems, from buying or selling a business to issues related to working at home. There are a few come-ons for American Express services, such as equipment financing, financial planning and, of course, applying for the well-known charge card. But the information is generally well-presented, factual and unbiased.

TRADE GROUPS AND ASSOCIATIONS

You're not in this alone. There are countless local and national organizations, both public and private, devoted to helping small businesses get up and running. They provide services ranging from low-rent facilities to financial assistance, from help in obtaining government contracts to help with basic business planning issues. Many of these services are provided for free or at nominal cost.

Plan Of Action

For more information, write to SCORE Association at 409 Third St. SW, 6th Fl., Washington, DC 20024, (800) 634-0245, www.score.org.

SCORE: The Service Corps of Retired Executives, known as SCORE, is a nonprofit group of mostly retired businesspeople who volunteer to provide counseling to small businesses at no charge. SCORE has been around since 1964 and has helped more than 3 million entrepreneurs and aspiring entrepreneurs. SCORE is a source for all kinds of business advice, from how to write a business plan to investigating marketing potential and managing cash flow.

SCORE counselors work out of nearly 400 local chapters throughout the United States. You can obtain a referral to a counselor in your local chapter by contacting the national office.

National Business Incubation Association: The NBIA is the national organization for business incubators, which are organizations specially set up to nurture young firms and help them survive and grow. Incubators provide leased office facilities on flexible terms, shared business services, management assistance, help in obtaining financing and technical support.

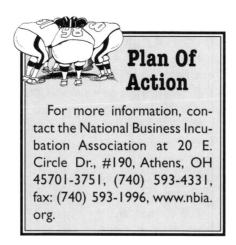

Plan Of Action

For more information, contact the National Business Incubation Association at 20 E. Circle Dr., #190, Athens, OH 45701-3751, (740) 593-4331, fax: (740) 593-1996, www.nbia.org.

NBIA says there are nearly 600 incubators in North America. Its services include providing a directory to local incubators and their services.

Chambers of commerce: The many chambers of commerce throughout the United States are organizations devoted to providing networking, lobbying, training and more. If you think chambers are all about having lunch with a bunch of community boosters, think again.

Plan Of Action

For more information, contact the U.S. Chamber of Commerce at 1615 H St. NW, Washington, DC 20062-2000, (202) 659-6000, fax: (202) 463.3190, www.uschamber.org.

Among the services the U.S. Chamber of Commerce offers is a Web-based business solutions program that provides online help with specific small-business needs, including planning, marketing and other tasks such as creating a press release, collecting a bad debt, recruiting employees or creating a retirement plan.

The U.S. Chamber of Commerce is the umbrella organization for local chambers, of which there are more than 1,000 in the United States. If you're planning on doing business overseas, don't forget to check for an American chamber of commerce in the countries where you hope to have a presence. They are set up to provide information and assistance to U.S. firms seeking to do business there. Many, but not all, countries have American chambers.

BUSINESS PLAN CONSULTANTS

Businesspeople tend to fall into two camps when it comes to consultants. Some believe strongly in the utility and value of hiring outside experts to bring new perspective and broad knowledge to challenging tasks. Others feel consultants are overpaid yes men brought in only to endorse plans already decided upon or to take the heat for unpopular but necessary decisions.

Who's right? Both are, depending on the consultant you hire and your purpose for hiring one. Most consultants are legitimate experts in specific or general business areas. And most consultants can be hired to help with all or part of the process of writing a business plan.

The downside is, you have to spend a lot of time on communication before and during the process of working with a consultant. Be sure you have fully explained and the consultant fully understands the nature of your business, your concept and strategy, your financial needs, and other matters such as control, future plans and so on. Refer to these important issues throughout the

Plan Pitfall

Working with a consultant isn't exactly like working with a member of your staff, a partner, an investor, or a banker, lawyer or other professional you're retaining. Consultants are often freelancers, moving from assignment to assignment without looking back. That helps them bring a valuable outside perspective, but it can also make them more difficult to manage.

process—you don't want to pay for a beautifully done plan that fits somebody else's business, not yours. And when the work is done, debrief the consultant to find out if there's anything you can learn that wasn't included in the plan.

BUSINESS PLAN COMPETITIONS

If you happen to be a business student, you may be able to enter your business plan in a college business plan competition. These competitions, of which there are more than three dozen in the United States, confer a measure of fame and even some money on the winners. A panel of plan experts including college professors, venture capitalists and bankers usually judges entries.

HIRE POWER

If you decide to hire a consultant to help you prepare your plan, take care that you select the right person. Here are guidelines:

1. **Get referrals.** Ask colleagues, acquaintances and professionals such as bankers, accountants and lawyers for the names of business plan consultants they recommend. A good referral goes a long way to easing concerns you may have. Few consultants advertise anyway, so referrals may be your only choice.

2. **Look for a fit.** Find a consultant who is expert in helping businesses like yours. Ideally, the consultant should have lots of experience with companies of similar size and age in similar industries. Avoid general business experts or those who lack experience in your field.

3. **Check references.** Get the names of at least three clients the consultant has helped to write plans. Call the former clients and ask about the consultant's performance. Was the consultant's final fee in line with the original estimate? Was the plan completed on time? Did it serve the intended purpose?

4. **Get it in writing.** Have a legal contract for the consultant's services. It should discuss in detail the fee, when it will be paid and under what circumstances. And make sure you get a detailed written description of what the consultant must do to earn the fee. Whether it's an hourly rate or flat fee isn't as important as each party knowing exactly what's expected.

Winners are the plans that best lay out a convincing case for a business's success. Judges can be tough; contestants can expect scathing criticism of poorly thought-out plans.

Moot Corp. is the name of the best known of the nation's business plan competitions. It's sponsored each May by the University of Texas at Austin. Moot Corp. calls itself the "Super Bowl of World Business-Plan Competition" and is the oldest of the approximately three dozen business school-sponsored plan competitions. More than two dozen plan-writing teams from as far away as Australia participate in the contest, which began in 1983. The winner of the UT competition receives $15,000 and a significant publicity boost.

The most financially rewarding contest is the $50,000 competition sponsored by the Massachusetts Institute of Technology. The MIT winner takes home $30,000, while the next two finishers take $10,000 each. Business schools such as Harvard University and the University of Chicago are among other prestigious business institutions sponsoring plan contests.

FROM SCHOOLHOUSE TO PENTHOUSE

A fair number of business plan competition winners go on to become real businesses that succeed in the real world, often helped by investors attracted by the competition. Here are a few:

1. **WebLine Communications Corp.**, an Internet technology firm, won the Massachusetts Institute of Technology business plan competition. In addition to the $30,000 prize, founder Pasha Roberts eventually raised more than $8 million from investors impressed with his plan's finish.

2. **Ampersand Art Supply**, an art supply distributor, won the University of Texas plan competition. Ampersand CEO Elaine Salazar's presentation impressed one competition judge so much he threw in his own investment of $300,000.

3. **1-800 Contacts**, a mail order contact lens firm, won the contest put on by Brigham Young University. Today the company has annual sales of nearly $4 million.

Not every contest-winning plan turns into a company. Entering could even be a negative. Some contestants say that if you don't win, investors consider it a strike against you, while even if you do, the academic connection may paint your plan as a mere ivory-tower exercise.

Sample Business Plans

The four sample plans in the following appendices were chosen to represent a cross section of different types of companies and also different reasons for writing a plan. These companies are fictional samples; their concepts may or may not be viable in the real world. For the purposes of this book, they're offered to provide examples of how plan writers may approach various issues relating to a plan, depending on the type of industry, size of the company, characteristics of the market and management and other factors.

Read the sample plans with an eye to seeing whether any of the approaches taken in them fit what you're trying to do. There are, in the end, few absolute taboos in business planning. Even having no plan at all is something that more than a few successful entrepreneurs admit to. So read these plans not so much with the intention of finding flaws in them, but of finding things you might like to incorporate in your own plan.

APPENDIX A

Business Plan For A Retailer Seeking Seed Capital

The following business plan is for WaterWorks Inc., a start-up retail food-service operation seeking seed capital.

This plan is succinct, carefully thought out and well-documented. Particular attention has been paid to studying the national sales trends for the beverages it will serve. The plan provides adequate financial data, including a three-year income statement projection and month-by-month cash flow projection for the first year.

This primary purpose of this plan is to help the partners obtain a $15,000 bank loan to let them open the doors and get through the first six months. After that point, the business should be able to sustain itself on cash flow. When the partners need additional financing to open their second location in a couple of years, they should have little difficulty in obtaining a second loan for expansion.

Pluses to this plan include the fact that the company management is experienced in the hospitality industry. The partners are also providing a significant portion of the start-up capital themselves, which will set well with a banker. It's also advantageous that demand for the products it will sell appears to be growing quite rapidly, and yet there is little or no direct competition in the market it will serve. Most important, from the bankers' viewpoint, the plan appears to generate ample cash to pay off the requested loan in 12 months.

On the negative side, the idea is unproven, at least in this geographic market. Also, the partners are paying themselves salaries. Some lenders would prefer to see borrowers do without salaries, at least in the beginning. This is somewhat offset by the facts that the partners are not taking a draw—a dividend out of profits paid to owners in addition to salary—and that the salaries will be modest.

BUSINESS PLAN

WaterWorks Inc.

12709 Enfield Terrace
Austin, TX 78704
(512) 555-1212

Allis Walter, President
Matthew Strang, CEO

Contents

I. Executive Summary

Market

Still (noncarbonated) water beverages are the trendiest new drinks since gourmet coffee. The market for still water drinks has been building greatly for three years and now appears ready to enter a new, accelerated period of growth.

Still water drinks are much different from the mass-produced carbonated beverages sold by the soft drink giants. They are usually produced in small quantities by entrepreneurial organizations. Quality is high. Still water drinks also include functional additives, including nutriceuticals, which further differentiate them from mass-market soft drinks and which appeal to health-conscious consumers of all groups.

Business Description

WaterWorks will sell still water beverages through a retail outlet in Austin, Texas. The outlet will consist of a bar and seating area as well as a service counter and will serve beverages prepared on the premises for consumption either there or off-site, as well as prepackaged products, including baked goods.

A retail business, including a small bar and seating area and drive-thru window area, will be located in an existing facility near the intersection of Loop 1 and Enfield Road in central Austin.

Products

The product line, all purchased from outside vendors, will consist of approximately 20 different still water beverages and functional beverages, in addition to a selection of freshly baked breads, muffins, cookies and other locally produced adjuncts.

Management

WaterWorks will be owned by Allis Walter and Matthew Strang. The business will be structured as an equal partnership, with Mr. Walter bearing the title of president and Mr. Strang operating as chief executive officer. Mr. Walter and Mr. Strang are experienced in retail restaurant bar operations.

Financing Needs

WaterWorks is seeking $15,000 in short-term bank financing to cover start-up costs, purchase needed equipment, and provide working capital until the business can support itself financially. The owners will invest $10,000 of their own cash. Borrowings will begin at $10,000 and increase to a maximum of $15,000 after 180 days. Interest payments will commence after the first month, and after 10 months, operations will generate sufficient cash to pay down the balance of the loan in two balloon payments. Payment will be complete by the end of the first year. The owners are prepared to pledge personal assets in the amount of the loan to collateralize the transaction.

II. Business Mission And Strategy

Mission Statement

WaterWorks will sell still water drinks and functional beverages to health-conscious consumers in Austin, Texas. Retail customers will consist of students, faculty and staff from the nearby University of Texas campus, the nation's largest, and residents of the well-educated, affluent surrounding neighborhoods.

Strategic Elements

The WaterWorks strategy embodies several key elements:

- The store will be the first of its kind in Austin, a major metro area of more than 1 million people.

- The location is near Sixth Street and Lamar Boulevard, one of the city's busiest intersections and hottest retail environments.

- Only products of the highest quality will be offered.

- Austin has one of the country's highest per-capita rates of consumption of natural foods and beverages.

Strategic Objectives

- To repay initial bank loans by the end of the second year of operation.

- To produce a net profit of at least $50,000 by the third year of operation.

- To expand to three additional retail locations by the end of the fifth year of operation.

- To explore additional expansion through the creation of more company-owned or possibly franchised outlets after year five.

III. Sources And Uses Of Funds

Start-up Costs Summary

Start-up costs will be approximately $27,500, which will include initial lease payments, leasehold improvements, inventory, permits and other expenses. Start-up costs will be financed primarily through a combination of bank borrowing and investment by the partners.

Sources And Uses Of Funds

USE OF FUNDS

Capital Expenditures

Leasehold Improvements	$5,000
Equipment	5,000
Total Capital Expenditures	**$10,000**

Working Capital

Legal	$500
Permits And Licenses	750
Printing	500
Graphic Design	500
Insurance	1,250
Rent (3 months)	5,000
Salaries	5,000
Start-up Inventory	2,500
Other Business Activities	1,500
Total Working Capital	**$17,500**

TOTAL USE OF FUNDS	**$27,500**

SOURCES OF FUNDS

Partner Investments	$10,000
Trade Credit	2,500
Bank Loan	15,000
Total Source Of Funds	**$27,500**

IV. Products

WaterWorks will sell still water drinks and baked goods to customers in Austin, Texas.

Company Locations and Facilities

WaterWorks will be located near the intersection of Loop 1 and Enfield Road in Austin, Texas, an attractive retail location near desirable residential areas, the state capitol complex and the University of Texas main campus.

An existing 900-square-foot facility with seating and a drive-up window will be leased. Improvements will include additions to the seating area, a water bar and landscaping.

A second location is planned to be added in the third year of operation at a suitable site to be determined.

Products

The primary products to be sold through the WaterWorks business will be functional still water drinks in three categories:

1. **Nutriceuticals**

Nutriceutical waters include still waters to which have been added minerals such as potassium and calcium; vitamins including A, C and D; and other substances such as caffeine.

2. **Bacteria-free Still Water**

Bacteria-free still waters are processed using techniques that eliminate microorganisms, including associated flavors and particles, from the water.

3. **Exotic Waters**

Exotic waters are bottled and imported from locations such as Alaska, Canada, France, Hawaii, Sweden and Russia.

V. Markets And Competition

Still Water Sales Trends

Still water is the fastest growing segment of the alternative beverage industry. Sales for 1996, the most recent year available, were up 25 percent, almost double the industry average of 13 percent. Other alternative beverage segments include juices, teas, sport drinks, sparkling waters and natural sodas.

Still water sales totaled 731 million cases, making the category by far the dominant in alternative beverages, whose total sales neared 1.9 billion cases. Still water's share of the alternative beverage market exceeded 39 percent, up 3.7 percent from the previous year, when 585 million cases of still waters were sold. Other strong categories included sport drinks and teas.

Source: Beverage Digest, *April 1997*

Industry Analysis

Alternative beverage producers include some of the beverage industry's largest companies. The following graph shows the top 10 alternative beverage producers and their market share percentages:

Suppliers

These products will be supplied by various vendors, including the following:

Aqua Health, Water for Life, H2Ah!, Nutri-Water, Hydration Technologies, Guava Cool, Soft Beverages and Millennium Moisture. These vendors supply a variety of beverages with features such as nutriceutical content; bacteria-free processing; and a number of natural, organic flavorings including berries, fruits and spices.

These suppliers are, for the most part, located in the continental United States. While they are not currently available for wholesale distribution in Austin, which partially explains the lack of local retail distribution, all operate existing distribution systems with representatives in other Texas cities, including Houston, San Antonio and Dallas. No problems in obtaining adequate supplies of important products are anticipated.

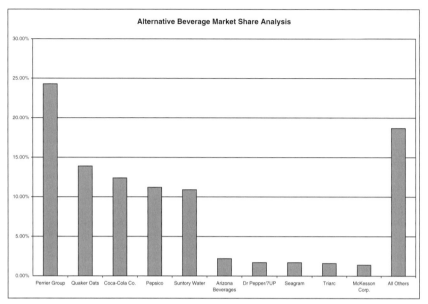

Source: Beverage Week

Market Analysis Summary

Austin is the capital of Texas, located near the center of the state approximately 70 miles north of San Antonio and 200 miles south of Dallas. The city has a population of roughly 500,000 and is the hub of a metropolitan area of more than 1 million people. It is home to the nation's largest university, as well as many offices related to the state government and also a booming business community, including the headquarters of Dell Computer Corp. and Whole Foods Market, the nation's largest retailer of natural foods.

Austin has one of the highest percentages of adults possessing a college degree of any American city, and is generally regarded as a center of progressive lifestyles in the Southwest.

WaterWorks is an ideal business for Austin given the market, including size and demographics. Based on average individual transactions of approximately $2.25, including functional still water drinks and ancillary products, the business has the potential to gross $300,000 in sales by the third year of operation.

Competitive Analysis

No other business in Austin focuses exclusively on the functional still water market. This will provide considerable flexibility in pricing and allow for the creation of a great deal of customer awareness and brand loyalty, erecting significant barriers to entry for potential competitors.

While no retail businesses devoted exclusively to functional water beverages exist in Austin, functional water beverages are sold at Whole Foods, Whole Earth Provision, Randall's Markets and other grocery retailers.

Research in San Francisco, California, indicated that six functional still water beverage retail locations existed. The oldest has been in operation for slightly more than two years. These businesses were thriving, selling functional still water drinks units at prices ranging from $1.25 for small counter-prepared beverages to be consumed on the premises, to $24.00 for larger bottles to be installed off-premises in water coolers.

The owner of one of the older San Francisco businesses indicated that first-year sales in his market, which, like the WaterWorks location is near a university and an affluent residential district, was selling 200 units per day, yielding a first-year revenue potential of $78,000, assuming minimal average transaction value of $1.25. Considerable price flexibility is likely to exist in markets where competition is less or absent. Research conducted in Ann Arbor, Michigan, a city more comparable to Austin in size, showed that in the two existing functional still water retailers, counter-prepared drinks sold for as high as $5.00 each.

Competition And Buying Patterns

Functional still water retailing will be new to Austin. Competitors primarily sell mass-market waters through grocery store-type locations and do not focus on the functional still water drinks market. There are no retail providers of counter-prepared still water beverages for consumption on the premises—so-called water bars.

WaterWorks' success will come from educating consumers about the appeal and benefits of functional still water beverages, and from providing a quality service and products not available in grocery stores. Price competition will be a minimal influence given current market conditions.

VI. Marketing

Marketing Strategy

WaterWorks' overall marketing strategy will be to educate consumers about the benefits of still water and functional water beverages, and to promote the availability through WaterWorks. Customers will be reached through fliers, newspaper advertisements, publicity efforts and special-event promotions.

Location will also play a crucial role in marketing and promotion. The business will be located near a high-traffic retail area in central Austin.

Target Markets And Market Segments

WaterWorks will target health-conscious, progressive and generally well-educated and affluent consumers who are interested in trying new products and experiences and are dissatisfied with the limited selection and lack of personal service found in grocery store-type water retailers.

Pricing Strategy

Functional still water fountain drinks will be offered at the following prices:

> *Small:* $1.00
>
> *Medium:* $1.50
>
> *Large:* $2.50

In addition, larger sizes of water will be sold for customer carryout or delivery. They will range from 1-liter bottles to 20-liter plastic jugs at prices ranging from $2.50 to $25.00.

Products will be sold on a cash basis to retail customers. Corporate customers, expected to represent an insignificant proportion of sales at the beginning, will be billed, payable in 30 days.

Promotion Strategy

WaterWorks will promote functional still water drinks to customers by:

- Regular newspaper advertisements focusing on education and information about the benefits of functional still water beverages
- A publicity campaign that will attempt to gain company owners'

appearances as experts on functional still water beverages on health-related TV and radio broadcasts, and as expert sources for print publications

- Distributing educational and promotional fliers to residences within a 1-mile radius

- Discounts offered to appropriate groups such as health food co-operatives, organic gardening clubs and cultural associations

Distribution Strategy

- Primary distribution of functional still water drinks will be through the retail facility.

- Secondary distribution will consist of deliveries of bottled water beverages to restaurants, retailers and corporate locations.

- Additional distribution will be accomplished through temporary booths set up at athletic and cultural events such as bicycle races and concerts.

Sales Projections

Sales will start in January 1999. Sales forecasts are based on experiences of similar start-up enterprises in San Francisco. Forecasts include retail sales projections in line with enterprises' experience in other markets with significant competition and may be considered conservative. Corporate sales include sales of bottles for office water coolers, beverages for corporate parties and the like. Special-events sales include products sold through booths set up at concerts, races and other events. Third-year sales are projected to include partial results from opening one new retail location.

Sales Forecast

Year	1999	2000	2001
Retail walk-in	$98,000	$122,000	$260,000
Corporate	0	4,000	8,000
Special events	10,000	12,000	20,000
Total	$108,000	$138,000	$288,000

VII. Management

Allis Walter has five years' experience in the retail restaurant industry. He has served as manager of the Lava Coffee Beanery and assistant manager of the Travis Bagel Shop. He is a 1994 graduate of the University of Texas at Austin business school.

Matthew Strang has seven years of experience in the hospitality industry. He has served as assistant general manager of the Hill Country Bed & Breakfast in Fredericksburg, Texas, and manager of Bee Cave Bar & Grill.

WaterWorks will hire one part-time employee to assist with the business. The partners will perform the bulk of the duties required to operate the initial store.

VIII. Financial Data

Financial Plan

WaterWorks will finance growth mainly through cash flow. Expansion will begin in year three and includes the planned opening of a second location, an expansion of corporate sales and added emphasis on special outside-event promotions.

Seasonal Data

Seasonal variations will be concentrated during the summer months of June, July and August. During these months, many between-term college students leave the city, causing a significant temporary reduction in the size of the potential market of consumers in Austin.

Break-Even Analysis

The following table and chart show the current break-even analysis. The operation will require sales of approximately $8,395 per month to break even during the first year of operation. Assumptions include average monthly fixed expenses of $6,296 and a gross profit margin of 75 percent.

Break-Even Analysis

$$\frac{\$6,296}{75\%} = \$8,395$$

Projected Profit And Loss

Profits for the next three years are projected to equal:

1999: $3,446

1998: $13,634

1999: $44,213

Projected Income Statement

Income Statement

	1999	2000	2001
INCOME			
Gross Sales	$108,000	$138,000	$288,000
Less Returns And Allowances	0	0	0
Net Sales	$108,000	$138,000	$288,000
Cost Of Sales	27,000	33,120	66,240
Gross Profit	$81,000	$104,880	$221,760
Gross Profit Margin	75%	76%	77%
OPERATING EXPENSES			
General & Administrative Expenses			
Salaries And Wages	$30,240	$36,500	$81,000
Employee Benefits	1,814	2,190	4,860
Payroll Taxes	1,512	1,825	4,050
Sales Commissions	0	0	0
Professional Services	1,150	1,150	1,600
Rent	19,600	19,600	39,200
Maintenance	900	900	1,500
Equipment Rental	1,100	1,500	2,250
Furniture And Equipment Purchase	1,250	1,600	2,250
Insurance	1,880	2,000	4,200
Interest Expenses	1,350	1,350	2,000
Utilities	2,150	2,250	2,560
Office Supplies	900	950	1,200
Postage	750	925	1,050
Marketing And Advertising	10,150	13,250	17,425
Travel	550	750	1,000
Entertainment	250	300	400
Bad Debt	0	0	0
Depreciation And Amortization	1,400	1,800	3,200
TOTAL OPERATING EXPENSES	**$76,946**	**$88,840**	**$169,745**
Net Income Before Taxes	$4,054	$16,040	$52,015
Provision For Taxes On Income	608	2,406	7,802
NET INCOME AFTER TAXES	**$3,446**	**$13,634**	**$44,213**

Notes to projected income statement:

1. Year 3 figures include added income and operating expenses from opening of second location.

2. Cost of Sales reflects slight but steady increase in gross profit margins.

4. Salaries and wages include one part-time employee the first two years of operation, three part-time employees the third year of operation, when two locations will be staffed, and the following annual salaries for each partner in lieu of draw:

1999: $12,000

2000: $15,000

2001: $30,000

Projected Cash Flow

Projected cash flow for the next three years are estimated as follows:

1999: $4,500

2000: $22,300

2001: $93,000

Projected Cash Flow Statement

Projected Cash Flow:
1999

	Jan.	Feb.	Mar.	Apr.	May	Jun.	Jul.	Aug.	Sep.	Oct.	Nov.	Dec.	TOTAL
CASH RECEIPTS													
Income From Sales													
Cash Sales	$2,000	$5,000	$7,000	$7,000	$11,000	$10,000	$10,000	$10,000	$11,000	$11,000	$12,000	$12,000	$108,000
Collections	0	0	0	0	0	0	0	0	0	0	0	0	$0
Total Cash From Sales	2,000	5,000	7,000	7,000	11,000	10,000	10,000	10,000	11,000	11,000	12,000	12,000	$108,000
Income From Financing													
Interest Income	0	0	0	0	0	0	0	0	0	0	0	0	$0
Loan Proceeds	10,000	0	0	2,500	0	0	2,500	0	0	0	0	0	$15,000
Total Cash From Financing	10,000	0	0	2,500	0	0	2,500	0	0	0	0	0	$15,000
Other Cash Receipts	10,000	0	0	0	0	0	0	0	0	0	0	0	$10,000
Total Cash Receipts	22,000	5,000	7,000	9,500	11,000	10,000	12,500	10,000	11,000	11,000	12,000	12,000	$133,000
CASH DISBURSEMENTS													
Expenses													
Cost Of Goods	500	1,250	1,750	1,750	2,750	2,500	2,500	2,500	2,750	2,750	3,000	3,000	$27,000
Operating Expenses	12,500	4,150	4,400	4,800	5,025	6,325	5,250	5,725	6,550	6,650	6,725	6,900	$75,000
Loan Payments	0	150	150	150	150	150	150	150	150	150	7,575	7,575	$16,500
Income Tax Payments	0	0	0	0	0	0	0	0	0	0	0	0	$0
Equipment Purchase	5,000	0	0	2,500	0	0	0	0	0	0	0	0	$7,500
Contingency	0	0	0	0	0	0	0	0	0	0	0	2,500	$2,500
Owners Draw	0	0	0	0	0	0	0	0	0	0	0	0	$0
Total Cash Disbursements	18,000	5,550	6,300	9,200	7,925	8,975	7,900	8,375	9,450	9,550	17,300	19,975	$128,500
Net Cash Flow	4,000	−550	700	300	3,075	1,025	4,600	1,625	1,550	1,450	−5,300	−7,975	$4,500
Opening Cash Balance	0	4,000	3,450	4,150	4,450	7,525	8,550	13,150	14,775	16,325	17,775	12,475	$0
Cash Receipts	22,000	5,000	7,000	9,500	11,000	10,000	12,500	10,000	11,000	11,000	12,000	12,000	$133,000
Cash Disbursements	−18,000	−5,550	−6,300	−9,200	−7,925	−8,975	−7,900	−8,375	−9,450	−9,550	−17,300	−19,975	−$128,500
Ending Cash Balance	$4,000	$3,450	$4,150	$4,450	$7,525	$8,550	$13,150	$14,775	$16,325	$17,775	$12,475	$4,500	

Notes to projected cash flow statement:

1. Cash sales reflect summer slowdown due to college students being out of town.

2. Other Cash Receipts consist of investment by partners.

3. Contingency fund set up at year-end to provide cash reserves.

4. Owners receive nominal salaries instead of draws.

5. Loan Payments cover interest at 10 percent on $15,000 loan until balance of principal and interest are repaid in two third-quarter balloon payments.

6. April equipment purchase is for trailer, portable equipment and booth to prepare for promotions at outdoor events.

Balance Sheet Projection

Projected shareholders' equity and net worth after one year of operation is $16,773.

Projected Balance Sheet

Projected Balance Sheet

WaterWorks Inc.

Year Ending December 31, 1999

ASSETS
Current Assets

Cash	$4,500
Accounts Receivable	0
Inventory	2,750
Prepaid Expenses	2,500
Total Current Assets	**$9,750**

Fixed Assets

Land	$0
Buildings	0
Equipment	2,000
Furniture	5,000
Fixtures	5,000
Less Accumulated Depreciation	2,250
Total Fixed Assets	**$9,750**

Other Assets	0
TOTAL ASSETS	**$19,500**

LIABILITIES
Current Liabilities

Accounts Payable	$2,750
Accrued Payroll	1,500
Taxes Payable	250
Short-Term Notes Payable	0
Total Current Liabilities	**$4,500**

Long-Term Liabilities

Long-Term Notes Payable	$0
Total Long-Term Liabilities	**$0**

Net Worth

Shareholders' Equity	$16,773
Retained Earnings	0
Total Net Worth	**$15,000**
TOTAL LIABILITIES & NET WORTH	**$19,500**

Note to projected balance sheet:

1. Accounts receivable will be minimal in year one, as all business will be conducted on a cash basis.

APPENDIX B

Business Plan For A High-tech Company Seeking Expansion Financing

T he following business plan is for a young high-tech company seeking a second round of financing to enable it to market and distribute its product nationwide.

The strongest parts of this plan are the industry analysis and management sections. Management is clearly experienced enough to be able to pull off its plan. And the industry's strong growth and trends favoring the introduction of such a product are convincing.

The plan's downsides relate primarily to the amount of money being requested. A half million dollars provides a more-than-ample cushion to the company, based on the rate it is going through. This may be comforting to management and owners, including the investors, but the high dollar amount requested reduces the expected return, based purely on net income projections, to a rate below that at which most venture capitalists are likely to be interested.

It's possible that another company might be interested in buying Palmistry out, or that the company may go public after a few more years. But the plan writer needs to make a stronger case for an enticing cash-out or to ask for less money.

Palmistry Productions Inc.

Productivity In The Palm Of Your Hand

26209 Fairfax Ave.
Cincinnati, OH 45207
(513) 555-7272

Bradley Regent, *CEO*

The information contained in this document is confidential. If you are not authorized to view it, return it to the above address immediately.

Table Of Contents

Executive Summary

Palmistry Productions is a 1-year-old producer of software-based productivity solutions for automobile dealers. The initial product is an inventory management system for portable palmtop computers.

Many automobile dealers complain about the lack of good inventory management systems. Current solutions involve paper stock cards, sales slips and invoice books, which are frequently out-of-date, inaccurate and time-consuming to maintain.

Additional problems with existing inventory management solutions include employees' inability to access inventory records while on the showroom floor or away from the office. This leads to missed sales opportunities, as employees must return to the office or call a prospect later to provide information about the availability of a particular model.

The PalmPal inventory management system produced by Palmistry Productions Inc. runs on PalmPilot portable computers. These pocket-sized machines have become the best-selling product in the history of the computer industry, producing sales of more than 3 million units since they were introduced in 1996 by what is now a division of 3Com. Many successful industry-specific software solutions running on the Pilot have been introduced.

Palmistry Productions was created specifically to produce Pilot-based software solutions for automobile dealers. The founder and CEO, Bradley Regent, spent approximately 10 years as an information systems manager for automobile dealerships in Ohio and Pennsylvania. Mr. Regent has considerable expertise in information systems, understanding of dealership information issues and contacts with the individuals responsible for purchasing information technology for dealerships. He has been joined by a team consisting of a marketing manager, a programmer and an office assistant.

After spending approximately nine months developing the PalmPal product, including market research, programming and testing, initial sales of the product have been encouraging. Several of the largest dealers in the Cincinnati area have tested the programs, and at least two regional chains are also trying them out.

The company was initially backed with $80,000 in funds provided by the founder. At this point, Palmistry is seeking an additional $500,000 to be used to market and distribute PalmPal nationwide. The company anticipates no difficulty raising this sum through a private equity placement of preferred stock, based on strong initial acceptance of the product and numerous pending sales.

The Palmistry Management Team

One of the strong points of Palmistry Productions is the industry experience possessed by members of its management team.

Bradley Regent
CEO

Prior to founding Palmistry, Mr. Regent worked for several large automobile dealerships as a programmer, systems analyst and information systems manager. Mr. Regent, a native of Cincinnati, graduated in 1985 with a degree in computer science from Ohio State University. Following two years with a large systems integrator in Cincinnati, Mr. Regent began working in the automobile dealership industry.

Mr. Regent has extensive experience in specifying, developing and maintaining inventory management systems for automobile dealerships. He's received professional training and certification as a developer in Oracle, SAP, Microsoft SQL and DB2 database environments. He has acted as manager of information systems departments of up to seven persons.

Mr. Regent's primary responsibilities at Palmistry will be formulating long-range strategy, participating in product development, managing the anticipated growth of the company, and interfacing with investors, customers and suppliers. Mr. Regent is the primary owner of Palmistry at present, holding 80 percent of the corporation's stock.

Wanda McIntire
Vice President Of Marketing

Ms. McIntire has worked for five years as a marketing specialist for two different companies serving the information systems needs of the automobile dealership industry in Kentucky and Indiana. Ms. McIntire has specialized experience in positioning and marketing new information systems products intended for automobile dealers. She was responsible for developing the initial marketing plan for Parts Perfect, a parts inventory management system developed by Autosoft Systems that is now in use by more than 500 dealerships nationwide. Ms. McIntire graduated from Tulsa University in 1992 with a degree in business.

Ms. McIntire's responsibilities at Palmistry consist of formulating and implementing marketing strategy, participating in product development and working with customers and prospects. She holds approximately 5 percent of the shares in the corporation.

Perry Honeywell
Program Developer

Mr. Honeywell was one of the first 20 employees of Helping Hand Systems, a Palo Alto, California, company that is now the largest third-party supplier of software for the PalmPilot computer system. He was responsible for leading the team that designed and produced Third Hand, a data collection system running on the PalmPilot that is now in use in ISO 9000 quality control programs around the world. He has received computer science degrees from the San Francisco University and the University of California at Berkeley.

Mr. Honeywell's responsibilities at Palmistry consist of overseeing program operation and interface design, and creating and testing code. He is the holder of approximately 10 percent of the corporation's shares.

Steven Wise
Human Resources and Administrative Manager

Mr. Wise has particular expertise in the interviewing, screening and hiring of applicants for positions with information systems firms. For the past three years, he has been in charge of staffing and administration for Staple Systems, a Cincinnati electronic commerce software firm that grew from three to more than 40 employees during the period in which he produced leading-edge software that has been well received in the marketplace.

Mr. Wise's responsibilities at Palmistry consist of managing office operations, including bookkeeping, accounts receivables and payables, as well as dealing with outside suppliers. As the company grows, he will be responsible for recruiting and hiring program designers, programmers, testers and other employees. Mr. Wise is the holder of approximately 5 percent of the company's shares.

The PalmPal Product

PalmPal is a compact, rugged, flexible and cost-effective software solution to the mobile inventory management needs of automobile dealerships. The program is constructed in the Palm OS environment, the operating system of the computing industry's most popular handheld computing device. The following table summarizes PalmPal features and benefits to customers.

PalmPal Features And Benefits

Features	Benefits
• Thoroughly tested software residing in a shock-resistant device that is pocket-sized and battery-operated	• Ready supply of inventory data in a portable, rugged and inexpensive package
• Highly customized application for quickly and easily transferring inventory information and updates both to and from desktop systems to a PalmPilot	• Ability of salespeople to provide customers with accurate availability information on specific automobile models even when off-site or away from a terminal
• Ability to interface with desktop-based inventory management systems from EDS, Dealer Solutions, ATP, Reynolds & Reynolds and others	• Design reflects intimate understanding of the needs of automobile dealerships

Palmistry believes that competing products, all of which are based on older laptop hardware designs or outdated paper systems, cannot match the PalmPal's combination of flexibility, convenience and integration.

PalmPal Marketing Strategy

Palmistry's marketing strategy takes advantage of two concurrent trends: the rapid growth of acceptance of palmtop computing systems in industrial and commercial vertical industry applications, and the increasing need for more sophisticated and flexible inventory management as the automobile dealership industry consolidates and grows in size.

Recent figures from the National Automobile Dealers Association show:

- Total auto dealership sales are more than $500 billion annually and growing.

- More than 22,500 new-car dealerships exist, a number that has dropped approximately 50 units annually for the past several years.

- The industry has consolidated drastically, with the number of smaller dealerships selling fewer than 150 vehicles annually shrinking from 13,100 in 1977 to 4,540 in 1997.

- Information systems have become steadily more important to the remaining larger dealerships, with special concern being paid to the need for open systems for information interchange and dealer purchase of hardware.

- The PalmPilot computing platform has become the fastest-selling computer device in the history of the industry. Facts include:

- More than 3 million units have been sold in approximately two years.

- Thousands of third-party software developers have written applications for many niche uses.

- The PalmPilot's ruggedness, versatility and extreme portability make it the most popular choice for industrial vertical application software developers.

Palmistry has priced its product to compete with both off-the-shelf general-purpose database and inventory management systems for the Pilot and with existing laptop-based inventory management systems specific to the auto dealership industry.

Pricing of approximately $10,000 for a five-unit site license, including five PalmPilot III computers, training, and an annual maintenance contract, has proved acceptable to dealerships, and is far below what competing products based on larger systems sell for.

Palmistry is using direct-mail marketing to auto dealership information systems managers, followed up with telemarketing and personal sales calls as its primary marketing modality. This approach takes maximum advantage of the company principals' reputation and visibility in the Ohio automobile dealership community.

As marketing for the PalmPal is rolled out nationwide to all 22,500 potential auto dealer customers, additional marketing dollars will be required to produce and deliver direct-mail marketing materials, conduct telemarketing follow-up calls and arrange for personal sales calls to especially promising prospects. A significant concern will be staffing these functions with appropriately skilled personnel.

Palmistry believes it can achieve a 9 percent market share within four years. System sales to approximately 2,000 dealerships, at an average purchase price of $10,000, indicates total sales through 2003 of approximately $2 million, with over half that amount occurring in the final year as the effect of prior marketing efforts begins to make itself felt.

Program Development And Operations

One of Palmistry's prime advantages is the combined expertise of its principals in the design, development and maintenance of software for portable applications and for the automobile dealer industry.

The principal technologists, Bradley Regent and Perry Honeywell, combine years of expertise in, respectively, auto dealership information systems and portable platform software development. In addition to extensive training in industry-standard database management systems, which allows Mr. Regent to effectively interface PalmPal data with existing dealership computer systems, he maintains a network of beta testers, consisting primarily of auto dealership IS managers, sales managers, salespeople and inventory management personnel, to help with testing, product development, feature refinement and other tasks.

Mr. Honeywell is a recognized expert in third-party PalmPilot software development. He serves on the advisory board for developing and maintaining standards for vertical industry software applications for the PalmPilot. His contacts and experience within the palmtop software field ensure that Palmistry will have continual access to the latest and best technology for developing its products.

Management believes this combination of industry-specific expertise and broad Palm application development experience make it unique among companies addressing the inventory management needs of automobile dealerships. Other competitors include EDS, Digital Dealership, Microsoft and SAP. All these companies are far larger than Palmistry and capable of bringing much greater resources to bear on the market. However, it is the opinion of Palmistry management that the company's lead time in developing applications for this market, plus the niche's small size in relation to the markets its competitors are primarily interested in will provide the company with a long-lasting opportunity to secure a solid market edge in the field.

Palmist operates out of offices at 26209 Fairfax Ave. in Cincinnati, Ohio. The offices, comprising approximately 5,000 square feet, offer adequate room for anticipated expansion over the next five years. Terms are flexible and management believes the rate is competitive with comparable office space in the city.

In addition to office furniture and fixtures, Palmistry's primary physical assets consist of five computer workstations used for application development. The company also maintains a varying number of PalmPilot models to be used for application testing and development.

Palmistry's inventory is limited to prepackaged versions of its software, and a small number of PalmPilots that are maintained in ready inventory for use in customer installations requiring rapid response. Most customer installations involve PalmPilots ordered from Palm Computing specifically for certain customers. This practice minimizes inventory carrying costs while maintaining an acceptable level of responsiveness in the majority of situations.

Historical Financial Statements And Projections

Palmistry's start-up was financed by $80,000 contributed by Bradley Regent. The current financial plan anticipates raising an additional $500,000 to be used to market and distribute PalmPal nationwide. Equity ownership would be distributed as shown below following this financing.

Pro Forma Statement Of Equity Ownership

Owner	Stock Class	Shares	Amount
Mr. Regent	Common	350,000	$660,000
Ms. McIntire	Common	2,000	44,000
Mr. Honeywell	Common	4,000	88,000
Mr. Wise	Common	2,000	44,000
Investors	Preferred	100,000	500,000
Total		458,000	$1,336,000

The proceeds of this financing will allow Palmistry to expand distribution and marketing of its PalmPal product nationwide.

Palmistry Income Statement

	1998	1999
Net Sales	$0	$55,600
COGS	0	32,475
Gross Margin	$0	$23,125
Operating Costs		
Development	$27,866	$13,887
SG&A	4,835	17,652
Other	1,325	1,796
Total Operating Costs	**$34,026**	**$33,335**
Operating Earnings	−34,026	−10,210
Interest Expense	−986	−1,425
Pretax Earnings	−35,012	−11,635
Income Tax	0	0
Net Income	**−$35,012**	**−$11,635**

Notes to income statement: Palmistry's income statement for the first two years of operations reflects no sales revenues the first year, when the founder's efforts were devoted to developing the product. Development costs that year were correspondingly high. Sales the second year took off nicely, and gross margin was also in line. However, heavy marketing expenses took their toll, and the company has produced a net loss of more than $42,000 for its first two years in operation.

Palmistry Balance Sheet

December 31, 1999

ASSETS	
Cash	$36,000
Accounts Receivable	11,853
Inventory	787
Prepaid Expenses	2,796
Other Current Assets	1,116
Total Current Assets	**$52,552**
Fixed Assets	17,564
Intangibles	1
Other Noncurrent Assets	0
Total Assets	**$70,117**

LIABILITIES

Notes Payable	$7,623
Accounts Payable	2,274
Interest Payable	783
Taxes Payable	652
Other Current Liabilities	1,584
Total Current Liabilities	**$12,916**
Long-term Debt	0
Other Noncurrent Liabilities	2,121
Total Liabilities	**$15,037**
Net Worth	**$55,080**
Total Liabilities & Net Worth	**$70,117**

Note to balance sheet: Assets included $36,000 in cash from the founder's $80,000 initial capitalization.

Palmistry Cash Flow Statement

Sources Of Cash	
Sales	$55,600
Total Cash In	**$55,600**
Uses Of Cash	
COGS	$32,475
SG&A	17,652
Other	1,796
Interest	1,425
Taxes	0
Equipment Purchase	4,320
Total Cash Out	**$57,668**
NET CHANGE IN CASH	**−$2,068**
Beginning Cash On Hand	**$37,201**
Ending Cash On Hand	**$35,133**

Palmistry Pro Forma Income Statement

INCOME PROJECTION

	2000	2001	2002	2003
INCOME				
Net Sales	$127,500	$191,250	$525,938	$1,051,876
Cost Of Sales	63,750	91,800	241,931	525,938
Gross Profit	**$63,750**	**$99,450**	**$284,007**	**$525,938**
OPERATING EXPENSES				
General & Administrative Expenses				
Salaries And Wages	$77,525	$95,625	$157,781	$175,375
Sales Commissions	6,375	9,563	26,297	52,594
Rent	3,200	3,360	3,528	3,704
Maintenance	1,275	1,339	1,406	1,476
Equipment Rental	1,125	1,181	1,240	1,302
Furniture And				
Equipment Purchase	6,000	2,222	1,562	2,640
Insurance	1,520	1,596	1,676	1,999
Interest Expenses	1,250	1,313	1,379	2,606
Utilities	1,100	1,155	1,213	1,274
Office Supplies	650	826	2,177	977
Marketing				
And Advertising	100,150	65,500	80,000	90,000
Travel	10,500	12,500	15,000	17,500
Entertainment	600	301	426	555
Bad Debt	500	191	526	323
Depreciation				
And Amortization	1,800	2,700	4,050	6,075
TOTAL OPERATING EXPENSES	**$213,570**	**$199,372**	**$298,261**	**$358,400**
Net Income				
Before Taxes	−$149,820	−$99,922	−$14,254	$167,538
Provision For				
Taxes On Income	0	0	0	25,131
NET INCOME AFTER TAXES	**−$149,820**	**−$99,922**	**−$14,254**	**$142,407**

Notes to income projections: Sales projections reflect assumptions of progressively greater rollout into the national market, with accordingly higher levels of sales. Heavy first-year marketing expenses level off as national distribution is achieved. Sales increase in subsequent years as the effect of initial marketing efforts is felt. Wage and salary increases reflect need to hire additional programmers, salespeople and administrative personnel to cope with higher sales.

Sustained profitability is achieved in 2003. Projected income tax reflects effects of applying net operating loss form prior years to 2003 profits.

Palmistry Pro Forma Balance Sheet

		1999	% Sales	2000 (projected)
	Sales	$55,600		$127,500
ASSETS				
Cash		$36,000	64.7%	$82,493
Accounts Receivable		11,853	21.3%	27,158
Inventory		787	1.4%	1,785
Prepaid Expenses		2,796	5.0%	6,375
Other Current Assets		1,116	2.0%	2,550
Total Current Assets		**$52,552**	94.5%	**$120,488**
Fixed Assets		17,564	31.6%	40,290
Intangibles		1	0.0%	0
Other Noncurrent Assets		0		0
Total Assets		**$34,117**		**$78,285**
LIABILITIES				
Notes Payable		$7,623	13.7%	$17,468
Accounts Payable		2,274	4.1%	5,228
Interest Payable		783	1.4%	1,785
Taxes Payable		652	1.2%	1,530
Other Current Liabilities		1,584		1,671
Total Current Liabilities		**$12,916**		**$27,682**
Long-term Debt		0		0
Other Noncurrent Liabilities		2,121		3,222
Total Liabilities		**$15,037**		**$30,904**
Net Worth		**$55,080**		**$129,874**
Total Liabilities & Net Worth		**$70,117**		**$160,778**

Note to balance sheet projection: Balance sheet projections were based on relationships among various items reflected in 1999 actual results. Intangibles include goodwill, proprietary technology and long-term service and maintenance contracts.

Palmistry Pro Forma Cash Flow Statement

Projected Cash Flow: 2000

	Jan.	Feb.	Mar.	Apr.	May	Jun.	Jul.	Aug.	Sep.	Oct.	Nov.	Dec.	TOTAL
CASH RECEIPTS													
Income From Sales													
Sales	$7,650	$7,650	$8,925	$8,925	$10,200	$10,200	$11,475	$11,475	$11,475	$12,750	$12,750	$14,025	$127,500
Total Cash From Sales	7,650	7,650	8,925	8,925	10,200	10,200	11,475	11,475	11,475	12,750	12,750	14,025	$127,500
Financing Income													
Net Offering Proceeds	433,000	0	0	2,500	0	0	0	0	0	0	0	0	$435,500
Interest Income	3,500	3,500	2,500	2,500	2,000	2,000	1,750	1,750	1,500	1,500	1,250	1,250	$25,000
Total Cash Receipts	444,150	11,150	11,425	13,925	12,200	12,200	13,225	13,225	12,975	14,250	14,000	15,275	$588,000
CASH DISBURSEMENTS													
Expenses													
COGS	3,825	3,825	4,462	4,462	5,099	5,099	5,737	5,737	5,737	6,374	6,374	7,012	$63,743
SG&A	12,100	10,555	9,228	6,025	8,750	8,222	9,557	9,525	9,222	10,500	8,750	9,685	$112,119
Taxes	0	0	0	0	0	0	0	0	0	0	0	0	$0
Equipment Purchase	8,000	0	0	0	0	0	4,000	0	0	0	0	0	$12,000
Dividends	0	0	0	0	0	0	0	0	0	0	0	0	$0
Total Cash Disbursements	23,925	14,380	13,690	10,487	13,849	13,321	19,294	15,262	14,959	16,874	15,124	16,697	$187,862
Net Cash Flow	$420,225	-$3,230	-$2,265	$3,438	-$1,649	-$1,121	-$6,069	-$2,037	-$1,984	-$2,624	-$1,124	-$1,422	$400,138
Opening Cash Balance	36,000	456,225	452,995	450,730	454,168	452,519	451,398	445,329	443,292	441,308	438,684	437,560	$0
Cash Receipts	444,150	11,150	11,425	13,925	12,200	12,200	13,225	13,225	12,975	14,250	14,000	15,275	$588,000
Cash Disbursements	-23,925	-14,380	-13,690	-10,487	-13,849	-13,321	-19,294	-15,262	-14,959	-16,874	-15,124	-16,697	-$187,862
Ending Cash Balance	$456,225	$452,995	$450,730	$454,168	$452,519	$451,398	$445,329	$443,292	$441,308	$438,684	$437,560	$436,138	

Note to cash flow projection: Cash flow projections for 2000 reflect offering proceeds, net of fees, of $433,000. Interest income is generated from investing excess proceeds of offering.

Business Plan For An Established Service Firm Seeking Working Capital

The following business plan is for an established company seeking working capital.

Draper Rains Associates has grown steadily for 15 years—it employs 109 people and has a solid base of customers and billings. Now, however, the company has embarked on an ambitious plan of expansion to attract new and larger clients. The result has been an increase in expenses and a greater need for working capital. The company is seeking a bank loan to provide the working capital it needs as it grows to a new level.

The indications are that the company is prudent in seeking additional working capital. Its cash flow is no more than adequate, and expenses can be expected to increase as its geographic expansion gathers steam.

Business Plan: Confidential

Draper Rains Associates

14479 Jackson St.
San Francisco, CA 94115
(415) 555-6968

Alice Draper, Chairman, President & CEO

Executive Summary

Draper Rains Associates is a 15-year-old public relations and marketing consultancy serving health-care clients in the San Francisco Bay Area.

Draper Rains offers integrated public relations and marketing consulting services to its clients, who consist of large hospitals, clinics and health maintenance organizations. While the majority of the services Draper Rains offers are available from other firms, the company believes its execution is superior. This is evidenced by the fact that the majority of its clients have been active with the firm for more than five years, some have been active more than 10 years, and one client has been with the firm since its founding.

After several years of steady growth as a regional services provider, the company is now poised to break out into the national scene. In pursuit of this strategy, the company has expended a substantial proportion of its capital reserves in opening new offices, increasing staff, and acquiring necessary equipment and technology.

The strategy has been successful so far, and the firm has acquired several national accounts whose billings are much larger than the average client the firm has worked with in the past. These larger clients, many of whom are also slower in cycling invoices than other clients, are causing increases in accounts payable and accounts receivable. As a result, the company is now seeking additional capital to provide working capital during this period of expansion.

Bank financing in the amount of $350,000 is being sought. The objective is a line of credit in that amount, with approximately $175,000 expected to be paid out immediately and the balance in equal quarterly installments for the next five quarters. At the end of two years, payments against principal will begin, with the entire principal amount due to be paid off after four years.

Product

Draper Rains provides integrated public relations and marketing services to large hospitals, clinics and health maintenance organizations.

The company's services consist of planning marketing strategy, writing and editing marketing materials and press releases, conducting publicity and media placement campaigns, media training for key executives, and related services. The company arranges for production of videotapes and printed materials, conducts on-premises briefings and seminars, and participates in high-level strategy sessions with its clients' executives.

The purpose of the company is to provide its clients with positive, integrated public images in the marketplace, with the ultimate goal of increasing client sales and profits.

Draper Rains competes with numerous other companies for customers. Many of these competitors provide similar services. However, the company believes that its reputation for quality service, and its long-established relationships with existing clients, will allow it to maintain and expand its current level of sales despite the competitive environment.

Industry

The health-care industry is undergoing monumental shifts as changes in payer policies, declining bed utilization rates and increasingly expensive new medical technology combine to make marketing much more important than it has been previously.

The marketing and public relations industry is also undergoing a period of consolidation as numerous global advertising and marketing firms establish large, United States-based public relations divisions. These same competitors are targeting health care, for much the same reasons Draper Rains is.

If current trends play out as expected, the business of providing marketing and public relations services to large health-care clients will become increasingly consolidated among a few sizable firms. As a result, Draper Rains feels that to compete for new, desirable large clients in the health-care field, the company must develop a national presence.

Draper Rains believes its best chance for remaining competitive in this industry environment is to grow and establish a national presence. To this end, it has pursued geographic expansion, opening new offices on the East and West Coasts as well as in the Midwest and Southeast. In addition, it has increased employee head count by approximately 25 percent, or 16 persons, to staff these offices. Management believes the recently conducted expansion will accomplish this objective.

Marketing

Draper Rains obtains clients almost exclusively through word-of-mouth. Because of the large size of its typical client—average clients are billed approximately $30,000 annually—and the longstanding conservatism of health-care institutions in matters of marketing, it is believed that personal referrals, informal testimonials and a generally sterling reputation among hospital administrators and professionals in the health-care marketing field continue to be the best marketing tools available.

Draper Rains has a formal program for generating and disseminating positive word-of-mouth, informal testimonials and referrals in the marketplace. This program is difficult to track for effectiveness. However, the company believes its program is effective and is continuing and expanding its use.

For the company to compete effectively in new geographic markets, it must establish and maintain a physical presence in those markets. To that end, the company has in the past year opened new offices in several cities, each of which serves as a hub for its region of the United States. New offices include Miami, Chicago, New York and Los Angeles.

The company's headquarters in San Francisco consists of approximately 8,000 square feet of leased space in a modern office building. Headquarters staff numbers approximately 80 persons. In each of the new cities the firm has begun with small facilities and small staffs. Offices average approximately 600 square feet and staffs average five persons. This was done to control operational and staffing expenses while providing a marketing foothold in the new markets. Each of the new offices has adjoining space suitable for expansion. Draper Rains has acquired formal options to lease adjoining space in New York, Miami and Los Angeles, and has an informal understanding with its landlord in Chicago.

In addition to establishing a physical presence in the new cities, Draper Rains is mounting a modest advertising campaign. The effort includes placing advertisements in the printed programs for meetings of local health-care marketing organizations, advertising groups and the like. The firm has purchased outdoor advertising space on one or more billboards in each of the cities for a term of approximately one year to build initial name recognition among its target group.

Another key element of the company's marketing campaign consists of personal sales calls by the principal and other personnel. These sales calls are scheduled with hospital administrators, hospital marketing directors,

HMO chief executives and marketing vice presidents and similar individuals. The initial intent of these sales calls is to introduce our firm to potential clients and to begin a dialogue. We anticipate these sales calls, the
increased frequency of which is indicated in the growing travel budget, will
yield significant numbers of new clients and increased billings over time.

Management

Alice Draper
Chairman, CEO And President

Draper Rains is led by Ms. Draper. Ms. Draper, a resident of San Rafael, California, since 1976, is one of the best-known figures in the field of public relations and marketing in the Bay Area. She is past president of Northern California Media Relations Professionals, was a delegate from the Public Relations Society of America to a global conference in London, England, in 1996, and has taught classes in the marketing curriculum at San Jose State University as an adjunct professor since 1994. Ms. Draper founded the firm as a homebased business in 1984 in San Francisco. Over the next 15 years, she grew the firm to its present size of 109 employees. She is a graduate of San Jose State University.

Charles Allen
Vice President, Marketing

Mr. Allen is the firm's chief marketing officer and handles many of the marketing duties that are beyond the scope of the president's duties. He and his staff are responsible for developing marketing strategy, preparing marketing plans and executing the marketing plan. Mr. Allen has been with Draper Rains for seven years. He is a graduate of the University of Colorado.

Cheryl Plant
Vice President, Technology

Ms. Plant is Draper Rains' chief information officer. She is responsible for developing technology strategies; selecting hardware, software and vendors; staffing the information office; and preparing a budget for information technology expenditures. Her role has become more important as information management becomes essential to providing the firm's services and as remote offices are incorporated into the firm's technology network. Ms. Plant joined the firm last year from Intel Corp., where she served as assistant director of information services for a major division. She is a graduate of Carnegie Mellon University.

Facilities

Draper Rains operates out of a headquarters at 14479 Jackson St. in San Francisco. Additional offices are located in New York, Miami, Chicago and Los Angeles. Until 1999, the firm's only office was in San Francisco. The additional offices were opened as part of the long-range expansion plan.

One of the company's key operational resources is the integrated communications and computing network that links all personnel in its headquarters, as well as those in the remote offices. This network allows the company to quickly and effectively compose, edit, reproduce and disseminate client marketing materials. The investment in technology provides the company with a significant edge over competitors in terms of increased quality and reduced turnaround time to complete assignments.

The company's physical assets primarily consist of the computers, modems, cabling and other equipment required to construct this network. Other assets consist of furniture, equipment and fixtures in its headquarters office. Most fixtures and furnishings in the new offices are leased rather than purchased.

Financials

Income Statement

Sales Receipts	$5,451,090
Interest Income	10,712
COGS	3,597,719
Gross Margin	1,864,083
Expenses	1,362,773
Depreciation	25,685
Operating Earnings	475,625
Interest Expense	75,658
Pretax Earnings	399,967
Income Tax	119,990
Net Income	**$279,977**

Balance Sheet

June 30, 1998

ASSETS

Cash	$178,532
Accounts Receivable	434,452
Prepaid Expenses	136,572
Other Current Assets	75,827
Total Current Assets	**$825,383**
Fixed Assets	256,854
Total Assets	**$1,082,237**

LIABILITIES

Notes Payable	$143,586
Accounts Payable	113,564
Interest Payable	6,305
Taxes Payable	29,998
Other Current Liabilities	986
Total Current Liabilities	**$294,439**
Long-term Debt	253,556
Other Noncurrent Liabilities	1,156
Total Liabilities	**$549,151**
Net Worth	**$533,087**
Total Liabilities & Net Worth	**$1,082,237**

Note to balance sheet: The company operates on a June 30 fiscal year.

Cash Flow Statement

Sources Of Cash

Sales	$5,178,536
Other Sources	
Interest	10,712
Short-term Borrowings	100,000
Total Cash In	**$5,289,248**

Uses Of Cash

COGS	$3,417,833
SG&A	1,362,773
Interest	75,658
Taxes	119,990
Equipment Purchase	53,542
Debt Principal Payments	25,842
Dividends	0
Total Cash Out	**$5,055,638**
NET CHANGE IN CASH	**$233,610**
Beginning Cash On Hand	**$54,387**
Ending Cash On Hand	**$287,997**

Note to cash flow statement: The company intends to reduce short-term borrowings in favor of less costly long-term debt.

Pro Forma Income Statement

INCOME PROJECTION

	1996	1997	1998	1999 (projected)
INCOME				
Net Sales	$4,919,609	$5,178,536	$5,451,090	$5,996,199
Interest Income	6,352	8,542	10,712	11,524
Cost Of Sales	3,197,746	3,366,048	3,597,719	3,897,529
Gross Profit	$1,728,215	$1,821,029	$1,864,083	$2,110,194

OPERATING EXPENSES

General And Administrative Expenses

Salaries And Wages	$646,437	$680,460	$705,644	$787,901
Sales Commissions	245,980	258,927	327,065	299,810
Rent	22,544	23,671	24,855	41,756
Maintenance	49,196	51,656	54,755	91,988
Equipment Rental	3,849	4,041	4,283	7,195
Furniture And Equipment Purchase	3,232	3,394	3,564	5,988
Insurance	6,978	8,722	10,902	13,082
Interest Expenses	36,250	38,158	75,658	142,994
Utilities	49,196	51,785	54,511	85,855
Office Supplies	31,977	33,660	35,977	35,078
Marketing And Advertising	83,633	88,035	92,669	9,204
Travel	17,443	21,804	27,255	1,000
Entertainment	14,759	15,536	16,353	555
Bad Debt	5,461	5,748	6,051	323
Depreciation And Amortization	16,438	20,548	25,685	38,528
TOTAL OPERATING EXPENSES	$1,233,373	$1,306,145	$1,465,227	$1,561,257
Net Income Before Taxes	$494,842	$514,885	$398,856	$548,937
Provision For Taxes On Income	148,453	154,466	119,990	164,681
NET INCOME AFTER TAXES	$346,389	$360,419	$278,866	$384,256

Pro Forma Balance Sheet

	1998	% Sales	1999 (projected)
Sales	$5,451,090		$5,996,199
ASSETS			
Cash	$178,532	3.3%	$197,875
Accounts Receivable	$434,452	8.0%	$479,696
Prepaid Expenses	136,572	2.5%	149,905
Other Current Assets	75,827	1.4%	83,947
Total Current Assets	**$825,383**	15.1%	**$905,426**
Fixed Assets	256,854	4.7%	281,821
Total Assets	**$903,705**		**$995,369**
LIABILITIES			
Notes Payable	$143,586	2.6%	$155,901
Accounts Payable	113,564	2.1%	125,920
Interest Payable	6,305	0.1%	5,996
Taxes Payable	29,998	0.6%	35,997
Other Current Liabilities	986	0.0%	0
Total Current Liabilities	**$294,439**	5.4%	**$323,794**
Long-term Debt	253,556	4.7%	281,821
Other Noncurrent Liabilities	1,156		1,468
Total Liabilities	**$549,151**		**$607,083**
Net Worth	**$533,087**		**$391,455**
Total Liabilities & Net Worth	**$1,082,237**		**$1,187,247**

Note to pro forma balance sheet: Long-term debt projected includes $175,000 in loan proceeds.

Pro Forma Cash Flow Statement

Projected Cash Flow: 2000

	Jan.	Feb.	Mar.	Apr.	May	Jun.	Jul.	Aug.	Sep.	Oct.	Nov.	Dec.	TOTAL
CASH RECEIPTS													
Income From Sales													
Cash Sales	$479,696	$437,723	$485,692	$533,662	$455,711	$509,677	$449,715	$527,666	$497,685	$545,654	$533,662	$545,654	$6,002,197
Total Cash From Sales	$479,696	$437,723	$485,692	$533,662	$455,711	$509,677	$449,715	$527,666	$497,685	$545,654	$533,622	$545,654	$6,002,197
Income From Financing													
Loan Proceeds	175,000	0	0	0	0	0	0	0	0	0	0	0	$175,000
Other Cash Receipts	960	960	960	960	960	960	960	960	960	960	960	960	$11,520
Total Cash Receipts	$655,656	$438,683	$486,652	$534,622	$456,671	$510,637	$450,675	$528,626	$498,645	$546,014	$534,622	$546,614	$6,188,717
CASH DISBURSEMENTS													
Expenses													
COGS	$316,599	$288,897	$320,557	$352,217	$300,769	$336,387	$296,812	$348,260	$328,472	$360,132	$352,217	$360,132	$3,961,451
SG&A	119,924	109,431	121,423	133,416	113,928	127,419	112,429	131,917	124,421	136,414	133,416	136,414	$1,500,552
Interest	11,916	11,916	11,916	11,916	11,916	11,916	11,916	11,916	11,916	11,916	11,916	11,916	$142,992
Taxes	13,723	13,723	13,723	13,723	13,723	13,723	13,723	13,723	13,723	13,723	13,723	13,723	$164,676
Equipment Purchase	5,500	0	5,500	0	5,500	0	5,500	0	5,500	0	5,500	0	$33,000
Debt Principal Payments	2,000	2,000	2,000	2,000	2,000	2,000	2,000	2,000	2,000	2,000	2,000	2,000	$24,000
Dividends	0	0	0	0	0	0	0	0	0	0	0	0	$0
Total Cash Disbursements	$469,662	$425,967	$475,119	$513,272	$447,836	$491,445	$442,380	$507,816	$486,032	$524,185	$518,772	$524,185	$5,826,671
Net Cash Flow	185,994	12,716	11,533	21,350	8,835	19,192	8,295	20,810	12,613	22,429	15,850	22,429	$362,046
Opening Cash Balance	178,532	364,526	377,242	388,775	410,125	418,960	438,152	446,447	467,257	479,870	502,299	518,149	$0
Cash Receipts	655,656	438,683	486,652	534,622	456,671	510,637	450,675	528,626	498,645	546,614	534,622	546,614	$6,188,717
Cash Disbursements	−469,662	−425,967	−475,119	−513,272	−447,836	−491,445	−442,380	−507,816	−486,032	−524,185	−518,772	−524,185	−$5,826,671
Ending Cash Balance	$364,526	$377,242	$388,775	$410,125	$418,960	$438,152	$446,447	$467,257	$479,870	$502,299	$518,149	$540,578	

Business Plan For A Manufacturer Seeking A Strategic Partner

The company in the following business plan is a manufacturer court-ing a strategic partner. The plan writer hopes to convince a larger company of the wisdom of joining the company in a strategic al-liance to manufacture and distribute its patented quick-connect device for coaxial cables.

The basic business strategy is sound. The company sees a mushrooming opportunity in the growth of the Internet and projected demand for cable modems and other devices requiring large numbers of coaxial cable con-nectors. The existing coaxial connectors on the market are cumbersome and inefficient compared with its improved design, and the company has hopes of snaring a significant market share amid rapidly growing demand.

The problem is that the opportunity is bigger than Kwiq-Kliq. The com-pany has only 24 employees and, while it's generating profits and cash flow sufficient for moderate growth, there's no way it can fund a big rollout of product from operations. In addition, it is carrying a fairly heavy debt load—its debt-to-equity ratio is approximately 4.3:1. That amount of leverage has apparently given Kwiq-Kliq's bankers pause, so the company is turning to an alternative means of conducting its expansion.

Kwiq-Kliq is proposing a modest degree of alliance. It's nothing so for-mal and long-term as a joint venture, just a manufacturing license and dis-tribution agreement. The company hopes that it will increase its market share dramatically, while giving up to its partner only a portion of profits it would make if it were able to conduct the expansion on its own.

Kwiq-Kliq Inc.

Cable Connectors
For All Purposes

16901 Rising Sun Ave.
Philadelphia, PA 19111
(215) 555-7227

Contact: Paula Bench, President

Executive Summary

Kwiq-Kliq Inc. designs and manufactures coaxial cable connectors for the cable TV, Internet access, broadcasting, security and data transmission industries.

The company's proprietary designs for quick-connect coaxial cable connectors have proved superior to existing products. Since their introduction in 1995, they have gained approximately 1 percent of the market.

Management feels that much larger sales gains and market share could be obtained, given the Kwiq-Kliq's demonstrable superiority to competitive designs. However, the company's existing production and distribution capacity offer significant constraints.

Management is seeking a strategic partner to license manufacture of the patented Kwiq-Kliq connector line and assist in providing or arranging distribution to a larger market. It is anticipated that the partner will not need to invest any funds in the company, with the exception of licensing fees.

Kwiq-Kliq's 24-person employee team includes persons with more than 60 combined years of experience in connector design, light manufacturing operations and industrial marketing.

The company feels the opportunity for obtaining a significantly increased market share is at hand. With a suitable strategic partner, this opportunity can be seized to the mutual benefit of Kwiq-Kliq and its partner.

Kwiq-Kliq Mission Statement

Connecting to the needs of customers, employees, suppliers and partners quickly, efficiently and effectively.

Industry

Kwiq-Kliq's opportunity is being driven by one of the fastest and most sweeping industrial and commercial revolutions in history. That revolution consists of the extremely rapid growth in the use and number of connections to the Internet. An increasing number of Internet users use coaxial cable to access the network, and each one of these connections, plus many more between the user and the infrastructure, is a candidate for a Kwiq-Kliq connector. Following are key industry statistics relating to Kwiq-Kliq's business plan:

- World Wide Web users, estimated to number approximately 35 million at the end of 1996, will grow to approximately 163 million by the year 2000.

- The number of Web users is currently increasing at a rate in excess of 1 million per month.

- Content is growing rapidly as well. The number of Internet hosts grew from approximately 1 million in 1992 to more than 10 million in 1996.

- The complexity of Internet content has increased to include real-time video, CD-quality audio and high-resolution graphics.

- The Internet network infrastructure is overburdened, as evidenced by headlines such as "No Shortage of Bottlenecks on the Information Superhighway" and "Explosive Growth Clogs Internet's Backbone."

- Cable-delivery systems are capable of delivering information to millions of Internet users at rates up to 1,000 times as rapid as traditional modems operating over twisted-pair telephone networks.

- Cable companies plan to invest about $14 billion in equipment upgrades through the end of the decade.

- Set-top boxes that will bring cable-delivered Internet services as well as movies on demand, on-screen program guides and other services are expected to be within the range of $300 to 400 per subscriber.

- Cable infrastructure already passes 97 percent of American homes, meaning the cable industry has an edge in becoming the Internet access provider of the next century.

- The number of Internet domains, or hosts, is also growing extremely rapidly, as is evidenced by the following graph based on a twice-yearly survey.

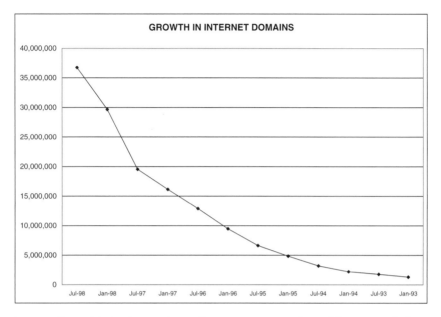

As a well-established supplier of connectors to the cable-TV and data-transmission industry, Kwiq-Kliq is positioned to take maximum advantage of the explosive growth potential in coaxial cable connector supply.

Management Team

Paula Bench
President

Paula Bench has served as president of Kwiq-Kliq since 1993. Her responsibilities include overseeing new-product development, setting long-range strategy, and building and maintaining relationships with key customers and suppliers. She previously was employed at the company, then known as Pennsylvania Connectors, in a variety of capacities, until the founder's retirement in 1993. Ms. Bench, then working as general manager, purchased the company from the founder and has served as sole owner and president since that time. Ms. Bench is past president of the Pennsylvania-Area Small Business Conclave. She is a 1985 graduate of Pennsylvania State University with a degree in engineering.

David Stone
Operations Vice President

David Stone has served as operations vice president of Kwiq-Kliq since 1994. His responsibilities include overseeing manufacturability of new Kwiq-Kliq product designs, setting up and running manufacturing operations, specifying new equipment purchase and installation, overseeing maintenance of the company's fleet of vehicles, and other duties relating to the manufacture and delivery of the company's products. Prior to joining Kwiq-Kliq, he was employed as manufacturing supervisor for Cable Manufacturing in Blue Bell, Pennsylvania. He is a 1983 graduate of Rensselaer Polytechnic Institute.

Peter August
Chief Financial Officer

Peter August has served as chief financial officer of Kwiq-Kliq since 1996. Prior to that time he served in various capacities as treasurer, controller and bookkeeper. He is a 1990 graduate of the University of Indiana.

Diane Paterson
Vice President, Marketing

Diane Paterson has served as marketing vice president of Kwiq-Kliq since 1992. Her duties include setting marketing strategy, pricing, product design, customer communications, staffing the sales function and other marketing-related duties.

Product Description

Cable modems connect TVs to the cable TV coaxial wiring and may also attach a personal computer via a standard Ethernet connection to the cable infrastructure. Internet appliances and similar devices, a few of which are already on the market, may provide access to many users in the near future. Cable modems are sold by a number of vendors, including Bay Networks, Hewlett-Packard, Motorola and several smaller manufacturers.

Kwiq-Kliq's patented easy-on connectors provide cable modem companies, cable installers, and cable TV and data service access providers with a rapid, secure method for completing the numerous connections associated with a typical installation of cable service to a home or business. These connectors use a proprietary, patented serrated-tooth locking mechanism to achieve a solid, radiation-secure attachment, which can nevertheless be completed with one hand, a significant convenience to installation personnel.

To be maximally effective, the company's cable connections must be installed on both the coaxial cable and the device being connected to. For that reason, the company has negotiated supply contracts with several smaller cable modem manufacturers. It is hoped that the presence of a larger partner will allow the negotiation of similar arrangements with a number of the larger device manufacturers.

In addition to offering significant improvement in functionality compared with traditional threaded connectors, Kwiq-Kliq's cable connectors are cost-competitive. When purchased in volume, the company's connectors are priced in the range of 5 cents to 7 cents per connection. Competing designs are priced at 4 cents to 6 cents. The price difference, when compared with the increase in usability and efficiency, has not proved sufficient to inhibit customer purchases to date, and the company sees no reason why it should.

Marketing

Kwiq-Kliq's marketing plan revolves around presenting the advantages of its fastening system to large cable operators, cable system installers and equipment manufacturers.

The intent with manufacturers is to obtain the specification of Kwiq-Kliq connectors for new devices to be connected to the cable infrastructure. Installers are approached in the same fashion, with the goal being to have Kwiq-Kliq connectors specified for new installations and retrofit projects. Cable system operators are invited to use Kwiq-Kliq connectors in their back-office operations, as well as to specify them for use by installers and end-user device manufacturers.

In all cases, Kwiq-Kliq's primary marketing method consists of personal sales calls to engineers, network architects, designers, maintenance managers and others responsible for specifying the use of coaxial connectors in cable systems and devices.

The company has experienced considerable success with this approach. It has exclusive supplier agreements with four of the top six cable system operators in Pennsylvania and three of the top five installation companies. In addition, the company has made good progress in presenting the advantages of the Kwiq-Kliq system to manufacturers of end-user devices, including set-top boxes and cable modems, and anticipates announcing a major new contract in this area shortly.

For example, the company recently agreed to be the exclusive supplier of cable connectors to NetCable, a Philadelphia provider of cable modem Internet access. NetCable has grown rapidly and promises to become one of the industry's premier providers. After less than two years of commercial availability, NetCable now serves approximately 127,000 cable modem subscribers across the Northeast, an increase of 53 percent from late 1998. NetCable's cable modem subscriber base has nearly tripled since the beginning of 1998. The base of homes with access to two-way upgraded systems increased to 9 million on December 31, 1999, from 7.7 million on March 31, 1999.

Given that the cable industry is moving strongly toward standardization of all aspects of plant, equipment and operation, many other service providers can be expected to follow NetCable's lead. As a result, Kwiq-Kliq anticipates further agreements with other leading operators will be concluded during the coming year.

Operations

Kwiq-Kliq operates out of a 10,000-square-foot manufacturing and head-quarters space in Philadelphia. The building and land are owned by the company. Various machines, including drill presses, metal stampers, extruding machines and packing equipment, are also owned or leased by the company.

The company uses industry-standard production machinery in all processes. Its materials are obtained from vendors who supply its competitors—no unusual materials are used in their construction. Likewise, the company employs no proprietary processes or technologies in the manufacture of its products.

The primary value-added feature in the company's products is the design, which applies to coaxial cable connection technology proven in other uses. This technology, on which the company holds patents for application in coaxial cable connections, requires only moderate retooling of machinery used by the majority of manufacturers to make industry-standard coaxial cable connectors.

The company's current production capacity amounts to approximately 1.5 million connectors monthly. While current production capacity is adequate to meet the existing level of orders, management believes additional sales could be procured if service, especially turnaround time on orders, were improved.

Achieving a significant improvement in service, including reducing turnaround, would require substantial investments in new, higher-capacity production equipment, plus the addition of an improved distribution center and, likely, geographically dispersed distribution centers to serve clients in far-off regions. It is the opinion of management that the company's financial structure will not support the added debt burden that would be necessary to accomplish these operational improvements. Therefore, the decision has been made to pursue a strategic alliance with an existing manufacturer who can license Kwiq-Kliq's designs and provide appropriately located distribution centers.

Financial Data

Income Statement

Sales Receipts	$1,197,000
Interest Income	3,579
COGS	790,020
Gross Margin	410,559
Expenses	311,220
Depreciation	20,268
Operating Earnings	79,071
Interest Expense	20,571
Pretax Earnings	58,500
Income Tax	17,550
Net Income	**$40,950**

Balance Sheet

June 30, 1998

ASSETS

Cash	$59,642
Accounts Receivable	95,401
Prepaid Expenses	25,935
Other Current Assets	25,827
Total Current Assets	**$206,805**
Fixed Assets	202,684
Total Assets	**$409,489**

LIABILITIES

Notes Payable	$123,584
Accounts Payable	25,935
Interest Payable	1,714
Taxes Payable	4,388
Other Current Liabilities	2,357
Total Current Liabilities	**$157,978**
Long-term Debt	153,566
Other Noncurrent Liabilities	2,298
Total Liabilities	**$313,842**
Net Worth	**$95,647**
Total Liabilities & Net Worth	**$409,489**

Cash Flow Statement

Sources Of Cash

Sales	$1,137,150

Other Sources

Interest	3,579
Short-term Borrowings	16,243
Total Cash In	**$1,156,972**

Uses Of Cash

COGS	$750,519
SG&A	311,220
Interest	20,571
Taxes	17,550
Equipment Purchase	35,212
Debt Principal Payments	10,824
Dividends	0
Total Cash Out	$1,145,896

NET CHANGE IN CASH	**$11,076**
Beginning Cash On Hand	**$59,642**
Ending Cash On Hand	**$70,718**

Income Projection

INCOME PROJECTION

	1997	1998	1999	2000 (projected)
INCOME				
Net Sales	$1,091,664	$1,149,120	$1,197,000	$1,388,520
Interest Income	1,792	2,415	3,579	3,005
Cost Of Sales	709,582	746,928	790,020	902,538
Gross Profit	$383,874	$404,607	$410,559	$488,987
OPERATING EXPENSES				
General & Administrative Expenses				
Salaries And Wages	$143,445	$150,994	$154,952	$182,452
Sales Commissions	54,583	57,456	71,820	69,426
Maintenance	10,917	11,463	12,151	20,414
Equipment Rental	3,849	4,041	4,283	7,195
Furniture And Equipment Purchase	3,232	3,394	3,564	5,988
Insurance	1,532	1,915	2,394	2,873
Interest Expenses	8,044	8,379	20,571	38,879
Utilities	10,917	11,491	11,970	18,853
Office Supplies	7,096	7,469	7,900	8,123
Marketing And Advertising	18,558	19,535	20,349	9,204
Travel	3,830	4,788	5,985	1,000
Bad Debt	1,212	1,276	1,329	323
Depreciation And Amortization	12,971	16,214	20,268	30,402
TOTAL OPERATING EXPENSES	$280,186	$298,415	$337,536	$395,132
Net Income Before Taxes	$103,688	$106,192	$73,023	$93,855
Provision For Taxes On Income	15,553	15,929	17,550	14,078
NET INCOME AFTER TAXES	$88,135	$90,263	$55,473	$79,777

Note: Sales projections include an estimated $100,000 from licensing fees.

Balance Sheet Projection

	1999	% Sales	2000 (projected)
Sales	$1,197,000		$1,388,520
ASSETS			
Cash	$59,642	5.0%	$69,426
Accounts Receivable	$95,401	8.0%	$111,082
Prepaid Expenses	25,935	2.2%	30,547
Other Current Assets	25,827	2.2%	30,547
Total Current Assets	$206,805	17.3%	$240,214
Fixed Assets	202,684	16.9%	234,660
Total Assets	$409,489		$474,874
LIABILITIES			
Notes Payable	$123,584	10.3%	$143,018
Accounts Payable	25,935	2.2%	30,547
Interest Payable	1,714	0.1%	1,389
Taxes Payable	4,388	0.4%	5,554
Other Current Liabilities	2,357	0.2%	2,777
Total Current Liabilities	$157,978	13.2%	$183,285
Long-term Debt	153,566	12.8%	177,731
Other Noncurrent Liabilities	2,298		1,895
Total Liabilities	$313,842		$362,911
Net Worth	$95,647		$102,243
Total Liabilities & Net Worth	$409,489		$474,874

Cash Flow Projection

Projected Cash Flow: 2000

	Jan.	Feb.	Mar.	Apr.	May	Jun.	Jul.	Aug.	Sep.	Oct.	Nov.	Dec.	TOTAL
CASH RECEIPTS													
Income From Sales													
Sales & Licensing Fees	$111,082	$109,693	$116,636	$118,024	$133,298	$99,973	$129,132	$112,470	$105,528	$131,909	$113,859	$99,973	$1,381,577
Total Cash From Sales	111,082	109,693	116,636	118,024	133,298	99,973	129,132	112,470	105,528	131,909	113,859	99,973	$1,381,577
Income From Financing													
Loan Proceeds	5,000	0	0	5,000	0	0	5,000	0	0	5,000	0	0	$20,000
Other Cash Receipts	0	0	0	0	0	0	0	0	0	0	0	0	$0
Total Cash Receipts	$116,082	$109,693	$116,636	$123,024	$133,298	$99,973	$134,132	$112,470	$105,528	$136,909	$113,859	$99,973	$1,401,577
CASH DISBURSEMENTS													
Expenses													
COGS	$73,314	$72,397	$76,980	$77,896	$87,977	$65,982	$85,227	$74,230	$69,648	$87,060	$75,147	$65,982	$911,840
SG&A	27,771	27,423	29,159	29,506	33,325	24,993	32,283	28,118	26,382	32,977	28,465	24,993	$345,395
Interest	3,240	3,240	3,240	3,240	3,240	3,240	3,240	3,240	3,240	3,240	3,240	3,240	$38,880
Taxes	1,173	1,173	1,173	1,173	1,173	1,173	1,173	1,173	1,173	1,173	1,173	1,173	$14,076
Equipment Purchase	1,497			1,497	0	1,497	1,497	0	0	0	1,497	0	$5,988
Debt Principal Payments	1,232	1,232	1,232	1,232	1,232	1,232	1,232	1,232	1,232	1,232	1,232	1,232	$14,784
Dividends	0	0	0	0	0	0	0	0	0	0	0	0	$0
Total Cash Disbursements	$108,227	$105,465	$111,784	$114,544	$126,947	$96,620	$124,652	$107,993	$101,675	$125,682	$110,754	$96,620	$1,330,963
Net Cash Flow	7,855	4,228	4,852	8,480	6,351	3,353	9,480	4,477	3,853	11,227	3,105	3,353	$70,614
Opening Cash Balance	59,642	67,497	71,725	76,577	85,057	91,408	94,761	104,241	108,718	112,571	123,798	126,903	$0
Cash Receipts	116,082	109,693	116,636	123,024	133,298	99,973	134,132	112,470	105,528	136,909	113,859	99,973	$1,401,577
Cash Disbursements	−108,227	−105,465	−111,784	−114,544	−126,947	−96,620	−124,652	−107,993	−101,675	−125,682	−110,754	−96,620	−$1,330,963
Ending Cash Balance	$67,497	$71,725	$76,577	$85,057	$91,408	$94,761	$104,241	$108,718	$112,571	$123,798	$126,903	$130,256	$130,256

APPENDIX E

GOVERNMENT LISTINGS

GOVERNMENT AGENCIES

◆ Copyright Clearance Center, 222 Rosewood Dr., Danvers, MA 01923, (978) 750-8400, fax: (978) 750-4470, www.copyright.com

◆ Copyright Office, Library of Congress, 101 Independence Ave. SE, Washington, DC 20559-6000, (202) 707-3000, fax: (202) 707-6859, www.loc.gov/copyright

◆ Department of Agriculture, 1400 and Independence Aves. SW, Washington, DC 20250, (202) 720-7420, www.fas.usda.gov

◆ Department of Commerce, 14th St. and Constitution Ave. NW, Washington, DC 20230, (202) 482-2000, fax: (202) 482-5270, www.doc.gov

◆ Department of Energy, 1000 Independence Ave. SW, Washington, DC 20585, (202) 586-5000, www.doe.gov

◆ Department of Interior, 1849 C St. NW, Washington, DC 20240, (202) 208-3100, www.doi.gov

◆ Department of Labor, 200 Constitution Ave. NW, Rm. S-1004, Washington, DC 20210, (202) 219-6666, www.dol.gov

◆ Department of Treasury, Main Treasury Bldg, 1500 Pennsylvania Ave. NW, Washington, DC 20220, (202) 622-2000, www.ustreas.gov

◆ Export-Import Bank of the United States, 811 Vermont Ave. NW, Washington, DC 20571, (202) 565-3946, fax: (202) 565-3380, www.exim.gov

◆ Internal Revenue Service, 1111 Constitution Ave. NW, Washington, DC 20224, (202) 622-5000, www.irs.ustreas.gov

◆ Patent and Trademark Office, Washington, DC 20231, (800) 786-9199, www.uspto.gov

◆ Printing Office, Superintendent of Documents, Washington, DC 20402, (202) 512-1800, fax: (202) 512-2250, www.access.gpo.gov/sudocs

◆ Securities and Exchange Commission, 450 Fifth St. NW, Washington, DC 20549, (202) 942-8088, www.sec.gov

◆ Small Business Administration, 409 Third St. SW, Washington, DC 20416, (800) 827-5722, www.sba.gov

SBA District Offices

The Small Business Administration has several types of field offices. Of these, the district offices offer the fullest range of services. To access all district office Web sites, go to www.sba.gov and then click on "Local SBA Resources."

◆ **Alabama:** 2121 Eighth Ave. N., #200, Birmingham, AL 35203-2398, (205) 731-1344, fax: (205) 731-1404

◆ **Alaska:** 222 W. Eighth Ave., Rm. A36, Anchorage, AK 99513-7559, (907) 271-4022, fax: (907) 271-4545

◆ **Arizona:** 2828 N. Central Ave., #800, Phoenix, AZ 85004-1093, (602) 640-2316, fax: (602) 640-2360

◆ **Arkansas:** 2120 Riverfront Dr., #100, Little Rock, AR 72202, (501) 324-5871, fax: (501) 324-5491

◆ **California:** 2719 Air Fresno Dr., #107, Fresno, CA 93727-1547, (209) 487-5189, fax: (209) 487-5803

330 N. Brand Blvd., #1200, Glendale, CA 91203-2304, (818) 552-3210, fax: (818) 552-3286

550 W. C St., #550, San Diego, CA 92101, (619) 557-7252, fax: (619) 557-5894

455 Market St., 6th Fl., San Francisco, CA 94105-1988, (415) 744-6801

660 J St., Rm. 215, Sacramento, CA 95814-2413, (916) 498-6410, fax: (916) 498-6422

200 W. Santa Ana Blvd., #700, Santa Ana, CA 92701-4134, (714) 550-7420, fax: (714) 550-0191

◆ **Colorado:** 721 19th St., #426, Denver, CO 80202-2599, (303) 844-3984, fax: (303) 844-6490

◆ **Connecticut:** 330 Main St., 2nd Fl., Hartford, CT 06106,
(860) 240-4700, fax: (860) 240-4659

◆ **Delaware:** 824 N. Market St., #610, Wilmington, DE 19801-3011,
(302) 573-6294

◆ **District of Columbia:** 1110 Vermont Ave. NW, #900, Washington,
DC 20005, (202) 606-4000, fax: (202) 606-4225

◆ **Florida:** 100 S. Biscayne Bl., 7th Fl., Miami, FL 3313-2011,
(305) 536-5521, fax: (305) 536-5058

7825 Baymeadows Wy., #100-B, Jacksonville, FL 32256-7504,
(904) 443-1900, fax: (904) 443-1980

◆ **Georgia:** 1720 Peachtree Rd. NW, 6th Fl., Atlanta, GA 30309,
(404) 529-9865, fax: (404) 347-0694

◆ **Hawaii:** 300 Ala Moana Blvd., Rm. 2-235, Honolulu, HI 96850-
4981, (808) 541-2990, fax: (808) 541-2976

◆ **Idaho:** 1020 Main St., #290, Boise, ID 83702-5745, (208) 334-1696,
fax: (208) 334-9353

◆ **Illinois:** 500 W. Madison St., #1250, Chicago, IL 60661-2511,
(312) 353-4528, fax: (312) 866-5688

511 W. Capitol Ave., #302, Springfield, IL 62704, (217) 492-4416

◆ **Indiana:** 429 N. Pennsylvania, #100, Indianapolis, IN 46204-1873,
(317) 226-7272, fax: (317) 226-7259

◆ **Iowa:** Mail Code 0736, 215 Fourth Ave. SE, #200, The Lattner Bldg.,
Cedar Rapids, IA 52401-1806, (319) 362-6405, fax: (319) 362-7861

210 Walnut St., Rm. 749, Des Moines, IA 50309-2186, (515) 284-
4422, fax: (515) 284-4572

◆ **Kansas:** 100 E. English St., #510, Wichita, KS 67202,
(316) 269-6616, fax: (316) 269-6499

◆ **Kentucky:** 600 Dr. Martin Luther King Jr. Pl., Rm. 188, Louisville, KY
40202, (502) 582-5971, fax: (502) 582-5009

◆ **Louisiana:** 365 Canal St., #2250, New Orleans, LA 70130,
(504) 589-6685, fax: (504) 589-2339

◆ **Maine:** 40 Western Ave., Rm. 512, Augusta, ME 04330,
(207) 622-8378, fax: (207) 622-8277

◆ **Maryland:** 10 S. Howard St., #6220, Baltimore, MD 21201-2525,
(410) 962-4392, fax: (410) 962-1805

- **Massachusetts:** 10 Causeway St., Rm. 265, Boston, MA 02222-1093, (617) 565-5590, fax: (617) 565-5597

- **Michigan:** 477 Michigan Ave., Rm. 515, Detroit, MI 48226, (313) 226-6075, fax: (313) 226-4769

- **Minnesota:** MC 0508, 610-C, Butler Square, 100 N. 6th St., Minneapolis, MN 55403-1563, (612) 370-2324, fax: (612) 370-2303

- **Mississippi:** 101 W. Capitol St., #400, Jackson, MS 39201, (601) 965-4378, fax: (601) 965-4294

- **Missouri:** 323 W. Eighth St., #501, Kansas City, MO 64105, (816) 374-6708, fax: (816) 374-6759

  815 Olive St., Rm. 242, St. Louis, MO 63101, (314) 539-6600, fax: (314) 539-3785

- **Montana:** 301 S. Park Ave., Rm. 334, Helena, MT 59626-0054, (406) 441-1081, fax: (406) 441-1090

- **Nebraska:** 11145 Mill Valley Rd., Omaha, NE 68154, (402) 221-4691, fax: (402) 221-3680

- **Nevada:** 300 S. Las Vegas Blvd., #1100, Las Vegas, NV 89101, (702) 388-6611, fax: (702) 933-6469

- **New Hampshire:** 143 N. Main St., #202, Concord, NH 03302-1248, (603) 225-1400, fax: (603) 225-1409

- **New Jersey:** 2 Gateway Center, 15th Fl., Newark, NJ 07102, (973) 645-2434, fax: (973) 645-6265

- **New Mexico:** 625 Silver SW, #320, Albuquerque, NM 87102, (505) 346-7909, fax: (505) 346-6711

- **New York:** 111 W. Huron St., Rm. 1311, Buffalo, NY 14202, (716) 551-4301, fax: (716) 551-4418

  26 Federal Plaza, #31-00, New York, NY 10278, (212) 264-1319, fax: (212) 264-7751

  401 S. Salina St., 5th Fl., Syracuse, NY 13202-2415, (315) 471-9272

- **North Carolina:** 200 N. College St., Ste. A-2015, Charlotte, NC 28202-2137, (704) 344-6563

- **North Dakota:** 657 Second Ave. N., Rm. 219, Fargo, ND 58102, (701) 239-5131, fax: (701) 239-5645

- **Ohio:** Superior Ave., #630, Cleveland, OH 44114-2507, (216) 522-4180, fax: (216) 522-2038

Nationwide Plaza, #1400, Columbus, OH 43215-2542, (614) 469-6860, fax: (614) 469-2391

◆ **Oklahoma:** 210 Park Ave., #1300, Oklahoma City, OK 73102, (405) 231-5521, fax: (405) 231-4876

◆ **Oregon:** 1515 SW Fifth Ave., #1050, Portland, OR 97201-6695, (503) 326-2682

◆ **Pennsylvania:** 900 Market St., 5th Fl., Philadelphia, PA 19107, (215) 580-2722, fax: (215) 580-2762

1000 Liberty Ave., Rm. 1128, Pittsburgh, PA 15222-4004, (412) 395-6560, fax: (412) 395-6562

◆ **Puerto Rico:** Citibank Tower, 252 Ponce de Leon Blvd., Rm. 201, Hato Rey, PR 00918, (787) 766-5572, fax: (787) 766-5309

◆ **Rhode Island:** 380 Westminster Mall, 5th Fl., Providence, RI 02903, (401) 528-4561, fax: (401) 528-4539

◆ **South Carolina:** 1835 Assembly St., Rm. 358, Columbia, SC 29201, (803) 765-5377, fax: (803) 765-5962

◆ **South Dakota:** 110 S. Phillips Ave., #200, Sioux Falls, SD 57102-1109, (605) 330-4231, fax: (605) 330-4215

◆ **Tennessee:** 50 Vantage Wy., #201, Nashville, TN 37228-1500, (615) 736-5881, fax: (615) 736-7232

◆ **Texas:** 4300 Amon Carter Blvd., #114, Ft. Worth, TX 76155, (817) 885-6500, fax: (817) 885-6543

9301 Southwest Fwy., #550, Houston, TX 77074-1591, (713) 773-6500, fax: (713) 773-6550

222 E. Van Buren St., Rm. 500, Harlingen, TX 78550-6855, (956) 427-8533, fax: (956) 427-8537

1611 Texas Ave., #408, Lubbock, TX 79401-2693, (806) 472-7462, fax: (806) 472-7487

727 E. Durango Blvd., Rm. A-527, San Antonio, TX 78206-1204, (210) 472-5900, fax: (210) 472-5935

◆ **Utah:** 125 S. State St., Rm. 2229, Salt Lake City, UT 84138-1195, (801) 524-5804

◆ **Vermont:** 87 State St., Rm. 205, Montpelier, VT 05602, (802) 828-4422

◆ **Virginia:** 1504 Santa Rosa Rd., #200, Richmond, VA 23229, (804) 771-2400, fax: (804) 771-8018

◆ **Washington:** 1200 Sixth Ave., #1700, Seattle, WA 98101-1128, (206) 553-7310, fax: (206) 553-7099

601 W. First Ave., 2nd Fl. West, Spokane, WA 99201-3826, (509) 353-2810, fax: (509) 353-2829

◆ **West Virginia:** 168 W. Main St., 6th Fl., Clarksburg, WV 26301, (304) 623-5631, fax: (304) 623-0023

◆ **Wisconsin:** 212 E. Washington Ave., Rm. 213, Madison, WI 53703, (608) 264-5261, fax: (608) 264-5500

◆ **Wyoming:** 100 E. B St., Rm. 4001, P.O. Box 2839, Casper, WY 82602-2839, (307) 261-6500

SMALL BUSINESS DEVELOPMENT CENTERS

The following state Small Business Development Centers (SBDCs) can direct you to the SBDC in your region. You can access all state SBDC Web sites at www.smallbiz.suny.edu/sbdcnet.htm.

◆ **Alabama:** Alabama Small Business Development Center, University of Alabama, Box 870397, Tuscaloosa, AL 35487, (205) 348-7011, fax: (205) 348-9644, www.cba.ua.edu./sbdc.htm

◆ **Alaska:** UAA Small Business Development Center, 430 W. Seventh Ave., #110, Anchorage, AK 99501, (907) 274-7232, fax: (907) 274-9524

◆ **Arizona:** Arizona Small Business Development Center Network, 2411 W. 14th St., #132, Tempe, AZ 85281, (602) 731-8720, fax: (602) 731-8729, www.dist.maricopa.edu/sdbdc

◆ **Arkansas:** Arkansas Small Business Development Center, 100 S. Main, #401, Little Rock, AR 72201, (501) 324-9043, fax: (501) 324-9049, www.ualr.edu/~sbdcdept

◆ **California:** California Small Business Development Center, Office of Small Business, 801 K St., #1700, Sacramento, CA 95814, (916) 324-5068, fax: (916) 322-5084, www.ca.gov/commerce/license/preface.htm

◆ **Colorado:** Colorado Business Assistance Center, 1625 Broadway, #805, Denver, CO 80202, (800) 333-7798, (303) 592-5720, fax: (303) 592-8107, www.state.co.us/govdir/obd/sbdc.htm

◆ **Connecticut:** Connecticut Small Business Development Center, University of Connecticut, 2 Bourn Pl., U-94, Storrs, CT 06269-5094, (860) 486-4135

◆ **Delaware:** Delaware Small Business Development Center, University of Delaware, 102 MBNA America Hall, Newark, DE 19716, (302) 831-2747, fax: (302) 831-1423, www.dleawaresbdc.org

◆ **District of Columbia:** Small Business Development Center, Howard University, School of Business, Rm. 128, 2600 Sixth St. NW, Washington, DC 20059, (202) 806-1550, fax: (202) 806-1777, husbdc@cldc.howard.edu

◆ **Florida:** Florida Small Business Development Center, 19 W. Garden St., #300, Pensacola, FL 32501, (850) 470-4980, (850) 595-6060, fax: (850) 595-6070, www.floridasbdc.com

◆ **Georgia:** Business Outreach Services, Small Business Development Center, Chicopee Complex, University of Georgia, 1180 E. Broad St., Athens, GA 30602-5412, (706) 542-6762, fax: (706) 542-6776, www.sbdc.uga.edu

◆ **Guam:** Pacific Islands Small Business Development Center Network, UOG Station, Mangilao, Guam 96923, (671) 735-2590, fax: (671) 734-2002, http://uog2.uog.edu/sbdc

◆ **Hawaii:** University of Hawaii at Hilo, Small Business Development Center Network, 200 W. Kawili St., Hilo, HI 96720-4091, (808) 974-7515, fax: (808) 974-7683, www.hawaii-sbdc.org

◆ **Idaho:** Idaho Small Business Development Center, Boise State University, 1910 University Dr., Boise, ID 83725-1655, (208) 426-1640, fax: (208) 426 3877, www.idbsu.edu/isbdc

◆ **Illinois:** Illinois Greater North Pulaski Small Business Development Center, 4054 W. North Ave., Chicago, IL 60639, (800) 252-2923 (in Illinois), (773) 384-2262

◆ **Indiana:** Indiana Small Business Development Center, 1 N. Capitol, #1275, Indianapolis, IN 46204, (317) 264-6871, fax: (317) 264-2806, www.isbdcorp.org

◆ **Iowa:** Iowa Small Business Development Center, 137 Lynn Ave., Ames, IA 50014, (515) 292-6351, fax: (515) 292-0020, www.iowasbdc.org

◆ **Kansas:** Small Business Development Center, 1501 S. Joplin, Pittsburg, KS 66762, (316) 235-4920, fax: (316) 235-4919, www.pittstate.edu/bti/sbdc/htm

◆ **Kentucky:** Kentucky Small Business Development Center, 225 Gatton College of Business and Economics, Lexington, KY 40506,

(606) 257-7668, fax: (606) 323-1907
http://gatton.gws.uky.edu/kentuckybusiness/ksbdc/ksbdc.htm

◆ **Louisiana:** Louisiana Small Business Development Center, College of
Business Administration, Northeast Louisiana University, Monroe, LA
71209-6435, (318) 342-5506, fax: (318) 342-5510,
www.lsbdc.net1.nlu.edu

◆ **Maine:** University of Southern Maine, Maine Small Business
Development Centers, 96 Falmouth St., P.O. Box 9300, Portland, ME
04104-9300, (207) 780-4420, fax: (207) 780-4810,
www.usm.maine.edu/~sbdc

◆ **Maryland:** Maryland Small Business Development Center, 7100 E.
Baltimore Ave., #401, College Park, MD 20740-3627, (301) 403-
8300

◆ **Massachusetts:** Massachusetts Small Business Development Center,
University of Massachusetts, P.O. Box 34935, Amherst, MA 01003,
(413) 545-6301, fax: (413) 545-1273, www.ump.edu/msbdc

◆ **Michigan:** Michigan Small Business Development Center, 2727
Second Ave., #107, Detroit, MI 48201, (313) 964-1798, fax: (313)
964-3648, http://bizserve.com/sbdc

◆ **Minnesota:** Minnesota Small Business Development Center, Dept. of
Trade and Economic Development, 500 Metro Square, 121 Seventh
Pl. E., St. Paul, MN 55101-2146, (651) 297-5773, fax: (651) 296-
1290, www.dted.state.mn.us

◆ **Mississippi:** Mississippi Small Business Development Center,
University of Mississippi, 216 Old Chemistry Bldg., University, MS
38677, (800) 725-7232 (in Mississippi), (601) 232-5001, fax: (601)
232-5650, www.olemiss.edu/depts/mssbdc

◆ **Missouri:** Missouri Small Business Development Center, 1205
University Ave., #300, Columbia, MO 65211, (573) 882-0344, fax:
(573) 884-4297, www.missouri:edu/~sbdwww

◆ **Montana:** Small Business Development Center, Department of
Commerce, 1424 Ninth Ave., Helena, MT 59620, (406) 444-4780,
fax: (406) 444-1872

◆ **Nebraska:** Nebraska Business Development Center, College of
Business Administration, University of Nebraska at Omaha, Rm. 407,
Omaha, NE 68182-0248, (402) 554-2521, fax: (402) 595-2385,
www.unomaha.edu

◆ **Nevada:** Nevada Small Business Development Center, University of

Nevada at Reno, College of Business Administration, MS 32, Reno, NV 89557-0100, (702) 784-1717, fax: (702) 784-4337, www.scs.unr.edu/nsbdc

◆ **New Hampshire:** New Hampshire Small Business Development Center, 1000 Elm St., 12th Fl., Manchester, NH 03101, (603) 624-2000, fax: (603) 647-4410, www.nhsbdc.org

◆ **New Jersey:** New Jersey Small Business Development Center, 49 Bleeker St., Newark, NJ 07102-1913, (973) 353-1927, fax: (973) 353-1110, www.nj.com/smallbusiness

◆ **New Mexico:** New Mexico Small Business Development Center, Santa Fe Community College, 6401 S. Richards Ave., Santa Fe, NM 87505, (800) 281-SBDC, (505) 428-1362, fax: (505) 428-1469, www.nmsbdc.org

◆ **New York:** New York Small Business Development Center, SUNY Plaza, S-523, Albany, NY 12246, (518) 443-5398, fax: (518) 465-4992, www.nys-sbdc.suny.edu

◆ **North Carolina:** North Carolina Small Business and Technology Development Center, 333 Fayetteville Street Mall, #1150, Raleigh, NC 27601, (800) 258-0862 (in North Carolina), (919) 715-7272, fax: (919) 715-7777, www.sbtdc.org

◆ **North Dakota:** North Dakota Small Business Development Center, University of North Dakota, P.O. Box 7308, Grand Forks, ND 58202, (701) 777-3700, fax: (701) 777-3225, www.und.nodak.edu/dept/ndsbdc

◆ **Ohio:** Ohio Small Business Development Center, P.O. Box 1001, Columbus, OH 43261-1001, (800) 848-1300, (614) 466-2480, fax: (614) 466-0829, www.odod.ohio.gov

◆ **Oklahoma:** Oklahoma Small Business Development Center, Stn. A, P.O. Box 2584, Durant, OK 74701, (580) 924-0277, fax: (580) 920-7471, www.osbdc.org

◆ **Oregon:** Oregon Small Business Development Center Network, 44 W. Broadway, #501, Eugene, OR 97401-3021, (541) 726-2250, fax: (541) 345-6006, www.efn.org/~osbdcn

◆ **Pennsylvania:** Pennsylvania Small Business Development Center, University of Pennsylvania, Vance Hall, 3733 Spruce St., 4th Fl., Philadelphia, PA 19104, (215) 898-1219, fax: (215) 573-2135, www.pasbdc.org

◆ **Rhode Island:** Rhode Island Small Business Development Center,

Bryant College, 1150 Douglas Pike, Smithfield, RI 02917, (401) 232-6111, fax: (401) 232-6933, www.risbdc.org

◆ **South Carolina:** South Carolina Small Business Development Center, The Darla Moore School of Business, University of South Carolina, Columbia, SC 29208, (803) 777-4907, fax: (803) 777-4403, http://sbdcweb.badm.sc.edu

◆ **South Dakota:** South Dakota Small Business Development Center, University of South Dakota, School of Business, 414 E. Clark St., Vermillion, SD 57069-2390, (605) 677-5498, fax: (605) 677-5427, www.usd.edu/brbinfo/sbdc

◆ **Tennessee:** Tennessee Small Business Development Center, University of Memphis, South Campus, Bldg. No. 1, Box 526324, Memphis, TN 38152, (901) 678-2500, fax: (901) 678-4072, www.tsbdc.memphis.edu

◆ **Texas:** Texas Small Business Development Center, 1100 Louisiana, #500, Houston, TX 77002, (713) 752-8400, fax: (713) 756-1500, http://smbizsolutions.uh.edu

◆ **Utah:** Utah Small Business Development Center, 125 S. State St., Salt Lake City, UT 84111, (801) 957-3840, fax: (801) 524-4160, www.sbaonline.sba.gov

◆ **Vermont:** Vermont Small Business Development Center, 60 Main St., #103, Burlington, VT 05401, (802) 658-9228, fax: (802) 860-1899, www.vtsbdc.org

◆ **Virginia:** Virginia Small Business Development Center, P.O. Box 446, Richmond, VA 23218-0446, (804) 371-8258, fax: (804) 225-3384, www.dba.state.va.us

◆ **Washington:** Washington Small Business Development Center, Washington State University, P.O. Box 644851, Pullman, WA 99164-4851, (509) 335-1576, fax: (509) 335-0949, www.sbdc.wsu.edu

◆ **West Virginia:** West Virginia Small Business Development Center, 950 Kanawha Blvd. E., #200, Charleston, WV 25301, (888) 982-7732, (304) 558-2960, fax: (304) 558-0127, www.wvsbdc.org

◆ **Wisconsin:** University of Wisconsin at Whitewater, Small Business Development Center, Carlson 2000, Whitewater, WI 53190, (414) 472-3217, fax: (414) 472-5692

◆ **Wyoming:** Wyoming Small Business Development Center, 111 W. Second St., #502, Casper, WY 82601, (307) 234-6683, fax: (307) 577-7014, www.sbdc@trib.com

State Commerce and Economic Development Departments

◆ **Alabama:** Alabama Development Office, 401 Adams Ave., Montgomery, AL 36130, (334) 242-0400, fax: (334) 242-2414, www.ado.state.al.us

◆ **Alaska:** Alaska State Dept. of Commerce and Economic Development, P.O. Box 110800, Juneau, AK 99811-0800, (907) 465-2500, fax: (907) 465-5442, www.commerce.state.ak.us

◆ **Arizona:** Arizona State Dept. of Commerce Business Assistance Center, 3800 N. Central Ave., Phoenix, AZ 85012, (800) 542-5684, (602) 280-1480, fax: (602) 280-1339, www.commerce.state.az.us/frabc.shtml

◆ **Arkansas:** Arkansas Economic Development Commission, Advocacy and Business Services, 1 State Capitol Mall, Little Rock, AR 72201, (501) 682-1060, fax: (501) 324-9856, www.aedc.state.ar.us

◆ **California:** California Trade and Commerce Agency, Office of Small Business, 801 K St., #1700, Sacramento, CA 95814, (916) 324-1295, fax: (916) 322-5084, www.smallbusiness.commerce.ca.gov

◆ **Colorado:** Colorado Office of Business Development, 1625 Broadway, #1710, Denver, CO 80202, (303) 892-3840, fax: (303) 892-3848, http://governor.state.co.us/govdir/obd/obd.htm.

◆ **Connecticut:** Connecticut Economic Resource Center, 805 Brook St., Bldg. 4, Rocky Hill, CT 06067, (860) 571-7136, fax: (860) 571-7150, www.cerc.com

◆ **Delaware:** Delaware Economic Development Office, 99 Kings Hwy., Dover, DE 19901, (302) 739-4271, fax: (302) 739-5749, www.state.de.us

◆ **District of Columbia:** Office of Economic Development, 441 Fourth St. NW, Ste. North-1140, Washington, DC 20001, (202) 727-6365, fax: (202) 727-6703

◆ **Florida:** Enterprise Florida, 390 N. Orange, #1300, Orlando, FL 32801, (407) 316-4600, fax: (407) 316-4599, www.floridabusiness.com

◆ **Georgia:** Georgia Dept. of Community Affairs, 60 Executive Park S. NE, Atlanta, GA 30329-2231, (404) 679-4940, fax: (404) 679-4940, www.dca.state.ga.us

◆ **Hawaii:** Business Action Center, 1130 N. Nimitz Hwy., 2nd Level,

Ste. A-254, Honolulu, HI 96817, (808) 586-2545, fax: (808) 586-2544, www.hawaii.gov/dbedt

◆ **Idaho:** Idaho State Dept. of Commerce, P.O. Box 83720, Boise, ID 83720-0093, (208) 334-2470, fax: (208) 334-2631, www.idoc.state.id.us

◆ **Illinois:** Illinois Dept. of Commerce and Community Affairs, 620 E. Adams St., Springfield, IL 62701, (217) 524-6293, www.commerce.state.il.us

◆ **Indiana:** Indiana State Dept. of Commerce, 1 N. Capitol, #700, Indianapolis, IN 46204-2288, (317) 232-8782, fax: (317) 233-5123, www.indbiz.com

◆ **Iowa:** Iowa Dept. of Economic Development, 200 E. Grand Ave, Des Moines, IA 50309, (800) 532-1216, (515) 242-4750, fax: (515) 242-4776, www.state.ia.us/sbro

◆ **Kansas:** Kansas Dept. of Commerce and Housing, Business Development Division, 700 SW Harrison St., #1300, Topeka, KS 66603, (785) 296-5298, fax: (785) 296-3490, www.kansascommerce.com

◆ **Kentucky:** Kentucky Cabinet for Economic Development, Business Information Clearinghouse, 22nd Fl., Capitol Plaza Tower, Frankfort, KY 40601, (800) 626-2250, fax: (502) 564-5932, www.state.ky.us/edc/bic.htm

◆ **Louisiana:** Louisiana Dept. of Economic Development, P.O. Box 94185, Baton Rouge, LA 70804-9185, (225) 342-5372, fax: (225) 342-5349, www.lded.state.la.us

◆ **Maine:** Business Answers, Dept. of Economic and Community Development, 33 Stone St., 59 Statehouse Station, Augusta, ME 04333-0059, (207) 287-2656, fax: (207) 287-2861, www.econdev.maine.com

◆ **Maryland:** Maryland Dept. of Business and Economic Development, Division of Regional Development, 217 E. Redwood St., 10th Fl., Baltimore, MD 21202, (410) 767-0095, fax: (410) 338-1836, www.mdbusiness.state.md.us

◆ **Massachusetts:** Massachusetts Office of Business Development, 1 Ashburton Pl., 21st Fl., Boston, MA 02108, (617) 727-3221, fax: (617) 727-8797, www.state.ma.us/mobd

◆ **Michigan:** Michigan Jobs Commission, Customer Assistance, 201 N.

Washington Square, Victor Office Center, 4th Fl., Lansing, MI 48913, (517) 373-9808, fax: (517) 335-0198, www.state.mi.us/mjc

◆ **Minnesota:** Minnesota Small Business Assistance Office, 500 Metro Square, 121 Seventh Pl. E., St. Paul, MN 55101, (800) 657-3858, (612) 282-2103, fax: (612) 296-1290, www.dted.state.mn.us

◆ **Mississippi:** Mississippi Dept. of Economic and Community Development, Division of Existing Industry and Business, New Business, P.O. Box 849, Jackson, MS 39205-0849, (601) 359-3593, fax: (601) 359-2116, www.decd.state.ms.us

◆ **Missouri:** Missouri Dept. of Economic Development, P.O. Box 118, Jefferson City, MO 65102, (573) 751-4982, fax: (573) 751-7384, www.ecodev.state.mo.us/mbac

◆ **Montana:** Dept. of Commerce, Economic Development Division, 1424 Ninth Ave., Helena, MT 59620, (406) 444-3814, fax: (406) 444-1872, http://commerce/mt.gov

◆ **Nebraska:** Dept. of Economic Development, 301 Centennial Mall S., P.O. Box 94666, Lincoln, NE 68509-4666, (402) 471-3782, www.ded.state.ne.us

◆ **Nevada:** Nevada State Dept. of Business and Industry, Center for Business Advocacy, 2501 E. Sahara Ave., #100, Las Vegas, NV 89104, (702) 486-4335, fax: (702) 486-4340, www.state.nv.us/b&i

◆ **New Hampshire:** New Hampshire Office of Business and Industrial Development, P.O. Box 1856, Concord, NH 03302-1856, (603) 271-2591, fax: (603) 271-6784, http://ded.state.nh.us/obid

◆ **New Jersey:** Dept. of Commerce and Economic Development, 20 State St., CN 820, Trenton, NJ 08625, (609) 292-2444, fax: (609) 292-9145, www.nj.com/business

◆ **New Mexico:** New Mexico Economic Development Dept., P.O. Box 20003-5003, Santa Fe, NM 87504, (505) 827-0300, fax: (505) 827-0300, www.edd.state.nm.us

◆ **New York:** Division for Small Business, Empire State Development, 1 Commerce Plaza, Albany, NY 12245, (518) 473-0499, fax: (518) 474-1512, www.empire.state.ny.us

◆ **North Carolina:** Small Business and Technology Development Center, 333 Fayetteville Street Mall, #1150, Raleigh, NC 27601-1742, (919) 715-7272, fax: (919) 715-7777, www.sbtdc.org

◆ **North Dakota:** Center for Innovation, Rural Technology Incubator,

P.O. Box 8372, Grand Forks, ND 58202, (701) 777-3132, fax: (701) 777-2339, www.innovators.net

◆ **Ohio:** Ohio One-Stop Business Center, 77 S. High St., 28th Fl., P.O. Box 1001, Columbus, OH 43216-1001, (614) 644-8748, fax: (614) 466-0829

◆ **Oklahoma:** Department of Commerce, P.O. Box 26980, Oklahoma City, OK 73126-0980, (405) 843-9770, fax: (405) 815-5142, www.odoc.state.ok.us

◆ **Oregon:** Oregon Economic Development Dept., 775 Summer St. NE, Salem, OR 97310, (503) 986-0123, fax: (503) 581-5115, www.econ.state.or.us

◆ **Pennsylvania:** Pennsylvania Small Business Resource Center, Rm. 374, Forum Bldg., Harrisburg, PA 17120, (717) 783-5700, fax: (717) 234-4560, www.dced.state.pa.us

◆ **Rhode Island:** Rhode Island Economic Development Corporation, 1 W. Exchange St., Providence, RI 02903, (401) 222-2601, fax: (401) 222-2102, www.riedc.com

◆ **South Carolina:** Enterprise Inc., P.O. Box 1149, Columbia, SC 29202, (803) 252-8806, fax: (803) 252-0455

◆ **South Dakota:** Governor's Office of Economic Development, 711 E. Wells Ave., Pierre, SD 57501-3369, (605) 773-5032, fax: (605) 773-3256, www.state.sd.us

◆ **Tennessee:** Small Business Service, Department of Economic and Community Development, 320 Sixth Ave. N., 7th Fl., Rachel Jackson Bldg., Nashville, TN 37243-0405, (615) 741-2626, fax: (615) 532-8715, www.state.tn.us/ecd

◆ **Texas:** Texas Dept. of Economic Development, Office of Small Business Assistance, P.O. Box 12728, Austin, TX 78711-2728, (512) 936-0223, fax: (512) 936-0435, www.tded.state.tx.us

◆ **Utah:** Utah Dept. of Community and Economic Development, 324 S. State St., #500, Salt Lake City, UT 84111, (801) 538-8775, fax: (801) 538-8888, www.dced.state.ut.us

◆ **Vermont:** Vermont Agency of Commerce and Community Development, Department of Economic Development, National Life Bldg., Drawer 20, Montpelier, VT 05620-0501, (802) 828-3211, fax: (802) 828-3258, www.state.vt.us/dca/economic/develp.htm

◆ **Virginia:** Dept. of Business Assistance, Small Business Development

Center Network, 901 E. Byrd St., #1400, Richmond, VA 23219, (804) 371-8253, fax: (804) 225-3384, www.dba.state.va.us

◆ **Washington:** Business Assistance Division, Community Trade and Economic Development, 906 Columbia St. SW, P.O. Box 48300, Olympia, WA 98504-8300, (360) 753-4900, fax: (360) 586-0873, www.wa.gov/cted/lda/access.htm

◆ **West Virginia:** West Virginia Development Office, 950 Kanawha Blvd., Charleston, WV 25301, (304) 558-2960, fax: (304) 558-0127, www.wvsbdc.org

◆ **Wisconsin:** Department of Commerce, 201 Washington Ave., Madison, WI 53703, (608) 266-9467, fax: (608) 267-2829, www.commerce.state.wi.us

◆ **Wyoming:** Wyoming Business Council, 2301 Central Ave., Cheyenne, WY 82002, (307) 777-5874, fax: (307) 777-6005, www.wyomingbusiness.org

APPENDIX F
SMALL-BUSINESS-FRIENDLY BANKS

Small businesses are in the best shape they've ever been in when it comes to obtaining microloans ($100,000 or less), according to a recent study by the SBA Office of Advocacy.

In fact, according to Jere Glover, the Advocacy Office's chief counsel, the number of loans approved in this category jumped 26.8 percent over a one-year period.

One reason for the rise is the increased use of business credit cards, which banks consider to be a revolving line of credit; this helps establish a credit history with the bank. "The other reason is credit-scoring," says Glover. "If you have a good personal credit record, banks are [more] willing to make you a small-business loan." The use of credit-scoring reduces paperwork and speeds up the loan process, resulting in lower costs for banks—and a greater willingness to lend.

The increase in the number of microloans is occurring even in the face of an industry seemingly consumed by mergers. "As the bank industry consolidates into fewer and fewer hands, a few people could make decisions to cut back [on small-business lending], and the effect on the business sector could be dramatic," Glover says, noting that so far the impact has been minimal.

Glover acknowledges that one reason small-business credit hasn't been affected may be the increasing number of smaller banking institutions setting up shop.

Another trend to watch is the increasing availability of loans online. But this will only work in certain situations, warns Glover. "It works for small amounts, when you can get a credit loan," he says.

The SBA's annual bank study shows an improving landscape for small-business lending, but with all the new forces being brought to bear on the industry, vigilance continues to be the watchword.

The following ranking lists the SBA's top two microbusiness-friendly banks in each state (where there were two) by the percentage of microbusiness loans per total assets. The listing also includes banks whose microloans-to-assets ratio was 40 percent or higher.

The four variables measured are:

1. microbusiness loans-to-assets ratio
2. microbusiness loans-to-total-business-loans ratio
3. dollar volume of microbusiness loans
4. total number of microbusiness loans

Alabama

Independent Bank of Oxford, P.O. Box 3363, Oxford, AL 36203, (205) 835-1776

West Alabama Bank & Trust, P.O. Box 310, Reform, AL 35481, (205) 375-6261

Alaska

First National Bank, P.O. Box 100720, Anchorage, AK 99510, (907) 276-6300

Arizona

Bank of Casa Grande Valley, 1300 E. Florence Blvd., Casa Grande, AZ 85222, (520) 836-4666

Frontier State Bank, P.O. Box 1030, Show Low, AZ 85901, (520) 537-2933

Arkansas

Caddo First National Bank, P.O. Box 47, Glenwood, AR 71943, (870) 356-3196

Fidelity National Bank, 330 W. Broadway, West Memphis, AR 72301, (870) 735-8700

California

Cupertino National Bank & Trust, 20230 Stevens Creek Blvd., Cupertino, CA 95014, (408) 996-1144

Kings River State Bank, P.O. Box 997, Reedley, CA 93654, (209) 638-8131

Colorado

Cheyenne Mountain Bank, 1580 E. Cheyenne Mountain Blvd., Colorado Springs, CO 80906, (719) 579-9150

Bank of Grand Junction, 2415 F Rd., Grand Junction, CO 81505, (970) 241-9000

Connecticut

Lafayette American Bank, 130 N. Main St., Southington, CT 06489, (860) 620-5000

The Equity Bank, 1160 Silas Deane Hwy., Wethersfield, CT 06109, (860) 571-7200

Delaware

PNC National Bank of Delaware, 300 Delaware Ave., Wilmington, DE 19899, (302) 429-2274

NationsBank of Delaware, P.O. Box 7028, Dover, DE 19901, (302) 741-1000

District Of Columbia

Franklin National Bank, 1722 Eye St. N.W., Washington, DC 20006, (202) 429-9888

Florida

Northside Bank of Tampa, 12233 N. Florida Ave., Tampa, FL 33612, (813) 933-2255

Fidelity Bank of Florida, P.O. Box 540160, Merritt Island, FL 32954-0160, (407) 452-0011

Georgia

The Coastal Bank, P.O. Box 529, Hinesville, GA 31310, (912) 368-2265

Community Trust Bank, P.O. Box 1700, Hiram, GA 30141, (770) 445-1014

Hawaii

City Bank, 201 Merchant St., Honolulu, HI 96813, (808) 535-2500

Idaho

Panhandle State Bank, P.O. Box 967, Sandpoint, ID 83864, (208) 263-0505

D. L. Evans Bank, 397 N. Overland Ave., Burley, ID 83318, (208) 678-9076

Illinois

First National Bank-Employee Owned, 485 Lake St., Antioch, IL 60002, (847) 838-2265

The State Bank of Geneva, 22 S. Fourth St., Geneva, IL 60134, (630) 232-3200

Indiana

Peoples Trust Co., P.O. Box 190, Linton, IN 47441, (812) 847-4457

Scott County State Bank, P.O. Box 158, Scottsburg, IN 47170, (812) 752-4501

Iowa

Hartford-Carlisle Savings Bank, 100 First St., Carlisle, IA 50047, (515) 989-3255

Peoples Bank & Trust, P.O. Box 158, Rock Valley, IA 51247, (712) 476-2746

Kansas

The First National Bank of Conway Springs, 214 W. Spring Ave., Conway Springs, KS 67031, (316) 456-2255

First National Bank, 402 Main St., Palco, KS 67657, (785) 737-2311

Peoples Bank & Trust, P.O. Box 1226, McPherson, KS 67460, (316) 241-8450

Kentucky

Bank of Mt. Vernon, P.O. Box 157, Mt. Vernon, KY 40456-0157, (606) 256-5141

South Central Bank, 208 S. Broadway, Glasgow, KY 42141, (502) 651-7466

Louisiana

Community Bank of La Fourche, 3160 Hwy. 1, Raceland, LA 70394, (504) 537-6402

Community Trust Bank, 3921 Elm St., Choudrant, LA 71227, (318) 768-2531

Maine

United Bank, 145 Exchange St., Bangor, ME 04401, (207) 942-5263

Katahdin Trust Co., P.O. Box I, Patten, ME 04765, (207) 528-2211

Maryland

Maryland Permanent Bank & Trust Co., 9612 Reisters Town Rd., Owings Mills, MD 21117, (410) 356-4411

Bank of the Eastern Shore, 301 Crusader Rd., Cambridge, MD 21613, (410) 228-5800

Massachusetts

Luzo Community Bank, 1724 Acushnet Ave., New Bedford, MA 02746, (508) 999-9980

Bank of Western Massachusetts, 29 State St., Springfield, MA 01103, (413) 781-2265

Michigan

1st Bank, P.O. Box 335, West Branch, MI 48661, (517) 345-7900

MFC First National Bank, 1205 Ludington St., Escanaba, MI 49829, (906) 786-5010

Minnesota

Pioneer National Bank of Duluth, 331 N. Central Ave., Duluth, MN 55807, (218) 624-3676

State Bank of Delano, P.O. Box 530, Delano, MN 55328, (612) 972-2935

Mississippi

Pike County National Bank, P.O. Box 1666, McComb, MS 39649, (601) 684-7575

First Bank, P.O. Box 808, McComb, MS 39648, (601) 684-2231

Missouri

First Midwest Bank of Dexter, 20 W. Stoddard, Dexter, MO 63841, (573) 624-3571

First State Bank of Joplin, 802 Main, Joplin, MO 64801, (417) 623-8860

Montana

Mountain West Bank of Helena, 1225 Cedar St., Helena, MT 59601, (406) 449-2265

Bitterroot Valley Bank, Lolo Shopping Center, P.O. Box 9, Lolo, MT 59847, (406) 273-2400

Mountain West Bank of Great Falls, 12 Third St. N.W., Great Falls, MT 59404, (406) 727-2265

Nebraska

Sapp City Bank, 9003 S. 145th St., Omaha, NE 68138, (402) 891-0003

Dakota County State Bank, 2024 Dakota Ave., South Sioux City, NE 68776, (402) 494-4215

Nevada

First National Bank of Ely, 595 Aultman St., Ely, NV 89301, (702) 289-4441

BankWest of Nevada, 2700 W. Sahara Ave., Las Vegas, NV 89102, (702) 248-4200

New Hampshire
Community Bank & Trust Co., 15 Varney Rd., Wolfeboro, NH 03894, (603) 569-8400

Bank of New Hampshire, 300 Franklin St., Manchester, NH 03101, (603) 624-6600

New Jersey
Panasia Bank, 183 Main St., Ft. Lee, NJ 07024, (201) 947-6666

Minotola National Bank, 1748 S. Lincoln Ave., Vineland, NJ 08361, (609) 696-8100

New Mexico
Peoples Bank, 1356 Paseo del Pueblo Sur, Taos, NM 87571, (505) 758-4500

Norwest Bank of New Mexico, P.O. Box 1107, Tucumcari, NM 88401, (505) 461-3602

New York
Olympian Bank, 512 86th St., Brooklyn, NY 11209, (718) 748-3500

Champlain National Bank, Court St., Elizabethtown, NY 12932, (518) 873-6347

North Carolina
Wilkes National Bank, 1600 Curtsbridge Rd., Wilkesboro, NC 28697, (336) 903-0600

Yadkin Valley Bank & Trust Co., P.O. Box 888, Elkin, NC 28621, (910) 526-6371

North Dakota
Kirkwood Bank & Trust Co., P.O. Box 6089, Bismarck, ND 58506, (701) 258-6550

Citizens State Bank, P.O. Box 127, Mohall, ND 58761, (701) 756-6365

Ohio
First National Bank of Pandora, 102 E. Main St., Pandora, OH 45877, (419) 384-3221

Citizens Banking Co., 10 E. Main St., Salineville, OH 43945, (330) 679-2321

Oklahoma
Bank of Cushing, P.O. Box 951, Cushing, OK 74023-0951, (918) 225-2010

Bank of Kremlin, P.O. Box 197, Kremlin, OK 73753, (580) 874-2244

Oregon
Community First Bank, P.O. Box 447, Prineville, OR 97754, (541) 447-4105

Security Bank P.O., Box 1350, Coos Bay, OR 97420, (541) 267-6611

Pennsylvania
Pennsylvania State Bank, 2148 Market St., Camp Hill, PA 17011, (717) 731-7272

Old Forge Bank, 216 S. Main St., Old Forge, PA 18518, (717) 457-8345

Rhode Island
Washington Trust Co., 23 Broad St., Westerly, RI 02891, (401) 351-6240

South Carolina
Bank of Walterboro, 1100 N. Jefferies Blvd., Walterboro, SC 29488, (803) 549-2265

First National South, 307 N. Main St., Marion, SC 29571, (803) 431-1000

South Dakota
F & M Bank, P.O. Box 877, Watertown, SD 57201, (605) 886-8401

First National Bank in Garretson, P.O. Box G, Garretson, SD 57030, (605) 594-3423

Tennessee
Volunteer Bank & Trust, 728 Broad St., Chattanooga, TN 37402, (423) 265-5001

First Bank of Rhea County, P.O. Box 99, Spring City, TN 37381, (423) 365-9551

Texas
Navigation Bank, P.O. Box 228, Houston, TX 77001, (713) 223-3400

First Commercial Bank, 1336 E. Court St., Seguin, TX 78155, (830) 379-8390

Midland American Bank, 401 W. Texas, #100, Midland, TX 79701, (915) 687-3013

Woodhaven National Bank, 6750 Bridge St., Fort Worth, TX 76112, (817) 496-6700

Utah
Advanta Financial, 11850 S. Election Rd., Draper, UT 84020, (801) 523-0858

First USA Payment Tech., P.O. Box 57510, Salt Lake City, UT 84157, (801) 281-5800

Vermont
Union Bank, P.O. Box 667, Morrisville, VT 05661, (802) 888-6600

Citizens Savings Bank & Trust Co., P.O. Box 219, Saint Johnsbury, VT 05819, (802) 748-3131

Virginia
Benchmark Community Bank, P.O. Box 569, Kenbridge, VA 23944, (804) 676-8444

Chesapeake Bank, P.O. Box 1419, Kilmarmock, VA 22482, (804) 435-1181

Washington
First Heritage Bank, P.O. Box 550, Snohomish, WA 98291-0550, (360) 568-0536

First National Bank of Port, Orchard P.O. Box 2629, Port Orchard, WA 98366, (360) 895-2265

West Virginia
West Bank of Paden City, P.O. Box 178, Paden City, WV 26159, (304)337-2205

First National Bank in Marlinton, P.O. Box 58, Marlington, WV 24954, (304) 799-4640

Wisconsin
Stephenson National Bank & Trust, P.O. Box 137, Marinette, WI 54143-0137, (715) 732-1650

First National Bank, Fox Valley P.O. Box 339, Menasha, WI 54952, (920) 729-6900

Wyoming
Western Bank of Cheyenne, P.O. Box 127, 1525 E. Pershing Blvd., Cheyenne, WY 82001, (307) 637-7333

First Interstate Bank of Commerce, 4 S. Main St., Sheridan, WY 82801, (307) 674-7411

GLOSSARY

Balloon payment: a single, usually final, payment on a loan that is much greater than the payments preceding it; some business loans, for example, require interest-only payments the first year or two, followed by a single large payment that repays all the principal

Branding: the marketing practice of creating a name, symbol or design that identifies and differentiates a product from other products; well-known brands include Tide, Dockers and Twinkies

Business concept: the basic idea around which a business is built; for instance, Federal Express is built on the idea of overnight delivery, while Amazon.com is built around the idea of selling books over the Internet

Cash conversion cycle: the amount of time it takes to transform your cash outlays into cash income; for a manufacturer, the number of days or weeks required to purchase raw materials and turn them into inventory, then sales and, finally, collections

Competitive advantage: factor or factors that make one company, product or service different from and better than other offerings; lower price, higher quality and better name recognition are examples

Co-op promotion: arrangement between two or more businesses to cross-promote their enterprises to customers

Current assets: assets likely to be turned into cash within a year

Current liabilities: amounts you owe and are to pay in less than a year, such as accounts payable to suppliers and short-term loans

Due diligence: actions an investor should do to check out an investment's worthiness; it has a legal definition when applied to the responsibilities of financial professionals, such as stockbrokers; in general, it includes such things as requiring audited financial statements and checking warehouses for claimed inventory stocks

EBIT: acronym for earnings before interest and taxes, an accounting term for a company's operational earnings separate from the effects of interest payments and taxation

Electronic commerce: selling products and services through sites on the World Wide Web; also called e-commerce

Electronic Data Interchange: a computer-to-computer linkup of ordering and inventory systems between manufacturers and retailers; also called EDI

Executive summary: section of a business plan that briefly describes what the rest of the plan contains

Factoring: the flip side of trade credit; what happens when a supplier sells its accounts receivables to a financial specialist called a factor; the factor immediately pays the amount of the receivables, less a discount, and receives the payments when they arrive from customers; an important form of finance in many industries

Goal: short-term objective, usually incorporating firm time deadlines and quantifiable measures

Kaizen: Japanese term, popular in the 1980s and early 1990s, that means continuous improvement that seeks to constantly obtain small gains in productivity and quality over a long period, producing greater long-term gains

Leverage: the use of borrowed funds to increase purchasing power

Lifestyle entrepreneur: someone who starts a business for the sake of ownership or flexibility, as opposed to the desire to build a large enterprise or become wealthy

Limited Liability Corporation: business legal structure resembling an S corporation but allowing owners more flexibility in dividing up profits while still providing protection from liability; abbreviated LLC

Liquidity: a description of a company's ability to convert noncash assets, such as inventory and accounts receivable, into cash; essentially, the company's ability to pay its bills

Logistics: the science of moving objects, such as product inventory, from one location to another

Mission statement: a sentence describing a company's function, markets and competitive advantages

Objectives: long-term aims, frequently representing the ultimate level to which you aspire

Organization, functional: a company or other entity with a structure that divides authority along functions such as marketing, finance, etc.; these functions cross product lines and other boundaries

Organization, line and staff: a company or other entity with a structure calling for staff managers, like planners and accountants, to act as advisors supporting a line manager, such as the operations vice president

Organization, line: a company or other entity with a structure divided by product lines, means of production, industries served, etc.; each line may have its own support staff for the various functions

Outsourcing: having a component or service performed or supplied by an outside firm such as a manufacturer, wholesaler or broker; used to reduce time and money costs for support work and add flexibility in production staffing

Positioning: marketing tool that describes a product or service in reference to its position in the marketplace; for example, the newest, smallest, cheapest, second-largest, etc.

Psychographics: market researchers' attempt to accurately measure lifestyle by classifying customers according to their activities, interest and opinions

Rate of return: the income or profit earned by an investor on capital invested into a company; usually expressed as an annual percentage

Rich Text Format: standard word processing format in which most plan-writing software allows you to export your work; also called RTF

Strategy: the steps you plan to implement to achieve your business objectives

Subordinated: term usually applied to a debt and meaning its claim on the debtor's assets comes second to another's claim; senior subordinated debt has a claim before junior subordinated debt; preferred debt is the opposite of subordinated—it gets first claim

Trade credit: accounts payable representing bills owed to suppliers; typical trade credit terms allow payment in 30 days without penalty; an important source of financing for many companies

Turnaround: a reversal in a company's fortunes, taking it from near death to robust health; for example, in the 1970s, Chrysler had to be bailed out by the federal government, then in the 1980s, Chrysler turned around and Daimler-Benz bought the revived company in what was then history's biggest industrial buyout

Unique selling proposition: the factor or consideration presented by a seller as the reason that one product or service is different from and better than the competition

Vision statement: a sentence or two describing a company's long-range aims, such as achieving dominant market share or attaining a reputation for world-class quality

Working capital: the amount of money a business has in cash, accounts receivable, inventory and other current assets; normally refers to net working capital, which is current assets minus current liabilities

INDEX

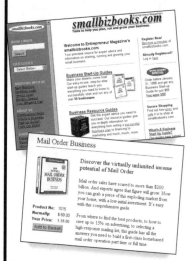

FREE ADVICE

When was the last time you got **free** advice that was worth something?

Entrepreneur Magazine, the leading small business authority, is loaded with free advice—advice that could be worth millions to you. Every issue gives you detailed, practical knowledge on how to start a business and run it successfully. Entrepreneur is the perfect resource to keep small business owners up-to-date, on track, and growing their business.

Get your **free issue** of Entrepreneur today!

Call 800-274-6229 Dept. 5G9J9, or fill out and mail the back of this card.

Entrepreneur
MAGAZINE

BREAK OUT

Business Start-Ups helps you **break** out of the 9–5 life!

Do you want to get out of the 9–5 routine and take control of your life? Business Start-Ups shows you the franchise and business opportunities that will give you the future you dream of. Every issue answers your questions, highlights hot trends, spotlights new ideas, and provides the inspiration and real-life information you need to succeed.

Get your **free issue** of Business Start-Ups today!

Call 800-274-8333 Dept. 5HBK2, or fill out and mail the back of this card.

Business Start-Ups

MILLION DOLLAR SECRETS

free issue!

Exercise your right to make it **big**.

Get into the small business authority—now at **80% off** the newsstand price!

Yes! Start my one year subscription and bill me for just $9.99. I get a full year of Entrepreneur and save 80% off the newsstand rate. If I choose not to subscribe, the free issue is mine to keep.

Name ☐ Mr. ☐ Mrs. _____
(please print)

Address _____

City_____ State _____ Zip _____

☐ BILL ME   ☐ PAYMENT ENCLOSED

Guaranteed. Or your money back. Every subscription to Entrepreneur comes with a 100% satisfaction guarantee: your money back whenever you like, for whatever reason, on all unmailed issues! Offer good in U.S. and possessions only. Please allow 4–6 weeks for mailing of first issue. Canadian and foreign: $39.97. U.S. funds only.

5G9J9

Mail this coupon to **Entrepreneur** MAGAZINE. P.O. Box 50368, Boulder, CO 80321-0368

OPPORTUNITY KNOCKS!!!

free issue!

save 72%!

Please enter my subscription to Business Start-Ups for one year. I will receive 12 issues for only $9.99. That's a savings of 72% off the news-stand price. The free issue is mine to keep, even if I choose not to subscribe.

Name ☐ Mr. ☐ Mrs. _____
(please print)

Address _____

City_____ State _____ Zip _____

☐ BILL ME   ☐ PAYMENT ENCLOSED

Guaranteed. Or your money back. Every subscription to Business Start-Ups comes with a 100% satisfaction guarantee: your money back whenever you like, for whatever reason, on all unmailed issues! Offer good in U.S. and possessions only. Please allow 4–6 weeks for mailing of first issue. Canadian and foreign: $34.97. U.S. funds only.

5HBK2

Mail this coupon to **Business Start-Ups** P.O. Box 50347, Boulder, CO 80321-0347